PRAISE FOR *LGBTQ FAMILY BUILDING*

LGBTQ readers who are thinking about parenthood but unsure about the best pathways to pursue will find this volume to be enormously helpful. Written by a respected researcher, the book offers up-to-date summaries of research and policy issues, as well as many other useful resources. For queer people who are thinking about becoming parents, this is the book to have!

—CHARLOTTE J. PATTERSON, PHD, PROFESSOR OF PSYCHOLOGY, UNIVERSITY OF VIRGINIA, CHARLOTTESVILLE

Dr. Goldberg is one of our foremost scholars of family diversity, and *LGBTQ Family Building* is her crowning glory. Blending sophisticated scholarship with practical recommendations in a format and tone ideal for parents, this book is a must if you are considering whether to parent or how to become a parent through adoption, donor insemination, or surrogacy. It's loaded with resources, helpful charts, and advice that's conveyed in an exquisitely readable format.

—RITCH C. SAVIN-WILLIAMS, PHD, PROFESSOR EMERITUS OF DEVELOPMENTAL PSYCHOLOGY, CORNELL UNIVERSITY, ITHACA, NY

Abbie Goldberg's book could not be timelier, as more and more LGBTQ individuals are becoming parents. Grounded in research findings and the lived experiences of participants from her LGBTQ Family Building Project, Goldberg, a highly respected clinical scholar, explores the complications, challenges, and satisfactions that LGBTQ individuals encounter as they embark on different pathways to parenthood through adoption, donor insemination, and surrogacy. She also highlights some of the unique parenting issues experienced by LGBTQ individuals as they transition to parenthood and raise their young children. Written in a warm, succinct, and accessible manner, this book will be a "must read" for clinicians working with LGBTQ clients.

—**DAVID BRODZINSKY, PHD,** PROFESSOR EMERITUS, RUTGERS UNIVERSITY, NEW BRUNSWICK, NJ

This is a book that so many of us have been waiting and hoping for! And not just LGBTQ advocates, but all members of LGBTQ families: children, siblings, parents, grandparents, and other extended family members. Goldberg manages a feat that very few psychologists successfully achieve: distilling complex evidence into easily understood and actionable guidance, with great empathy and eloquence, and with forthright acknowledgment of how much we still have to learn. I would joyfully place this book into the hands of every single LGBTQ person who has ever considered parenthood.

—**LISA M. DIAMOND, PHD,** PROFESSOR OF PSYCHOLOGY AND GENDER STUDIES, UNIVERSITY OF UTAH, SALT LAKE CITY

LGBTQ FAMILY BUILDING

LGBTQ FAMILY BUILDING

A GUIDE FOR PROSPECTIVE PARENTS

ABBIE E. GOLDBERG, PHD

 AMERICAN PSYCHOLOGICAL ASSOCIATION

Published by
American Psychological Association
750 First Street, NE
Washington, DC 20002
https://www.apa.org

Order Department
https://www.apa.org/pubs/books
order@apa.org

In the U.K., Europe, Africa, and the Middle East, copies may be ordered from Eurospan
https://www.eurospanbookstore.com/apa
info@eurospangroup.com

Typeset in Sabon by Circle Graphics, Inc., Reisterstown, MD

Printer: Sheridan Books, Chelsea, MI
Cover Designer: Mark Karis

Library of Congress Cataloging-in-Publication Data

Names: Goldberg, Abbie E., author. | American Psychological Association
Title: LGBTQ family building : a guide for prospective parents / BY Abbie
   E. Goldberg.
Description: Washington, DC : American Psychological Association, 2022. |
   Includes bibliographical references and index.
Identifiers: LCCN 2021047275 (print) | LCCN 2021047276 (ebook) | ISBN
   9781433833922 (paperback) | ISBN 9781433839542 (ebook)
Subjects: LCSH: Sexual minority parents. | Sexual minorities' families. |
   Parenthood.
Classification: LCC HQ75.27 .G64 2022 (print) | LCC HQ75.27 (ebook) | DDC
   306.874086/6—dc23/eng/20211013
LC record available at https://lccn.loc.gov/2021047275
LC ebook record available at https://lccn.loc.gov/2021047276

https://doi.org/10.1037/0000291-000

Printed in the United States of America

10 9 8 7 6 5 4 3 2 1

CONTENTS

Contents

PREFACE

I have written many journal articles and even a few books about lesbian, gay, bisexual, transgender (trans), queer (LGBTQ) parenthood, including building families through adoption and insemination. Yet over the years, it became increasingly obvious to me that my undergraduate and graduate students, friends, family members, and acquaintances—who sometimes asked me for input or advice about family building—were simply not going to pick up these materials, which were too academic, hard to access, or expensive. My passion lies in making the process of building families easier for LGBTQ folks, and it was evident to me I was not very successful in "giving psychology away" (or "giving research away")—at least not as successful as I would like to be. As I began to write more accessible books and articles, I realized that I could indeed write an accessible book that was not "fluffy" and overly simplistic but actually grounded in research findings and my accumulated knowledge. This is my attempt to do just that.

This book is ultimately the culmination of years of work and numerous collaborative relationships. I am ever grateful to the more than 500 research participants who took the LGBTQ Family Building Project Survey (Goldberg, 2021) and generously shared their experiences and perspectives, often recounting powerful and, in some cases, painful details of their lives. It is my privilege to be able to read your words and share your voices in this book.

I am also grateful to the hundreds of LGBTQ research participants who have been a part of my life and my work for the past 20 years, including my longitudinal study of the transition to parenthood among female couples using donor insemination; my longitudinal, ongoing study of the transition to adoptive parenthood; my study of families' experiences using reproductive technologies and different types of sperm donors; and my study of trans adults' educational and family-building plans and desires. You have made a difference.

ACKNOWLEDGMENTS

I am wildly indebted to Chris Kelaher, Tyler Aune, and Katherine Lenz, my editorial team at the American Psychological Association (APA). Chris and I spent several years talking about the possibility of doing a book like this, and it was his gentle prodding and dedicated faith in me that finally pushed me to seriously contemplate it and ultimately commit to it. I am grateful to these three powerhouses and the rest of the APA staff for their consistently positive yet constructive feedback. They supported my vision for this book and helped me to make it a reality.

I am also grateful to the three anonymous reviewers for the original proposal for this book. They provided me with important formative feedback, which I took seriously.

A separate group of three anonymous reviewers provided me with feedback on the book itself. These three reviewers clearly possessed different vantage points, areas of expertise, and disciplinary backgrounds as well as different social locations and identities. I benefited immensely from their unique perspectives, thoughtful and careful engagement with the book, and insightful feedback. I feel incredibly lucky to have received their generous input.

Throughout the writing of the book, I was fortunate to benefit from the feedback of several friends and colleagues. Davis Chandler blessed me with insightful feedback on every chapter of this book, drawing from their personal experience as a nonbinary and queer gestational parent as well as a therapist who specializes in working with lesbian, gay, bisexual, transgender (trans), queer (LGBTQ) parents and youths. I could not ask for a more generous and thoughtful reader and thinker. I consider Davis to be a thought partner in this book. Davis is also a coauthor with Damon M. Constantinides and Shannon L. Sennott of the 2019 book *Sex Therapy With Erotically Marginalized Clients: Nine Principles of Clinical Support*. Indeed, this book also benefited from important, engaging conversations with, and thoughtful input by, Shannon Sennott, a writer, scholar, and therapist who also specializes in working with LGBTQ people. I am grateful to Joanna Scheib, who directs the research program at The Sperm Bank of California and who is well known for her scholarship on the psychosocial issues involved in the use of reproductive technologies. Joanna provided input on several chapters in this book, which were inevitably strengthened by her extensive knowledge and sensitivity regarding reproductive technologies and the people who use them.

Although less tangible and specific, the generous contributions of my friends and family have also enabled me to write this book. I am incredibly lucky to be inspired by multiple LGBTQ members of my family whose parenthood statuses include "yes," "nope," and "remains to be seen." For those in the last category—in my family and beyond it—I write this book for you. May you have choices, and may you feel empowered to make the best choice for yourself.

LGBTQ
FAMILY
BUILDING

INTRODUCTION

The path to becoming a parent is complicated for LGBTQ[1] people. Some LGBTQ people are inhibited from seriously considering parenthood because of societal stereotypes and obstacles that make parenthood seem inaccessible or even impossible. Some are interested in parenthood but unsure about the first steps to take, uncertain what path is the best fit for them, or lack certain resources they feel are important to acquire (e.g., financial stability, a partner) before actively pursuing parenthood. Some LGBTQ people feel they would be good parents (e.g., they have a lot to offer, they have always wanted to be parents) but are discouraged by the attitudes of their family, community, or religion that have treated their gender identity or sexual orientation as liabilities, and they are made to feel that becoming a parent would be "unfair" to a child.

---

[1]The abbreviation "LGBTQ" refers to lesbian, gay, bisexual, transgender (trans), and queer people. *Transgender*, or *trans*, refers to people who have a gender identity that differs from the sex that they were assigned at birth. *Nonbinary* people, who may consider themselves to be trans or part of the trans community, are people whose gender identities fall outside of or beyond the gender binary of male/female.

Yet research points to the many strengths that LGBTQ people bring to parenthood, including freedom to define their own roles as parents, a tendency to share parenting responsibilities more equally than cisgender[2] (cis[3]) heterosexual folks, a deep appreciation for (i.e., not "taking for granted") the possibility of parenthood, and personal experiences with stigma and discrimination that may foster resilience and empathy (e.g., toward their children; Brown et al., 2009; Goldberg, Gartrell, & Gates, 2014; Titlestad & Robinson, 2019). Furthermore, research is consistent in finding that children with LGBTQ parents are not "disadvantaged" by their parents' sexual orientation and gender identity; in fact, the children may benefit in unique ways (e.g., they may be more open to and tolerant of various aspects of difference or diversity; Goldberg, Gartrell, & Gates, 2014; Goldberg & Smith, 2013; Perrin et al., 2013). Rather, the key challenges and barriers that LGBTQ parent families face are societal—in the form of laws, policies, and attitudes that stigmatize LGBTQ people and their families. But LGBTQ people who wish to pursue parenthood do need to consider a variety of unique factors and be prepared for a potentially complex set of decisions and steps. Furthermore, the process of becoming a parent may differ in important ways from that of most heterosexual, cisgender (cis) folks—and there may be more challenges and stumbling blocks along the way.

---

[2]The *Oxford English Dictionary* describes *cisgender* as an adjective and defines it as "designating a person whose sense of personal identity corresponds to the sex and gender assigned to him or her at birth" (Green, 2015, para. 3). For an interesting history and commentary on the word's inclusion in the *Oxford English Dictionary*, see Brydum's (2015) article "The True Meaning of the Word 'Cisgender'" in *The Advocate*.

[3]*Cis* describes a person whose gender identity aligns with what they were assigned at birth. *Heterosexual*, or "straight," generally refers to attraction to people of a different gender.

Most books on family building, becoming a parent, and early parenthood are aimed at heterosexual couples in which both partners identify as cis. These books also typically assume biological parenthood. Certainly, books like *What to Expect When You're Expecting* (Murkoff et al., 2018) are useful and play an important role in preparing for various aspects of parenthood, such as swaddling, diapering, and feeding. But they typically do not address the unique family-building decisions, pathways, and experiences of LGBTQ people. Furthermore, they make assumptions and use language that may be invalidating to LGBTQ people. They also rarely address considerations like choosing a sperm donor; deciding who should become pregnant (when both people in a couple are capable of becoming pregnant); evaluating adoption options; establishing and maintaining contact with birth families in open adoptions; choosing LGBTQ-friendly health care providers, adoption agencies, and day care providers; and addressing many other topics that are relevant to the LGBTQ family-building experience.

In this book, you will learn about the various steps and decision points in becoming a parent. You will also be offered a variety of self-assessment tools—for example, questions to ask yourself to help aid introspection related to family-building desires, motivations, and options. Becoming a parent is a major life decision, and this book is designed to help you engage with that decision: the "if," the "how," the "when," and all that comes after. Likewise, you will find a variety of questions and checklists to help you evaluate the LGBTQ friendliness and overall "fit" of adoption agencies, health care providers, day cares, and other institutions.

In this book, you will also learn about the research findings on LGBTQ family building. This research can be an important tool when trying to battle stereotypes or myths about LGBTQ parenting—either those you hear, or have internalized, from society, your community, your religion, or your parents. For example, maybe you have the idea that you shouldn't be a parent or don't deserve to be a parent. As one parent in my LGBTQ Family Building Project (which you will learn about in a moment), shared,

> I came from a very conservative, Evangelical Christian background, and was told that I was a danger to children when I came out. When deciding to become a parent, fostering and adopting domestically [seemed right] for me. I [rationalized] it as, "I can't really be a big danger to children who have had intense abuse and neglect as their other parenting option." I think I felt that my mother and sibling would react better to that than private adoption—an "undamaged" child—or to insemination strategies—clearly against the "natural" order of things.

This book offers parents and prospective parents evidence-based knowledge that directly challenges the kinds of beliefs that this participant refers to—beliefs that have frequently been weaponized against LGBTQ people, often discouraging or preventing them from becoming parents.

STRUCTURE OF THE BOOK

Each chapter in this book begins with a vignette of LGBTQ prospective parents or parents at different stages of their family-building and parenting journey and ends with a list of further resources.[4]

Chapter 1 addresses the process of deciding to become a parent, motivations for parenthood, potential barriers to parenthood, and resources for parenthood.

---

[4]The case studies are composites of research participants, interviewees, and therapy clients, and all names and relevant identifying information have been disguised to protect confidentiality.

Chapter 2 addresses choosing adoption, as well as choosing among public domestic, private domestic, and international adoption. It also examines race, gender, and other preferences in adoption, and it provides a brief overview of legal issues.

Chapter 3 explores the choice of donor insemination over adoption, choosing who will be pregnant or be genetically related to the child, choosing a sperm donor, and finding LGBTQ-competent providers. It provides an overview of specific considerations for nonbinary and trans masculine folks who pursue pregnancy.

Chapter 4 addresses the choice of surrogacy and the process of pursuing it. It also covers how to manage genetic asymmetry between parents and other parenthood routes not addressed elsewhere, namely, coparenting arrangements, cis/heteronormative sex,[5] and stepparenting.

Chapter 5 discusses choosing adoption agencies, fertility centers, ob-gyns, and midwives. In particular, the discussion attends to LGBTQ inclusiveness but also addresses other considerations (e.g., agency/clinic effectiveness, professional ethics).

Chapter 6 explores the transition to parenthood. It considers shifts in mental health, relationship quality, division of labor, and social support, including friends and family.

Chapter 7 addresses choosing day cares and schools, preparing for and preparing children for heterosexist bias, and navigating gender normativity pressures in society. It also discusses how to deal with other parenting challenges in early parenthood.[6]

---

[5]*Cis/heteronormative sex* refers to sexual (penile–vaginal) intercourse.
[6]Because this book is primarily aimed at addressing issues related to family building as opposed to parenting older children and adolescents, Chapter 7 ends with resources on parenting children at later stages of the family life cycle.

THE LGBTQ FAMILY BUILDING PROJECT

Throughout the book, you will be presented with data—numbers and quotes—from LGBTQ parents themselves. These data are from the LGBTQ Family Building Project (Goldberg, 2021), a survey that I undertook specifically *for* this book. I wanted to be able to supplement the research and guidance and tools that I discuss with contemporary data gathered from LGBTQ parents who took diverse routes to parenthood.

Importantly, the data were gathered July 2020 through February 2021 during a period of notable transition and upheaval in the United States—the COVID-19 pandemic and also before, during, and after, the 2020 election of President Joseph R. Biden Jr., and the subsequent departure of President Donald J. Trump from the White House. This is important context, given that the COVID-19 pandemic has had widespread impacts on the well-being of families in general but LGBTQ parent families in particular, who may be even more vulnerable to the economic and mental health consequences of the pandemic amid preexisting income inequities, discrimination burden, and parenting stress (Goldberg et al., 2021; Medina & Mahowald, 2021). Furthermore, LGBTQ parent families have been deeply affected by living through 4 years of a Trump administration—an administration that was characterized by near constant attacks on LGBTQ people's rights and liberties (Human Rights Campaign, n.d.-c).

Details about the LGBTQ Family Building Project and the 543 participants who completed the survey appear in Appendix A. A little more than two thirds of participants were cisgender women, 17.5% were cisgender men, and 14.5% were trans or nonbinary. A total of 82% were White, and 18% were of color, including biracial and multiracial. Among the 88% of participants with partners, 72% of their partners were White and 28% were of color. A total of 42% of participants identified as lesbians; 20%, as queer; 19%, as gay; 14%, as bisexual; 3%, as pansexual;[7] 1%, as asexual;[8] and the remainder, as something else. More than three quarters of participants worked full-time, and 90% had at least a college education. They lived in 44 U.S. states, with a small number (fewer than 5%) living outside the United States, predominantly in Canada and Europe. Participants had between one and six children: 47.5% had one child, 40.5% had two, 7% had three, and the remainder had from four to six children. Regarding child age, 42.5% had at least one child aged 5 years or younger, 36% had at least one child aged 6 to 10 years old, 35% had at least one child aged 11 to 15 years, 10.5% had at least one child aged 16 to 18 years, and 9% had at least one child older than 18. Of the participants, 60% used donor insemination or surrogacy to become parents, 32% used adoption or foster care, 6% used cis/heteronormative sex, and 5% were stepparents.

OTHER KEY FEATURES OF THE BOOK

This book contains not only data from the LGBTQ Family Building Project, but it is grounded in the empirical research on LGBTQ family building more broadly. It offers a variety of assessment tools, questions to ask yourself or your partner(s), fast facts about the different aspects of LGBTQ family building and parenting, and numerous resources to further your knowledge and understanding of the many aspects of LGBTQ parenting. The book also emphasizes specific considerations for trans and nonbinary prospective parents and parents.

---

[7] *Pansexual* refers to attraction (physical, emotional, or romantic) to people of all genders. It can be contrasted with *bisexual*, which means being attracted to more than one gender; being pansexual means being attracted to all gender identities or attracted to people independent or regardless of gender.
[8] Asexuality exists on a spectrum, but, in general, people who identify as *asexual* experience little or no sexual attraction to other people.

In recognition of the important history of LGBTQ parenting—including legal milestones and key figures in the battle for LGBTQ parenting rights—Appendix B contains a time line of key events in the history of LGBTQ parenting. This time line was compiled by Dana Rudolph, the creator and founder of Mombian (see https://mombian.com), one of the longest running LGBTQ parenting blogs that also serves as a clearinghouse for a wide range of resources and articles related to LGBTQ parenting. (For folks interested in a more in-depth account of LGBTQ parenting dating back to the 1950s, see Daniel Winunwe Rivers's 2013 book *Radical Relations: Lesbian Mothers, Gay Fathers, & Their Children in the United States Since World War II.* The book does not address bisexual or trans parents in depth, but it does provide a detailed account of the early struggles and triumphs as well as a largely hidden history of lesbian and gay parents.)

ONWARD . . .

As you explore the following pages, remember that this book is the beginning—and not the end—of your parenting journey. There are many choices and decisions to make, as well as much to consider. But, thanks to the pioneering LGBTQ parents who have made this journey over the past 5 decades in particular, you are well positioned to learn from their experiences and forge the road ahead with confidence. As Chapter 1 details, more and more LGBTQ young people are considering parenthood for themselves. Indeed, the possibilities for parenthood are expanding, and it's time to get started.

CHAPTER 1

DECIDING TO BECOME
A PARENT

THIS CHAPTER COVERS:

> deciding to become a parent for LGBTQ people
> motivations for parenthood
> obstacles to parenthood
> resources for parenthood

Marion and Ellie are a lesbian couple who have been together for 5 years and live outside of a major city on the East Coast. Marion, a White, cisgender, 33-year-old social worker, has always known she wanted to be a parent. She has several younger siblings and spent much of her childhood babysitting them and other neighborhood children. Ellie, a biracial (White/Latinx), cisgender, 29-year-old retail manager, never considered becoming a parent until she met Marion. She enjoys her status as "Auntie" to her brothers' children but worries about what she will lose if she is to become a parent, including an active social life and her involvement in a local cycling club.

For a long time, Marion and Ellie discussed parenthood only as a future "hypothetical." However, when Marion turned 33, she began to feel a greater sense of urgency regarding parenthood and the possibility of getting pregnant. One day, after they attended a friend's baby shower, Marion told Ellie that she wanted to become a parent "within the next year." Ellie was taken aback. She reiterated her concerns about all that she would have to give up if they were to become parents together and acknowledged that she really had never seen herself as a parent. However, Ellie emphasized that she loved and was committed to Marion and agreed to give it some thought. A few days later, Ellie said that she was open to "giving it a try" but stressed that she had "no interest" in being pregnant herself.

Marion is excited about Ellie's willingness to consider parenthood but is also concerned that Ellie may not be equally committed to parenthood. Marion feels stuck: Should they move forward or hit pause? Should they go to couples therapy? Should Marion go to individual therapy to figure out if she should even stay in the relationship if, indeed, Ellie is not fully on board with becoming a parent?

WHO WANTS TO BE A PARENT?

The reality is that lesbian, gay, bisexual, transgender (trans), and queer (LGBTQ) people are increasingly interested in becoming, and being, parents. As therapists Arlene Istar Lev and Shannon Sennott (Lev & Sennott, 2020) pointed out, contemporary LGBTQ young adults are growing up in an era when LGBTQ parenthood is more visible and achievable than in decades past, making it more of an issue of "Do I want to?" than "Can I?" (more on that later). *The Fosters* (Paige et al., 2013–2018) and *Modern Family* (Levitan et al., 2009–2020) are two contemporary TV shows that feature lesbian, gay, bisexual, and queer (LGBQ) parent (and multiracial) families, with LGBQ parenting also receiving airtime—albeit less centrally—on earlier shows, such as *Friends* (Bright et al., 1994–2004), *The L Word* (Chaiken et al., 2004–2009), and *Six Feet Under* (Greenblatt et al., 2001–2005). Trans parenthood has received more limited attention, such as in *Transparent* (Soloway et al., 2014–2019), a contemporary TV show that ran for 6 years. In turn, children born in the past 2 decades are being exposed to greater media representation of LGBTQ parenting than in decades past, thus modeling various pathways to parenthood as well as serving to normalize the notion of LGBTQ parenthood more broadly.

Contemporary LGBTQ young adults and adults may be less likely to aspire or intend to become parents than their heterosexual cis counterparts, but this gap is narrowing (Riskind & Tornello, 2017; Shenkman et al., 2019; Tate et al., 2019). A 2019 survey of LGBTQ adults by the organization Family Equality (Harris & Winn, 2019) found that about half of LGBTQ people between the ages of 18 to 35 planned to become parents for the first time or add more children to their family compared with 55% among heterosexual cis people—a much smaller gap than in prior decades. Furthermore, the survey determined similar rates of family planning across income levels, suggesting that the desire to have children is not bounded by financial security—although finances are clearly a factor in determining which parenthood route individuals pursue and their success in doing so. Although individuals making less than $25,000 per year were considering becoming a parent at similar rates as those making more than $100,000 per year, individuals in the upper income bracket were much more likely to consider private adoption or in vitro fertilization (IVF)[1] than those in the lower income bracket,

---

[1]*IVF* is a procedure in which the egg and sperm meet outside of the body in a petri dish and then the fertilized egg is placed into the uterus, usually in cases of infertility and always by a health care provider. Other forms of artificial insemination (also historically referred to as "alternative insemination") include *intrauterine insemination*, in which the sperm is placed into the uterus via a small tube that is passed up the cervix and into the uterus by a health care provider. The sperm need to be "washed" by a sperm bank to remove dead sperm and proteins that would cause cramping when inserted. *Intracervical insemination* involves placing the sperm into the cervix via a

who were predominantly considering cis/heteronormative sex, foster care, and adoption.

Yet, even as it becomes seen as more "normative" in society, LGBTQ family building typically *does* involve considerable consideration, deliberation, and planning. The path to becoming a parent involves a number of steps, which can be complex—but which you will learn more about in this book.

WHY DO YOU WANT TO BECOME A PARENT?

This is a simple question, yet one that cisgender heterosexual folks might not fully engage with. After all, parenthood as a valued life goal is frequently assumed—so much so that a cis heterosexual person who declares that they do *not* want to become a parent may be treated with suspicion or even derision. Of course, the assumption that people want to become parents and the assumption that it is easy to do so reveal the power of heteronormativity. *Heteronormativity* is a system that seeks to uphold heterosexuality as the only "normal"—and therefore taken-for-granted—sexual orientation. Heteronormativity entails a convergence of three sets of binary "opposites": (a) males and females versus gender deviants, (b) normal or natural (hetero)sexuality versus sexual deviants, and (c) normal or natural (heterosexual, biological) parent families versus deviant families (Oswald et al., 2005). The heteronormative family is traditionally gendered, White, and middle- to upper middle-class, and is characterized by biological parent–child relationships (Smith,

---

small tube. It can be done by a health care provider or at home using a specially designed syringe. In this procedure, the sperm does not need to be washed. *Intravaginal insemination* occurs when the sperm is placed into the vagina with a syringe; this is often done at home by the individual or with the help of partner(s). For more details, see Spalding (2019).

1993). In turn, people in general are assumed to be heterosexual; expected to marry people of the "other" gender; and expected to procreate with their monogamous, different-gender partners.

LGBTQ people by their very nature exist outside of the sexual (and perhaps gender) binary and, often, the family binary in that any families they create will be considered "deviant"—that is, if their children are not conceived by a "real" man and a "real" woman in a heterosexual procreative context. Likewise, LGBTQ people are not assumed to *want* to be parents as cis heterosexual people are. This lack of assumed parenthood, coupled with various obstacles to parenthood for LGBTQ people, means that LGBTQ people may be more likely to engage in self-exploration regarding the "ifs, hows, and whys" of becoming parents. This process of questioning and exploration, however, is one that perhaps all people should engage in: No one should assume parenthood as the default—for themselves or for others—because parenthood just isn't right for everyone! Yet parenthood is not simply less of a "given" for LGBTQ folks. Indeed, one of the inevitable downsides of developing and living within a heteronormative world is that becoming a parent is also much harder for LGBTQ folks because medical institutions— including those that control access to reproductive technologies—as well as adoption agencies, the legal system, and other systems are often rooted in heteronormative assumptions and practices that disadvantage LGBTQ parent families.

Motivation

Ultimately, LGBTQ people who decide to become parents do so for many of the same reasons as cis heterosexual people. But, by virtue of not being expected to pursue parenthood in the same way that heterosexual people are, as well as the extra work that may be required to make parenthood a reality, they often engage in an intentional, deliberate decision-making process related to parent-hood. In turn, their motivations for parenthood and the obstacles they can face in pursuing it may differ in meaningful ways from those experienced by cis heterosexual people.

A 2012 study (Goldberg, Downing, & Moyer, 2012) provided insight into reasons for wanting to become a parent among LGBQ people. To answer the question "How do gay men choose to become parents?" the research team interviewed 70 men in same-gender relationships who had recently become parents through adoption. Most men explained that they wanted to become parents because they believed it would be psychologically and personally rewarding. They discussed their valuing of family connections, enjoyment of children, sense that raising children is a natural part of life, desire to give a child a good home, and interest in teaching a child tolerance as key motivations to parent. Significantly, the first three of these reasons (valuing of family, love of children, belief that children are a part of life) are common to heterosexual parents as well as lesbian parents (Dion, 1995; Langdridge et al., 2005; Lewin, 1993; Siegenthaler & Bigner, 2000). The desire to give a child a good home was seemingly specific to the men's chosen route to parenthood or adoption, and the desire to have an effect on the world by raising a tolerant child was seemingly—at least in part—specific to their status as sexual minorities. A small number of men also said that they were becoming a parent because it was their partner's dream or goal, and a few men said that concern for their future security and well-being impacted their decision to pursue parenthood.

So, what about LGBQ women who also exist outside of the heteronormative parenting ideal by typically pursuing parenthood alone or with another woman (or person with a uterus)? Their parenting motivations look similar to those of the gay men in this 2012 study (Goldberg, Downing, & Moyer, 2012) but also differ in ways that may reflect their gendered socialization as women. A 1993 study (Lewin, 1993) of 73 lesbian mothers and 62 heterosexual mothers found that both groups articulated psychologically oriented reasons, such as the belief in parenthood as an important part of personal development. But the participants in this study also endorsed gender-related reasons, such as the belief that motherhood enables one to achieve the status of a complete woman. Likewise, a 2000 study (Siegenthaler & Bigner, 2000) of 25 lesbian mothers and 25 heterosexual mothers found that both groups emphasized happiness and affection and role-related reasons as motives for parenthood, but lesbians were less focused on "generativity" (i.e., the continuation of one's genetic line through childbearing) and "the passing on of family tradition" than heterosexual women. Thus, lesbians' motivations for parenthood may be less tied to heteronormative notions regarding motherhood as a necessary aspect of female identity development.

Research shows that LGBTQ people may also want to become parents for a variety of other reasons (Goldberg & Scheib, 2015). They may wish to be experience pregnancy or birth (something we return to later). They may wish to participate in the "queering" of parenthood, whereby gendered and heteronormative models for building families and rearing children are destabilized. They may also wish to become parents simply because they believe they have the personal qualities (e.g., accepting, empathic, affirming) to raise confident and tolerant "good citizens" of the world (Goldberg, 2010a; Goldberg & Scheib, 2015; Lev, 2004; Riggs, 2007). Some LGBTQ people—like cis heterosexual people—find the question of why they want to become a parent challenging to answer. It is hard to articulate the incalculable and visceral desire to be a parent that characterizes some people's experience. "I just wanted to," "It was something I always wanted to do," and "My biological clock was ticking," for example, were all common responses by participants in the LGBTQ Family Building Project (Goldberg, 2021).[2] The limited research on trans and nonbinary people's parenthood aspirations and motivations also highlights how, for many, parenthood is a lifelong dream or fantasy that is difficult to put into words—and is further complicated for trans and nonbinary folks, who especially wrestle with the reality that dominant ideas of parenthood are inherently gendered (mother/father) and potentially at odds with their own ideas of parenthood for themselves (Tasker & Gato, 2020).

Other Considerations: Questions to Ask Yourself

As important as it is to articulate all of the very good reasons why LGBTQ people might want to become parents, it is also worthwhile to consider what all people, including LGBTQ people, are giving up or forgoing when they become parents. In considering parenthood, it may be useful for you to consider the following questions alone or with your partner(s), if relevant (Rosenhaus, 2020):

- Do I enjoy spending time with children? Do I enjoy guiding and caring for others?
- Am I ready to put a child's needs before my own?
- Do I have a stable job and housing situation?
- Am I financially prepared to be a parent, including taking on the costs of becoming a parent as well as raising a child?
- If partnered: Is my relationship strong and stable? Is my partner similarly committed and willing to embark on this journey with me? Are we prepared for the changes that a child will introduce into our relationship?

---

[2]The LGBTQ Family Building Project is the study outlined in the Introduction to this book in which Goldberg (2021) surveyed more than 500 LGBTQ parents. For more information, see Appendix A.

- Will I need to rely on family or friends for housing or help raising a child?
- What are my long-term goals and how do they dovetail with raising a child?
- How will a child impact my life? What will change? Am I ready to make these changes?
- Will I experience regret or loss if I do not become a parent?

You might also wish to engage in a number of different exercises to help you to determine whether you want to become a parent (Gibson, 2019). For example:

- Live in the "yes" for a week (imagine that you have decided to become a parent) and then live in the "no" for a week (imagine that you have decided not to). Write down all of your thoughts, feelings, and questions as they come up.
- Write in a journal, using one color when you have a feeling of excitement or joy about becoming a parent and using a different color when you are considering reasons not to become, or are leaning toward not becoming, a parent. After a week or two, consider both the frequency and type of feelings that you are having surrounding parenthood.

Returning to the opening vignette, it might be beneficial for Marion and Ellie to individually engage in these exercises. They also might discuss their findings with a trained couples therapist.

OBSTACLES TO PARENTHOOD

LGBTQ people may be increasingly likely to consider or aspire to parenthood, but they are also more likely than cis heterosexual people to expect that they might not achieve it because of various

Barriers to Pursuing Parenthood

In the LGBTQ Family Building Project (Goldberg, 2021), more than 500 parents were asked about a variety of potential barriers or obstacles to parenthood. Here is what they endorsed:

Stigma and Support-Related Barriers

- Worries about teasing/harm for children: 35%
- Worries about other stressors (e.g., racism) for children: 22%
- Worries about discrimination in the family-building process: 30%
- Lack of LGBTQ role models: 25%
- Lack of support from family: 22%
- Internalized homophobia/biphobia/transphobia: 12%
- Lack of support from employer/work: 11%
- Lack of support from therapists/health providers: 10%
- Lack of support from friends: 8%

Structural/Practical Barriers

- Financial considerations: 58%
- Geographic considerations (e.g., LGBTQ-hostile or unsafe area): 18%
- Employment status: 15%
- Living situation (e.g., apartment, with roommates): 11%

Personal Circumstances

- Personal maturity/readiness: 22%
- Health concerns: 19%
- Partner uninterested in parenthood: 10%
- No partner: 9%

Other Barriers

Age ("felt we were too old"), work–family balance concerns, live far from family, worries about political climate, legal barriers, partner's mental health issues, health insurance issues

> "My partner and me were born in the late 70s and early 80s. Some of our earliest memories of gay representation were the AIDS crisis. Other than that, we never [had] any real representation as young children [of] gay relationships in a positive light, where it didn't end in pain, death, and sadness.
>
> And gay families? Not even a conversation. There was no representation for what gay relationships or families looked like. Nothing positive. But my partner and I both always wanted kids, and we were fortunate enough to have amazing families that rallied around us and gave us support, love, and acceptance. And we told ourselves: We will be the role model if that's what needs to happen."
>
> —PARTICIPANT IN THE LGBTQ FAMILY BUILDING PROJECT

challenges and barriers (Tate & Patterson, 2019). LGBTQ people face a number of obstacles to becoming a parent, with some common to parenthood in general and some specific to particular family-building routes.

Sexual Stigma and Discrimination

A primary barrier to parenthood for LGBTQ people is sexual stigma and discrimination, which operate on multiple levels and create a stressful social environment for LGBTQ people, possibly leading to expectations of discrimination and rejection, concealment of sexual orientation or gender identity, internalized stigma, and other negative outcomes (Meyer, 2003). This stigma manifests itself in discriminatory laws and policies, such as in faith-based adoption agencies' explicit disallowing of LGBTQ applicants, as well as institutional practices, such as health care professionals' failure to consider that patients might not be cis or heterosexual, or health insurance carriers' coverage of infertility-related procedures only when there is evidence of a lengthy period of "unprotected sex" between partners. Stigma also manifests itself in the attitudes and behaviors of LGBTQ people's friends and family members and may also be internalized by LGBTQ people themselves. One example or manifestation of sexual stigma (Herek, 2007) is the heteronormative belief that all children need a mother and a father to grow up to be successful, healthy, and productive adults, not to mention "normal" (i.e., heterosexual and cisgender). The accompanying presumption is often that LGBTQ people cannot be good parents and thus do not deserve to be parents. But resistance to LGBTQ people becoming parents is not simply rooted in the societal preference for a mother–father home and the corresponding panic about the development, sexual orientation, and gender identity of children raised by two moms, two dads, or parents who identify outside the gender binary. Resistance to queer and trans parenthood is also grounded in erroneous conflations of homosexuality, bisexuality, and trans identification with mental illness, unstable relationships, and even pedophilia. Decades of empirical research have been important in debunking such associations and consistently showing the positive qualities and characteristics of LGBTQ parents and their children (Goldberg, 2010a; Goldberg, Gartrell, & Gates, 2014), but stereotypes and ignorance prevail, and such myths still characterize and invade the belief systems of various institutions and individuals.

Internalized Stigmas

This kind of stigma may be internalized by LGBTQ people and can, therefore, act as a barrier to parenthood. LGBTQ people may wonder about—and even, on some level, *believe*—negative stereotypes of LGBTQ people, including that they are fundamentally "broken," deviant, or unstable; that they will not be good parents; and that their children will be angry at them for bringing them into the world or adopting them. In the LGBTQ Family Building Project, 12% of parents said that internalized homophobia/biphobia/transphobia was a barrier to pursuing parenthood (e.g., they worried they would be "less good" as a queer parent). In addition, more than one third (35%) said that worries about teasing or harm that a child of LGBTQ parents might endure was a barrier, and 22% identified worries about other stressors that a child might deal with (e.g., racism, classism, anti-Semitism) as a barrier.

Before moving forward in becoming parents, you should examine your own internalized stigmas and consider how they have played out over the course of your life. For example, what stigmatizing beliefs about LGBTQ people were you exposed to as a youth and young adult? How have these stigmas impacted your sense of self and behaviors? How have you managed to challenge such stigmas? Consider, for example, whether any of the following are true for you (Eliason & Schope, 2007; D. M. Frost & Meyer, 2009; Revel & Riot, n.d.):

- You have felt contempt, disgust, or shame toward LGBTQ people who don't "blend in."
- You have engaged in *gender policing*, that is, shaming others for not fitting into sexual/gender binaries.
- You find yourself judging or feeling embarrassed by celebrities who are "too" gay or "too" butch.
- You have experienced shame about your sexual experiences or attractions.
- You have tried to or wished to change your sexual orientation.
- You have asked a partner to keep secrets for you or stay in the closet with you or for you.

Individuals who realize early in life that they are LGBTQ but lack affirming family members and friends and access to an LGBTQ community are more likely to experience internalized sexual/gender stigma. Access to supports, including positive LGBTQ role models, are necessary to offset the harm done by living in a heterosexist, homophobic, biphobic, and transphobic society. Likewise, LGBTQ individuals who have affirming parents, live in geographic regions with LGBTQ-inclusive laws and policies, attend LGBTQ-inclusive schools, or are part of an active and affirming LGBTQ community may be less vulnerable to internalizing such negative societal attitudes (Bhattacharya et al., 2021).

Internalized homophobia (or homonegativity), biphobia (binegativity), and transphobia (transnegativity) are also impacted by a range of personal identities and social locations, including race, ethnicity, socioeconomic status, religion, religiosity, gender identity, gender expression, and (dis)ability status. For example, a gender nonconforming Black gay man who was raised in an Evangelical church may experience a unique set of internalized beliefs surrounding homosexuality/queer sexualities that are affected by their various identities and community influences. Furthermore, gender and sexuality intersect to shape the nature of internalized stigmas. A gay man must grapple with the unique historical stigmas surrounding gay men, including myths of gay men as child predators and myths of HIV/AIDS as a "gay disease," whereas a bisexual woman must navigate stereotypes unique to bisexuality, such as the idea that bisexual people are indecisive and hypersexual, as well as the erasure and invisibility of bisexuality within broader society and the LGBTQ community specifically.

To effectively deal with and overcome internalized stigma, you can engage in a variety of exercises and activities. These include (Revel & Riot, n.d.)

- thinking critically about the role of internalized stigma in your life rather than simply rejecting its relevance outright;

- reading memoirs, blogs, and other texts written by LGBTQ people, in which they narrate their process of exploring and accepting their sexual orientation and gender identity;
- building a community network of LGBTQ people and allies to access and receive compassion, insight, support, and mentorship;
- learning about the history of the LGBTQ rights movement to gain insight into its diverse voices and histories;
- finding an LGBTQ-affirming or LGBTQ-identified therapist;
- considering a departure from your religion or religious institution if it is not accepting;
- removing yourself from invalidating influences, including family, religion, and friends;
- practicing self-awareness, including any critical or judgmental inner dialogue about oneself or others related to sexuality, sexual orientation, or gender identity and expression, and exploring the source of such negative self-talk;
- recognizing that internalized stigmas are not your fault and originated elsewhere; and
- appreciating and respecting the diversity and visibility of the LGBTQ community.

It is especially crucial to examine internalized stigmas as they relate to parenthood. LGBTQ people may internalize the notion that LGBTQ people are not good parents or don't deserve to take on that role, and they will inevitably raise children who themselves will be distressed or damaged by having LGBTQ parents. In a 2014 study of adoptive parents in Britain, some lesbian, gay, bisexual parents recalled feeling "worried that their children might be disadvantaged or stigmatized" and "concerned that fulfilling their desire to parent would not be in the best interests of a child" (Jennings et al., 2014, p. 215). And, again, more than one third of LGBTQ people in the LGBTQ Family Building Project voiced worries related to children's being teased or otherwise experiencing harm because of their family structure as a barrier to becoming a parent, with more than one in five endorsing concerns about other forms of stigma, such as racism ("I was worried about my children experiencing discrimination/ bullying for having two mothers on top of [being] adopted and being of different ethnicities and races").

It is important for LGBTQ people to acknowledge these worries or beliefs; recognize where they come from; and seek out information, resources, and research that counter them. This book, for example, offers parents and prospective parents evidence-based knowledge that directly challenges these beliefs, which have often been wielded against LGBTQ people to discourage or undermine their parenting aspirations. It is also important to recognize that even after becoming a parent, you may still be plagued by these beliefs. As one parent in the LGBTQ Family Building Project said, "Even today, I often question my parenting choices. It's taken me a while to believe in my own ability as a dad."

Discrimination, Lack of Encouragement

In addition to internalized stigma, LGBTQ people who wish to become parents may face a variety of other obstacles to doing so. They may be concerned about discrimination in the family-building process, such as from adoption agencies or health providers; 30% of parents in the LGBTQ Family Building Project identified this as a barrier. A lack of encouragement and support from various sources in LGBTQ people's lives may also affect their decision making surrounding parenthood. Participants in the LGBTQ Family Building Project, for example, cited lack of support from family (22%), one's employer, supervisor, or colleagues (11%), therapists and other health care providers (10%), and friends (8%) as barriers or obstacles to parenthood.

Partner Disinterest in Parenthood

A partner's hesitation, ambivalence, or even hostility toward the possibility of parenthood may also be a barrier. Ten percent of participants in the LGBTQ Family Building Project said that this was, at some point in their lives, a barrier to pursuing parenthood. LGBTQ people—like cis heterosexual people—who are more interested in parenthood than their partner(s) should be aware that they have several options.

CHOOSE NOT TO BECOME A PARENT

LGBTQ people who choose this option may ultimately find other ways to be involved in children's lives in meaningful and important ways, such as acting as a foster parent—especially if one's partner(s) live(s) separately—or taking on a central role in the lives of nieces, nephews, or friends' children. Some individuals also find meaning in caring for children in their professional roles, such as teachers or therapists.

WAIT FOR THE HESITANT OR RELUCTANT PARENT TO BECOME MORE OPEN TO THE POSSIBILITY OF PARENTHOOD

Some degree of hesitation, ambivalence, reluctance, or fear is to be expected for many people, especially LGBTQ people, who may not have thought of themselves as parents or potential parents. Seeing a relationship therapist may be helpful in facilitating communication and perspective-taking, in general, and regarding parenthood, specifically. As therapist Arlene Istar Lev noted in her classic 2004 book *The Complete Lesbian & Gay Parenting Guide*,

> When partners feel differently about becoming parents, these issues are not easily resolved. Even when both partners desire

children, they may not agree on how to bring children into their lives [or] the number of children they want to raise. . . . In facing the important and sometimes staggering questions of whether to have children and how to do it, couples need and deserve support in learning to compromise and resolve differences. It is often useful to consider a support group for other wanna-be parents or couple counseling with a therapist trained in gay and lesbian family issues. (pp. 33–34)

Indeed, a participant in the LGBTQ Family Building Project shared this:

> Although I got baby fever when I was 25, my spouse wasn't interested in parenthood. We went to couples counseling to address the issue, and that eventually turned into a decision to pursue public adoption. In the end, we ended up in an open private newborn adoption. We chose adoption as a primary means for adding to our family because it was affordable— less so when we ended up in a private adoption, however!— because both of us had health concerns from our families, and because neither of us was interested in giving birth.

An initially reluctant partner's agreement to finally "get on board," however, does not always mean happily ever after. Another participant shared, "When I decided I was ready, I chose a partner who was not. I decided to have a kid anyway, and my partner was on board for a couple years, but it proved too much."

BECOME A PARENT ALONE

For some LGBTQ folks, a partner's lack of interest in parenthood is a sign that the relationship has an expiration date. Ending that relationship can sometimes be the beginning of one's parenthood pursuits. As one participant in the LGBTQ Family Building Project said, "I always wanted to be a parent and to adopt. My previous partner didn't want to adopt. When we separated, I started the process." Becoming a single LGBTQ parent can be challenging in unique ways. It requires having or establishing a strong support network—parents, siblings, friends, other single parents, or child care providers—as well as, ideally, a supportive and flexible workplace and financial stability.

Lack of Resources

Another possible barrier is a lack of LGBTQ parenting resources in one's immediate geographic area. In the absence of LGBTQ-friendly fertility services, adoption agencies, and the like, it is easy to feel invisible as a prospective parent or to experience fear or anxiety about potential mistreatment by local family-building services and supports. Prospective LGBTQ parents who are of color, are in consensually nonmonogamous relationships, or have disabilities may experience additional hurdles as they navigate their journey to parenthood and interface with various systems and services. (Future chapters provide questions that you can ask to gauge providers' attitudes and inclusiveness as well as suggestions that you can provide to providers to better serve you.)

Of course, it is important to emphasize that you (or a partner) may experience reluctance or lack of interest in parenthood that stems from considerations unrelated to LGBTQ-related stigmas and barriers. Perhaps you experienced family instability and chaos as a child, and you worry about how the absence of good role models for parenthood might affect your ability to be a good parent. Perhaps you have a history of mental health challenges and are concerned about how this might impact you as a parent, especially during times of intense stress. Such concerns may be worth discussing or exploring with a trusted therapist or mental health care provider.

Factors Impacting the Timing of Parenthood

A variety of factors may affect the timing of parenthood—that is, the "when." Waiting for a partner to get on board with parenting is one factor that might affect the timing of parenthood, ultimately delaying it. Age is another factor that may impact the timing of parenthood. LGBTQ people typically want to experience parenthood when they are still physically healthy and capable of being available to their children for all major life milestones. Fertility declines with age, and the likelihood of achieving a pregnancy (especially without fertility medications) decreases after age 30 and especially after age 35—and precipitously after age 40.

Finances also affect the timing of parenthood. LGBTQ people may wish to achieve some degree of financial stability, and, relatedly, housing stability (e.g., buying their own home). Some degree of savings may also be ideal—or necessary—depending on what route to parenthood LGBTQ people choose. "The financial burden of pursuing donor insemination was a major barrier, and we had to save money for a few years before starting," said one participant in the LGBTQ Family Building Project. Completion of educational goals, such as graduate school, or achieving job stability or security may also impact the timing of parenthood. In some cases, securing employment with certain health insurance benefits (e.g., fertility treatment coverage) may be viewed as a prerequisite to family building and thus impact the timing of parenthood. And, of course, personal readiness and emotional stability are key factors in determining the "when" of parenthood: People often want to be certain that they are at a stage in their personal development at which they can be generous and unselfish with their time and energy and also emotionally prepared to manage the many unexpected challenges of parenthood. In the opening vignette, some of Ellie's concerns about parenthood seemed to stem from worries about what she would have to give up in becoming a parent. It will be important for her to explore her feelings surrounding some degree of loss of freedom and autonomy, time alone and with friends, and so on.

Sometimes, too, LGBTQ folks may want to delay parenthood until they are able to move to a more LGBTQ-affirming neighborhood, state, or region to the extent that they have control over their geographic mobility at all. As one participant in the LGBTQ Family Building Project said, "We intentionally chose to move to Massachusetts for access to reproductive health care and legal protection to build a family." Sometimes, LGBTQ folks may prioritize other geographic factors that impact the timing of parenthood, such as community racial diversity, neighborhood safety, or access to "good schools."

PATHWAYS TO PARENTHOOD: A PREVIEW

Obviously, figuring out *how* to become a parent is a major decision. LGBTQ folks may consider various reproductive technologies, adoption pathways (e.g., foster care, private domestic adoption), and other pathways, with some providing fewer options and choices than others.

Choosing Reproductive Technologies

LGBQ women and trans/nonbinary folks with uteruses who have a strong desire to be pregnant, give birth, nurse/chestfeed, or be genetically connected to one's child, or whose partner has these desires, often choose to pursue parenthood with the use of reproductive technologies: donor insemination and, if necessary and deemed ethically acceptable and financially feasible, IVF, intrauterine insemination (IUI), surrogacy, or egg donation. Individuals may also wish to have biological children because they desire control over and knowledge of their children's health and development, and they are concerned about the various "unknowns" involved in adoption. Individuals with negative impressions or personal experiences of adoption or foster care, such as within their own extended family or friendship network, may also be oriented toward biological parenthood. They may consider ease and expediency, and conclude that, for example, it is easier to inseminate at home with the sperm of either a known donor[3] or sperm from a sperm bank than to pursue adoption. Adoption involves interfacing with adoption agencies, lawyers, and social workers as well as undergoing a formal evaluation and completing paperwork and programming to obtain approval of one's suitability to parent, not to mention enduring an often lengthy waiting period before being placed with a child(ren).

Gay, bisexual, and queer (GBQ) cis men who have a strong desire to be biogenetically connected to their children are similarly likely to be more oriented to surrogacy than adoption, but surrogacy is often not an option because of its high cost (more than $100,000) as well as the fact that it is not legal in all countries or states within the United States. In turn, GBQ men with a strong desire for biogenetic

---

[3]People with uteruses may opt to inseminate at home with sperm from a known donor as opposed to working with traditional medical systems because federal regulations recommend quarantining of known donor sperm (i.e., a person who is not one's spouse) for 6 months to rule out the presence of infectious disease. A downside of home insemination is that it may be less effective or successful. Of course, individuals who are pursuing IUI or IVF must necessarily work within the medical system and, in turn, need to be aware that if they are using sperm from a known donor, federal regulations recommend quarantining such sperm. This is ultimately fairly costly: A full panel of infectious disease testing is more than $1,000. For further details, see Boston IVF (n.d.) and Practice Committee of the American Society for Reproductive Medicine and the Practice Committee for the Society of Assisted Reproductive Technology (2021).

children, who also have significant financial resources and live in a place where compensated surrogacy (also called commercial surrogacy) is legal, are the most likely to pursue surrogacy.[4] Some male couples decide ahead of time which partner will provide the sperm, whereas others choose to form embryos with both partners' sperm and let fate decide who will be the biological father—or, if both will be if multiple embryos are implanted (see Chapter 4).

Choosing Adoption

Turning to adoption, people who choose to become adoptive parents often place less value on biogenetic connections than those who pursue parenthood with the help of reproductive technologies. Some LGBQ cis women and trans/nonbinary folks with uteruses, however, do arrive at adoption because their efforts to conceive are unsuccessful, or reproductive options are no longer financially feasible. Infertility can be a significant stressor that may warrant individual and couples therapy to work through feelings of grief, loss, disappointment, anger, and fear as well as the decisions that often accompany or follow this work, such as whether the other partner should try to become pregnant, whether the couple should cease family-building efforts temporarily or permanently, or whether to pursue adoption. Also, some LGBTQ folks who are older or who doubt that biological

---

[4]There are two main types of surrogacy: (a) *genetic (traditional) surrogacy* in which the sperm of a prospective gay, bisexual, queer (GBQ) father is used to fertilize the surrogate's egg in an artificial insemination procedure and (b) *gestational surrogacy* in which a donor's egg(s)—that is, not the surrogate's—are fertilized with the sperm of a prospective GBQ father by means of an IVF procedure in a laboratory. Afterward, the embryo is transferred to the surrogate's womb. GBQ men who want to become parents through surrogacy usually opt for gestational surrogacy.

family-building efforts are likely to be successful may opt for adoption right from the get-go. Likewise, GBQ men who might prefer but cannot afford surrogacy may move to considering adoption fairly quickly (Craven, 2019; Goldberg, 2012; Goldberg et al., 2009). LGBTQ people who pursue adoption may be motivated by altruism—that is, they want to parent a child who otherwise would not have a parent or set of parents. They are driven by a sense of moral or ethical commitment to redressing systemic inequalities or using their personal resources to "give back" to society.

LGBTQ people who choose adoption must decide among public domestic adoption, private domestic adoption, and international adoption. Individuals and couples with fewer resources and an interest in or willingness to adopt an older child, a child with special needs, or an otherwise "hard to place child" may be more oriented toward *public adoption*—also referred to as adoption via foster care or adoption via the child welfare system. Individuals and couples who wish to adopt a newborn or to have as much influence as possible on a child may be more drawn to *private domestic adoption*, which is characterized by placement of a child, typically at birth, in a family chosen by the birth parent(s). This type of adoption typically is facilitated by an adoption agency or a lawyer. LGBTQ people who strongly desire a child of a particular race that is not well represented in the pool of children available within the United States (e.g., an Asian child) may be more oriented toward international adoption. Note, though, that international adoption is increasingly not an option for LGBTQ people, given that many countries overwhelmingly prioritize different-gender couples as potential adoptive parents (Considering Adoption, n.d.; Hillis, 1998).

For LGBTQ prospective parents, Chapter 2 describes in greater detail the experiences of and the obstacles to adopting through each of these avenues. Chapter 3 discusses the experiences of and obstacles to pursuing donor insemination and surrogacy.

Choosing Other Pathways

In addition to building families through reproductive technologies and adoption, LGBTQ people become parents in a number of other ways. For example, they may become parents via cis/heteronormative sex in the context of different-gender relationships—such as in the case of a bisexual cis woman partnered with a cis man. They may also become parents in the context of stepparenting—for example, by partnering with a same-gender partner who has children. As one participant in the LGBTQ Family Building Project said, "I fell in love with someone who had kids, so it just sort of happened. Boom! Instant family." Another participant mused,

> I met my current partner, and I loved him and really wanted to build a life with him, and he had a child from a previous relationship. It was like I actively chose my partner, and stepparenthood was just the automatic result of that. The parenting came second.

LGBTQ people may become parents in the context of intentional coparenting arrangements. For example, a single GBQ man or couple and a single LGBQ woman or couple might decide to have and raise a child together: One or both men contribute sperm, and one woman inseminates/becomes pregnant. In such circumstances, drawing up legal coparenting agreements with an attorney is advised (Dodge, 2020).

Choosing an Adoption Pathway

In trying to determine what adoption option is the best fit, prospective parents are encouraged to consider questions, such as the following (Caughman & Motley, n.d.-a; Child Welfare Information Gateway, 2015):

- **How important is it for me to adopt a newborn/be a parent from birth?** If it is very important, private domestic adoption may be the best option. Otherwise, it may be worthwhile to consider adoption via the foster care system, in which children range widely in age; newborn adoptions are also possible but atypical.

- **How do I "look" to prospective birth parents and social workers (e.g., in terms of age, financial stability)?** In private domestic adoptions, both social workers and birth parents tend to have a preference for middle-class couples in their late 20s to late 30s. Individuals older than 50 are rarely chosen to adopt a newborn via private domestic adoption.
- **How do I feel about openness in adoption?** Most private domestic adoptions are open in that the birth parents and adoptive parents have some degree of contact—at the very least, before the placement, when the birth parents choose the adoptive parents.
- **How important is it to me to adopt a child who otherwise might not have a home?** Whereas there are thousands of children waiting for families in the U.S. foster care system, there are far fewer children available to be adopted via private domestic and especially international adoption. International adoption is currently not an option for many LGBTQ people at all.

FAMILY-BUILDING RESOURCES

Fortunately, there are an increasing number of resources, both physical (e.g., in people's communities) and online, that cater to supporting LGBTQ people in their journey to become parents. Participants in the LGBTQ Family Building Project identified a range of resources as important sources of information and support as they considered parenthood and explored various routes to parenthood. National organizations, such as Rainbow Families (https://rainbowfamilies.org/), were frequently cited as key sources of education and connection as well as the conferences, workshops, and trainings that these and local community centers held (e.g., "Maybe Baby" workshops, "Introduction to Foster Care" trainings). Queer- and trans-affirming or identified therapists, midwives, doulas, ob-gyns, and adoption agency personnel were also emphasized as resources. In online spaces, Facebook groups (e.g., for trans and queer parents, for transmasculine gestational parents, for LGBTQ people trying to conceive) were highlighted as central in their parenthood journeys as were various groups hosted by the BabyCenter platform (https://www.babycenter.com/; e.g., LGBTQ conception groups, queer parents groups). Various podcasts, blogs, and books were emphasized as were incidental encounters that were educational and transformative (e.g., "We learned about reciprocal IVF from a lesbian couple being interviewed . . . on NPR," "[We learned about family building] in a discussion at Michigan Womyn's Music Festival"). Friends and acquaintances also were highlighted as important sources of support and information about various parenthood paths (e.g., open adoption, IVF).

Among the books that were most frequently mentioned by participants were these:

- *The Kid (What Happened When My Boyfriend and I Decided to Get Pregnant): An Adoption Story*, by Dan Savage (2000)
- *The New Essential Guide to Lesbian Conception, Pregnancy, & Birth*, by Stephanie Brill (2006)
- *The Ultimate Guide to Pregnancy for Lesbians: How to Stay Sane and Care for Yourself From Pre-Conception to Birth*, by Rachel Pepper (2005)
- *The Lesbian Parenting Book: A Guide to Creating Families and Raising Children*, by D. Merilee Clunis and G. Dorsey Green (2004)
- *What to Expect When You're Expecting*, by Heidi Murkoff et al. (2018)

CONCLUSION

As the opening vignette illustrates, LGBTQ people may experience hesitation and fear surrounding parenthood. Such hesitation and fear can come from a variety of places, including internalized stigmas surrounding LGBTQ parenthood and a lack of LGBTQ parent role models. Working through such feelings with an LGBTQ-competent therapist, either in individual or couples therapy, may be useful. Knowledge of the positive outcomes and joys experienced by LGBTQ parents and the many strengths that LGBTQ people bring to parenthood (Rostosky & Riggle, 2017; Titlestad & Robinson, 2019) may also help to offset such worries.

In addition to engaging in personal exploration and enhancing one's knowledge of the research on LGBTQ parenting, investigating various family-building options may be helpful. Fortunately, the resources for LGBTQ folks who are considering parenthood are expanding. Still, the process can be overwhelming—a real roller-coaster ride with many decisions and choice points along the way. Let's move on to Chapter 2 to explore one key family-building route: adoption.

RESOURCES

Child Welfare Information Gateway. (2015). *Adoption options: Where do I start?* U.S. Department of Health and Human Services, Children's Bureau. https://www.childwelfare.gov/pubPDFs/f_adoptoption.pdf

Dodge, D. (2020, April 17). Legal basics for L.G.B.T.Q. parents. *The New York Times.* https://www.nytimes.com/article/legal-basics-for-lgbtq-parents.html

Gibson, C. (2019, March 15). Deciding whether to have kids has never been more complex. Enter parenthood indecision therapists. *The Washington Post.* https://www.washingtonpost.com/lifestyle/on-parenting/deciding-whether-to-have-kids-has-never-been-more-complex-enter-parenthood-indecision-therapists/2019/03/15/e69231da-44d7-11e9-8aab-95b8d80a1e4f_story.html

Harris, E., & Winn, A. (2019, December). *Building LGBTQ+ families: The price of parenthood.* Family Equality. https://www.familyequality.org/resources/building-lgbtq-families-price-parenthood/

Revel & Riot. (n.d.). *Internalized homophobia.* https://www.revelandriot.com/resources/internalized-homophobia/

CHAPTER 2

CONSIDERING AND CHOOSING ADOPTION

THIS CHAPTER COVERS:

> choosing adoption
> choosing a type of adoption
> public, private domestic, and international adoption
> race, gender, age, and other preferences in the adoption process
> legal issues in adoption

Corey, age 34, and Elliot, age 29, are a White, gay male couple, both cis, living in an urban area on the East Coast. They had been together for 7 years when they began their parenting journey. They started by attending a local parenting course for lesbian, gay, bisexual, transgender (trans), and queer (LGBTQ) people that assisted participants in clarifying their reasons for and obstacles to parenting, identifying methods of family formation, and locating the resources needed to help them achieve their goal of parenthood. Early in the course, Corey and Elliot cemented their desire to adopt rather than pursue other means of achieving parenthood, such as surrogacy. Both men were uncomfortable with bringing another child into the world when there were already children in need of homes.

At that time, they also began to consider myriad questions about the type of adoption to pursue. Each option seemed to have its own costs and benefits. They ultimately settled on domestic private adoption because both men strongly wished to parent a child from birth. Then they had to make other decisions, such as whether they were willing to accept a child who may have been exposed to drugs or alcohol prenatally and whether they were open to adopting a child of color.

Initially, both men were reluctant to share their feelings regarding adopting a child of another race, fearing that they would be judged by adoption social workers, who reassured them that such explorations were important for their best interests as well as the child's. Corey shared with social workers that the couple had begun to consider adopting a Black child but were uncertain how, as a White gay couple, they could socialize a child to prepare for and cope with societal racism.

As the couple further explored the issue, they became increasingly unsure. Elliot said,

> I started reading stuff about transracial parenting and how hard it is, and then we did a lot of thinking. We weren't sure if we were capable of handling a Black boy because of the sort of racial stuff that goes with Black men. Neither one of us feels equipped to explain the racial history of this country to an African American male child.

Elliot also disclosed, with some probing, that his greatest fear was of rejection of their family by Black parents. In particular, he worried that, as gay, White men, they would be judged by Black parents as unfit to raise a Black child. Elliot also shared his concerns about how some members of his family of origin might respond to their adopting a Black child: "I don't expect outright rejection of our family or our child, but I expect that there would be a lot of growing pains, and that doesn't feel fair to put on a child."

As they moved forward with adoption, the couple became acquainted with another gay couple who had successfully adopted a Latinx child. Corey noted that the area in which he

---

Choosing Adoption Over Other Reproductive Options

Of the participants in the LGBTQ Family Building Project (Goldberg, 2021), 154 had adopted or fostered at least one child. When asked why they chose adoption over donor insemination or surrogacy, here's what they said:

- 58%: altruism, or the desire to give a home or "forever family" to a child
- 49%: genetic connection not important
- 36%: cost—adoption is less expensive
- 27%: moral/ethical issues with donor insemination/surrogacy
- 18%: positive experiences with adoption (e.g., family members were adopted)
- 15%: failed donor insemination attempts
- 7%: failed in vitro fertilization attempts
- 5%: friend or family member passed away; their child/children needed a home

---

and Elliot lived had "a large Latino population . . ., and both Elliot and I speak some Spanish. My brother is married to a woman who is half Latina. So there is something that feels really accessible about adopting a Latino child."[1]

CHOOSING ADOPTION

LGBTQ people appear to be at least 4 times—and possibly as much as 10 times—more likely to adopt their children than are heterosexual people (Gates, 2013). This speaks to a general tendency for LGBTQ people to be less "tied" to traditional or heteronormative ideas of family building but also hints at the barriers that LGBTQ people may face in family building using other routes, such as those

---

[1]Part of this vignette is adapted from one presented in Goldberg and Gianino (2012).

that involve reproductive technologies (Goldberg, 2010a; Human Rights Campaign [HRC], n.d.-a).

While adoption is a great option for many individuals, it may not be ideal for everybody. The decision to adopt merits serious reflection and deliberation. For instance, some female same-gender couples arrive at adoption because of fertility issues, namely, a lack of success in getting pregnant and sometimes an inability to afford[2] some of the more expensive fertility treatments, such as in vitro fertilization (IVF; Goldberg et al., 2009). For example, in the LGBTQ Family Building Project (Goldberg, 2021), 26% of female cis and trans and nonbinary participants said that they had pursued adoption in part because of failed donor insemination or IVF attempts. One or both partners may have complex or unresolved feelings about infertility, which are important to address as couples actively move toward adoption. For example, the partner who tried to conceive may continue to experience feelings of anger, grief, loss, and disappointment surrounding their inability to carry and bear a child. This can place strain on the relationship, creating feelings of alienation and tension that may carry over into the adoption process if not directly addressed (Goldberg et al., 2009).

Such feelings of grief and loss may be amplified for LGBTQ folks because of discrimination or insensitivity among health care professionals, family, or friends, who may minimize the inability to conceive (and pregnancy losses specifically) as less valid or important because they are LGBTQ (Craven, 2019). Furthermore, there are few resources to support LGBTQ people in getting through such loss. As one participant

---

[2]Fertility coverage for LGBTQ people varies. Same-gender couples have been excluded in almost every state-mandated fertility treatment coverage plan, but some companies (e.g., Starbucks) are expanding fertility insurance coverage to be inclusive of LGBTQ employees. For more details on fertility insurance coverage and LGBTQ people, see Leondires (2020).

in the LGBTQ Family Building Project said, "We lost our first child at 20.5 weeks. There were limited resources available for same-sex couples undergoing a later pregnancy loss." Trans and nonbinary individuals who experience pregnancy loss may face even greater discrimination and insensitivity, and there may be even fewer outlets for in-person and online support, exacerbating social isolation in the wake of such loss (Craven, 2019; Ellis et al., 2015; Riggs et al., 2020).

Gay, bisexual, and queer (GBQ) men may also arrive at adoption not because they prefer it over surrogacy but because surrogacy is not financially attainable or, rarely, because of unsuccessful surrogacy attempts (Berkowitz, 2020). Likewise, for all LGBTQ people, adoption may seem to be the only family-building option available to them because by the time they are emotionally or financially ready to pursue parenthood, or have met the right person with whom to pursue it, they are too old to become parents via reproductive technologies. The need to address individual and couple issues related to the loss of genetic parenthood before fully committing to adoption is not specific to queer and trans people; this is also a salient issue among cis heterosexual folks as well (Brodzinsky, 1997; Center for Advanced Reproductive Services, n.d.).

Other LGBTQ people choose to adopt because they do not feel strongly about having a genetically related child or experiencing pregnancy and childbirth (almost 50% in the LGBTQ Family Building Project) or because they want to avoid genetic inequities, whereby one parent has a genetic connection to the child, and one does not.[3] The situation involving genetic connection can invite others to view one parent as more of the "real" parent, and some

---

[3]It is possible for one partner to provide the egg and one partner to be pregnant. This is called *reciprocal IVF* (or partner IVF, or comaternity) and is desirable to some couples because it allows both partners to be involved physically in the pregnancy. This is discussed in greater detail in Chapter 3.

couples may be concerned about their family and friends failing to respect or appreciate both partners' equal relationship to the child in such a scenario (Goldberg, 2012; Goldberg et al., 2009).

Single LGBTQ people may choose to adopt for reasons similar to those of their coupled counterparts and of cis heterosexual people, including fulfilling a lifelong desire to parent; the altruistic urge to provide a child with a loving and stable home; and, in some cases, an inability to become a genetic parent (e.g., because of age or after unsuccessful attempts to achieve pregnancy). However, single prospective parents, whether LGBTQ or not, face unique challenges. For instance, they may question whether they possess the emotional and financial resources to care for a child on their own, particularly if they lack family and friend support. They also may wonder whether parenthood will curtail their options for future relationships or professional advancement. One participant in the LGBTQ Family Building Project, for example, shared that concerns about "money and employment, including lack of paid leave" and worries about having enough of a "community of support" were key points of hesitation before pursuing parenthood.

You should consider family-building options counseling or preadoption consultation (IAC Counseling Center, n.d.) if you are seriously considering adoption but are also experiencing lingering intra- or interpersonal issues or questions. Working with a therapist or counselor who has expertise or at least experience in working with LGBTQ people and is also competent in family-building issues and options can help address any or all of the following:

- anxiety, uncertainty, or partner conflicts related to family-building options, or adoption specifically;
- grief, loss, and frustrations related to infertility;
- the inability to find the right partner with whom to pursue parenthood;

- health, age, and fertility-related issues that inhibit biological routes to parenthood;
- emotional and practical preparation for being an LGBTQ single parent;
- emotional and practical preparation for adoption and the journey that precedes it;
- identification of problematic or unrealistic beliefs and expectations about adoption; and
- key strengths in your or your partner's approach to, or framing of, adoption.

Such counseling, however, may not be possible because of financial or geographic constraints. In such cases, it may be especially helpful for LGBTQ folks to explore online resources, information, and guidance. Several large-scale organizations, such as RESOLVE: The National Infertility Association (see https://resolve.org/), have robust websites with many links to resources for LGBTQ folks. In addition, several books address infertility, loss, and adoption options for LGBTQ people, including Christa Craven's 2019 book *Reproductive Losses: Challenges to LGBTQ Family-Making*.

CHOOSING WHAT TYPE OF ADOPTION TO PURSUE

Among LGBTQ people who do choose adoption, they must decide among public domestic adoption (also known as "foster care adoption" or adoption through the child welfare system), private domestic adoption, and international adoption.

Public Domestic Adoption

Adoption through the child welfare system may be especially attractive to individuals and couples who are hoping or at least willing to adopt an older child, a child with special needs, or an otherwise "hard-to-place" child. Financial constraints may also lead LGBTQ folks to consider child welfare adoption because adopting a child from foster care is often funded by the state, and, in most cases, there are few or even no fees. States often provide ongoing financial assistance via monthly payments or certain reimbursements to families who adopt through foster care. It is important for individuals and couples who are considering child welfare adoption to be familiar with the basic characteristics of children in foster care as well as the legal issues inherent to adopting through the child welfare system. For example, consider these statistics from 2019 (U.S. Department of Health & Human Services, 2019):

- Of the children in foster care, 52% were boys.
- Children in foster care were 8 years old, on average.
- Fewer than half (44%) of children were White, 23% were Black/African American, 21% were Hispanic (of any race), and 8% were two or more races.
- Children had spent 19.7 months in foster care, on average, with the goal being reunification with birth family in 56% of cases and adoption in 27% of cases.
- The most common reasons for placement were neglect (62%), drug abuse (36%), caretaker inability to cope (14%), physical abuse (13%), and housing (10%).
- Among children adopted via foster care, the average age was 6 years; the length of time between termination of parental rights and adoption was 11.6 months; and the relationship of parent to child was foster parent (52%), relative (36%), or nonrelative (12%).

It is beyond the scope of this chapter to delve into the many problems with the child welfare system (see, e.g., *"When the Welfare*

People Come": *Race and Class in the US Child Protection System*, by Don Lash, 2017, and *Shattered Bonds: The Color of Child Welfare*, by Dorothy Roberts, 2002). But, it is worth noting that the child welfare system has historically overpoliced poor communities and communities of color, and its focus is often on child removal and permanency planning rather than on investing in the types of supports and services that would reduce the likelihood of removal in the first place (e.g., financial, housing, mental health supports for families). There is a clear need for states to prioritize family preservation and family support services so that children are not removed from their homes because of caregiver difficulties that could be effectively addressed with emotional, practical, and financial support (Child Welfare Information Gateway, n.d.-a).

Because of the risk factors associated with children's placement in foster care (e.g., neglect, poverty, parental drug abuse), it is perhaps not surprising that these children are at a greater risk for depression, anxiety, attention-deficit/hyperactivity disorder, and behavioral challenges than children living with two biological parents. Children with a history of foster care involvement are also disproportionately more likely to struggle in school, have difficulties finding employment, and abuse drugs and alcohol as young adults (Turney & Wildeman, 2016). Children in the child welfare system may also have physical or medical challenges or needs, some of which are related to prenatal drug exposure (Szilagyi et al., 2015). They may struggle with attachment problems after enduring caregiving transitions during their childhood. Yet it is essential to remember that these averages describe overarching patterns but not individual data points; there is wide variability in how children formerly in foster care fare in emotional, health, and academic domains.

Furthermore, the environment in which children are raised and the resources that are available to them can have a profound effect on their childhood and adult outcomes (Child Welfare

Information Gateway, 2018; Leslie et al., 2005). Many (35%–68%) of the preschool-aged children involved with child welfare show developmental delays, including neurological, language, and cognitive delays (Johnson-Motoyama et al., 2016). However, early intervention can help to offset or minimize such delays, improving children's physical and mental health, language and cognitive development, and social and emotional development (Child Welfare Information Gateway, 2018; Fisher et al., 1999; Ramey & Ramey, 1999).

You should be aware that not all children in the child welfare system are *legally free*, meaning that their parents' rights have been terminated or relinquished, and they are, therefore, legally available for adoption. Some people foster a child or children whom they ultimately wish to adopt but whose parents of origin have not yet legally relinquished their parental rights or had their parental rights terminated. The goal may indeed be reunification between child and parents of origin, and thus prospective adoptive parents may live with legal insecurity and uncertainty about the future for months or even years until either the parents' rights are terminated and the child can be adopted or the parent(s) and child are reunified.

Having a child removed from one's home to return to their parents of origin or another family member is not uncommon and can be emotionally devastating. More than one fifth—22%—of the participants in the LGBTQ Family Building Project who had fostered or adopted children via the child welfare system had this experience. As one participant said,

> It was really one of the worst experiences of our lives. I didn't think our marriage was going to make it. We knew the risks going into the foster-to-adopt process, but it was so hard after we lost our first placement. . . . We had her for 1 month. . . . We were off the list for about 9 months before we got back on.

Another participant said,

> [It was a] devastating experience. What helped me was my
> drive to provide a second child a permanent home—and support
> from the professionals who supported me in my grief over the
> disruption and had faith that I could be a good parent to a
> different child.

Significantly, there is little widespread recognition and awareness
of the difficult emotions and grieving that foster parents frequently
experience following the removal of foster children from their home.
As another participant shared,

> Losing a very high needs . . . child during the adoption process
> was one of—if not the most—painful experiences of my life.
> It was most difficult because the state treated our 2 years of
> parenting—the longest the child had ever been with anyone—
> as mere professional work. There was no attempt to ensure we
> remained in contact or that the bond was supported. Person-
> ally, the loss was intense but didn't have a name or a formally
> acknowledged grieving process. No work leave, no one know-
> ing how to respond to our grief, no clear symbol like a grave to
> acknowledge the loss. I began going to a . . . meditation group
> and learned to accept the pain.

It is notable that among the things that participants mentioned
helped them to move through the experience of a failed placement
were therapy (individual and couples); support from friends/family;
podcasts and online support spaces; and talking, emailing, or mes-
saging with people who had experienced similar losses. Depending
on where you live, such supports for foster parents may be available.
For example, in Massachusetts, All Our Kids (https://fosteringaok.org/)
is a volunteer-run organization that engages, supports, and connects
foster parents.

You should ask yourself the following questions before actively pursuing adoption through the child welfare system, which involves a *home study*—a formal evaluation of the prospective adoptive parents and their home—and many hours of training and paperwork:

- How willing am I to take on a child with special physical, medical, cognitive, emotional, or behavioral needs?
- How able am I to handle those challenges?
- If I were not afraid of seeming selfish or rigid, would I willingly adopt
    - a child with physical, medical, cognitive, emotional, or behavioral needs?
    - an older child?
    - a child of a different race?
    - a child who was exposed to drugs prenatally?
    - a child with a history of physical abuse? sexual abuse? neglect?
- Am I prepared to raise a child who might need a lot of attention or specialized services?
- Am I prepared to make the financial commitment that may be necessary to provide for a child with serious or specific special needs?
- Is my house equipped to accommodate specific physical needs? For example, is it wheelchair accessible, or could it be modified accordingly?
- Will my family and friends support my decision to adopt
    - a child with special physical, medical, cognitive, emotional, or behavioral needs?
    - a child of a different race?
    - a child of [insert racial, ethnic, and cultural background here]?

- What neighborhood and community resources in my area are available for
  - children with physical, medical, cognitive, emotional, or behavioral needs?
  - children of various racial, ethnic, and cultural backgrounds?

It might be of interest to know how participants in a study of more than 2,700 LGBTQ people across the United States expressed an openness to adoption:

- Of the participants, 34% of GBQ men, 41% of lesbian, gay, bisexual, and queer (LGBQ) women, and 58% of trans people were open to adopting a child older than 12 years.
- Thirty-seven percent of GBQ men, 47% of LGBQ women, and 49% of trans people were open to adopting a sibling group.
- Of the participants, 28% of GBQ men, 41% of LGBQ women, and 57% of trans people were open to adopting a child with a mental health diagnosis.
- Of the participants, 21% of GBQ men, 31% of LGBQ women, and 46% of trans people were open to adopting a child with a physical (dis)ability (Goldberg, Tornello, et al., 2020).

These numbers can be seen as highlighting LGBTQ people as an important and valuable resource for adoption of children with

> "When we first did finish all the fostering classes and started getting foster placements, I got the distinct sense that the social workers placed the 'hard-to-place' kids with us and saved the easy babies for others. I may be wrong. It could be that we were also more competent, especially later, when we clearly showed we were."
>
> —PARTICIPANT IN THE LGBTQ FAMILY BUILDING PROJECT

special needs and challenges. However, they also raise the question of whether LGBTQ people, to varying degrees, experience a sense of pressure to indicate openness to, and to eventually adopt, children with challenges—perhaps because they hope to make themselves as attractive as possible to social workers or because they believe they will be unsuccessful in adopting if they do not indicate such openness. This possibility should be on your radar as you consider, explore, and ultimately assert what types of children you are open to adopting.

It is also worth noting that LGBTQ adults may be especially sought after for one particular overrepresented and hard-to-place group: LGBTQ teenagers (Child Welfare Information Gateway, 2013). LGBTQ teens are disproportionately represented in the foster care population (Wilson et al., 2014). Many have been rejected by their families of origin, and LGBTQ individuals and couples are seen as a potentially powerful source of corrective support and acceptance. LGBTQ individuals and couples who offer a stable, supportive, and accepting family environment can play an important role in enhancing the safety, health, and well-being of vulnerable LGBTQ teens. Some adoption agencies and organizations have launched campaigns aimed at encouraging LGBTQ adults to consider adopting LGBTQ teens. For example, in 2014, You Gotta Believe (YGB, n.d.) launched the YGB Pride Initiative, which aims to connect LGBTQ prospective adoptive parents with LGBTQ youths in foster care who are in need of permanent homes.

There is no doubt that LGBTQ are an important resource in adopting from the child welfare system in general and offer many unique strengths in this regard. These include a strong motivation to help and support children with special needs or difficult circumstances as well as a willingness to seek out services and supports for their children and families, if needed (Brown et al., 2009; Downing et al., 2009; Goldberg, Frost, & Black, 2017).

Private Domestic Adoption

Individuals and couples who wish to adopt a newborn and be involved in a child's life from birth may be more drawn to private domestic adoption. This approach is characterized by placement of a child, typically at birth, in a family chosen by the birth parent(s) and is most often facilitated by an adoption agency or lawyer. Most private adoptions are *open adoptions*, which means that there is contact before or after the adoptive placement, or both, either direct (i.e., between parents of origin—birth families—and adoptive families) or mediated through the adoption agency (Child Welfare Information Gateway, 2019; Goldberg, 2019). Such contact may be virtual, in-person, or in the form of photos and letters. Openness in adoption can provide children with valuable connections to their birth family members—connections that may emerge as more or less important at different stages of an individual's life. Importantly, there is an increasing movement toward openness in foster care adoptions as well: If children have birth family members in their lives with whom they share a healthy and important connection, it may be beneficial for children to maintain some contact with those family members postadoption (Child Welfare Information Gateway, n.d.-b, 2019).

No single open adoption arrangement is best for everyone, and open adoption relationships—like all relationships—tend to change and evolve over time such that level and type of communication and contact shift according to the needs, interests, and life circumstances of birth family members, adoptive family members, and the child. If you go the private domestic adoption route, it is important to think carefully about the level and type of openness you desire while you maintain a child-focused approach such that children's needs and well-being are centered. It is also important you and your partner(s), if relevant, come to a shared sense of what you envision as workable for your family. Getting clear on your preferences and values as an individual and couple will better position you to evaluate the potential "fit" of various potential matches with birth parents.

The following are a few myths (America Adopts, n.d.; Goldberg, 2019; Spence-Chapin, 2018) about open adoptions that are important to challenge before moving on:

- **Myth:** Open adoption is a relationship in which the adoptive family and birth family have regular in-person visits with each other or in which adoptive parents and birth parents coparent the child.

  Correction: Open adoption is not a coparenting relationship. The adoptive parents have legal decision-making authority. Some birth families and adoptive families do have visits and phone calls, but those vary in frequency and regularity. Some birth families and adoptive families do not have either type of contact, at least not regularly. Rather, they may have contact via mail (e.g., pictures, letters), email, video calls, or text messages, and the frequency of any contact varies widely. It all depends on what the two parties agree to, and that may change over time.

- **Myth:** Most birth parents want a great deal of ongoing contact, and, thus, adoptive parents frequently find themselves in a position of agreeing to or having more contact than they would prefer.

  Correction: Many prospective birth parents want to have a personal relationship with the adoptive parents and often want to exchange email addresses and phone numbers for contact before and after placement. But some prefer or are content with receiving photos and updates about the child several times a year. Some prefer limited contact initially but find themselves wanting more openness as the years unfold.

"Demands" for frequent visits that the adoptive parents do not want is a rarity. Frequently, adoptive parents end up wanting more contact than they initially envisioned or asserted being comfortable with (Goldberg, 2019). A general point to remember is that contact and relationships between birth and adoptive families are dynamic and diverse, and they vary across families and over time.

- **Myth:** Open adoption is confusing for the child. They won't know who their parents are!
  Correction: Considerable research suggests that this is just not true. Even if, on some level, children understand that they have "three moms" (e.g., a birth mom and two adoptive moms), they will understand the complexity and nuance of these relationships, recognizing the differences between the mother who was pregnant with them and the mothers who raise them (America Adopts, n.d.; Goldberg, 2019). Both the child and the parents will understand the different roles and responsibilities of each parent.

Understandably, many LGBTQ people wonder if they will be disadvantaged in the open adoption process. They worry about societal heterosexism, homophobia, and transphobia as well as whether they will really be chosen by prospective birth parents to adopt their children. There are no systematic data collection efforts that address this issue, but adoption agencies across the United States routinely match birth parents to LGBTQ adoptive parents. Some anecdotal evidence even suggests that younger birth parents may be especially interested in placing children with LGBTQ parents, especially male couples, for example, because they want to place their child with individuals who are highly invested in parenthood but who would otherwise not have the opportunity to be parents (Goldberg, 2012, 2019).

A typical adoption agency response to the question "Will I have to wait longer than other prospective parents that want to adopt?" is as follows:

> AT [Adoptions Together] shares profiles[4] of [prospective] families in the order that they have been waiting. [However,] ultimately the choice and selection of adoptive parents is left to the birthparents or birthmother of the child. In the event that the birthparents choose to not participate in the selection process, our agency will place the child based on a number of factors that include the length of time adoptive parents have been waiting and the quality of the match. Historically many of our birthparents have been open to same sex couples and single adoptive parents. (Adoptions Together, n.d., para. 7)

Some agencies do caution that single people may very well wait longer than couples. Adoptions From the Heart (AFTH; https://afth. org/), for example, acknowledged that although many expectant parents and birth parents are open to viewing profiles for LGBTQ parent families, and, in turn, the agency does not see significant differences in wait times between same-gender and heterosexual couples, single people hoping to adopt—regardless of parent gender—seem to have the longest wait times. AFTH also noted that wait times are likely longer for people with more stringent criteria—for example, if they

---

[4]Part of the profile involves a "Dear Expectant Parent/s" letter (often referred to as a "Dear Birth Mother" letter) that is written by the prospective adoptive parents. This letter serves to outline who the adoptive parents are and what their life is like, thereby giving the expectant parent(s) as a sense of them and whether it would be a good "match." Many resources online outline how to write such letters and what to include in them (e.g., photos) as well as tone to take (i.e., positive, authentic, simple). See, for example, Mills (2018) and Adoptive Families (n.d.-b).

are not open to in-person visits in open adoptions, adopting a child of a different race, or adopting a child with some possibility of prenatal drug/alcohol exposure.

Regardless of wait time, it is important to be aware that the process of waiting for a potential "match" with birth parents can be nerve-wracking—an emotional roller-coaster. Furthermore, matches can sometimes fall through. In the LGBTQ Family Building Project, of the 97 participants who adopted at least one child via private domestic adoption, about one in five reported having had a match dissolve postmatch but prebirth—that is, the birth parent(s) decided not to place the child. And about one in five had a match dissolve postbirth—that is, the birth parent(s) decided to parent the child after the child was born. Thus, it is best to approach a match with cautious optimism, recognizing that a match that falls through may be painful ("It was anxiety provoking, sad, and discouraging," said one participant) but ultimately in the child's best interests. As one participant shared,

> Ultimately, we knew it was the decision of the birth family, and the situation was just not meant to be. It was difficult, but having a child-centered view of the situation made moving on after a significant emotional investment easier.

Trans prospective adopters may face unique issues in relation to birth parents (Farr & Goldberg, 2018). A couple may appear to be or present as a heterosexual couple (male/female), but one member may be trans. In a truly open adoption, birth parents should ideally know about both members' gender identity. But, of course, there are risks associated with disclosure, such as a prospective birth mother wavering in or withdrawing interest in a couple as prospective adoptive parents once learning of one or both partners' gender identities. LGBTQ people may more easily embrace the idea and reality of open adoption as well as the idea of expanding one's family to include people outside of the immediate nuclear nest insomuch as LGBTQ people are particularly likely to view nonfamily members as kin (Goldberg et al., 2011; Oswald, 2002). Indeed, research with lesbian, gay, and heterosexual cis parents in open adoption arrangements suggested that lesbian and gay parents were more likely to use inclusive language in regard to birth parents (e.g., referring to the birth mother as part of their extended family; Goldberg et al., 2011). This can be viewed as a unique strength.

International Adoption

International adoption is increasingly not an option for LGBTQ people. (Indeed, in the LGBTQ Family Building Project, few participants reported having adopted internationally, and all had adopted before 2015, with most indicating that they adopted before 2010.) Several mentioned that they pursued international adoption at a time when they were more fearful of discrimination against LGBTQ people in the domestic adoption system (e.g., they feared that they would never be chosen by birth parents because they were gay). Most countries that have children for adoption and that are open to adoption by people from other countries are prejudiced against LGBTQ people. They tend to have either societal or cultural "codes" or mandates against LGBTQ adoption, or strict laws or policies against LGBTQ adoption. Few U.S.- based adoption agencies are willing to represent LGBTQ individuals for international adoption because of such obstacles, coupled with the general barriers that cis heterosexual people and couples are facing in adopting from abroad amid increasingly strict regulations and laws governing international adoption (HRC, n.d.-a).

Importantly, international adoption has historically involved a fair amount of secrecy and concealment of individuals' sexuality and same-gender relationship status, such that one individual in a same-gender couple is typically selected to adopt as a single parent, and the home study is written up such that the other partner is depicted as a roommate or housemate. Having just one partner be recognized as the prospective parent (e.g., during adoption classes, during travel to the host country) can create stress and tension for both partners and in the relationship.

Currently, Colombia and Brazil are two of the few countries that are open to adoptions by lesbian, gay, bisexual, queer (LGBQ) people from the United States specifically. In Colombia, preference is given to prospective adoptive parents of any sexual orientation who are of Colombian heritage (i.e., this expedites wait time; Wide Horizons for Children, n.d.). Wide Horizons for Children is one adoption agency offering specific guidance to LGBQ people seeking to adopt from Colombia (Wide Horizons for Children, n.d.). Notably, their website mentions "gay or lesbian applicants" (Wide Horizons for Children, n.d., "Eligibility" section), which is a common example of agencies' erasure of bisexual and queer identities by adoption agencies as well as the conflation of relationship configuration (same- versus different-gender) with sexual identity. The description of who is eligible to adopt from abroad also explicitly leaves out trans or gender nonconforming adopters, suggesting that trans adopters have not historically been served by the agency.

CHOOSING AN ADOPTION AGENCY

Even though major strides have been made over the past decade regarding LGBTQ people's ability to achieve legal recognition as parents, legal and practical barriers remain, including some religiously affiliated adoption agencies' unwillingness to serve LGBTQ prospective adopters as clients (Moreau, 2020). Furthermore, even if adoption agencies are, on paper, "open" to LGBTQ clients, this does not mean that they will actively advocate for their LGBTQ clients (Bayless, 2018). It is important that LGBTQ people search out LGBTQ-friendly adoption agencies to the extent possible (e.g., amid geographic and financial limitations). As a first step, you should do the following (more detailed guidance is offered in Chapter 5):

- Look at the agency mission statement for an explicit anti-discrimination clause about placing children with same-gender couples or LGBTQ-identified people. If you are trans or gender diverse, look for explicit mention of gender identity or expression. The agency Adoptions From the Heart, for example, explicitly states on their website that they welcome trans individuals and couples interested in adoption (AFTH Marketing, 2020).
- Check out the stock photos used in brochures, posters, and on the website. Are ostensibly same-gender couples portrayed or only heterosexual couples? Are a range of gender expressions portrayed? Or are all individuals fairly gender conforming?
- Go on LGBTQ family-building social media pages (e.g., via Facebook, Instagram, Twitter) and see what agency names are repeatedly coming up as go-to sources.
- Evaluate the agency's paperwork. What type of language is used? (Is it inclusive of different relationship configurations, such as Prospective Parent 1 and Prospective Parent 2? Are gender options beyond male and female listed?)
- Call agencies and ask if they work with LGBTQ people. Ask for referrals of current or former clients you can call to ask about their experiences with that agency. This is especially important because it gets beyond the potentially savvy marketing to

LGBTQ people and is a test of whether they are indeed "walking the walk" with regard to inclusive practices.

CONSIDERING PREFERENCES IN ADOPTION

Prospective adopters are asked to think carefully about their preferences regarding race, age, and gender and to assert those preferences during the adoption process. In adoption via the foster care system, all three of these domains are relevant because there is variability and therefore choice regarding all three.

Racial Preferences

Racial preferences are arguably the most complex of these three domains. In the United States, adoptive parents are disproportionately more likely to be White (vs. other racial groups), and children available for adoption are disproportionately more likely to be of color—that is, not exclusively White (Vandivere et al., 2009). As a prospective adopter, you should evaluate your level of preparation for and commitment to becoming a multiracial family, assuming you aren't one already. You should, like Elliot and Corey in the opening vignette, honestly and deeply interrogate your own beliefs, feelings, and preferences regarding race and ethnicity in general and in the context of parenting. If you are a person of color, questions of whether you are willing and prepared to adopt across racial lines still apply, of course (e.g., are you prepared, as a Latinx person, to adopt a Black child? A multiracial child? A White child?) and may be answered differently, in part, based on your partner's race, if applicable.

Exercises to Explore and Identify Racial Preferences

It is important to seek out learning opportunities during the process of exploring and articulating your specific racial preferences. If you are a considering adopting a child of a different race/ethnicity than you, consider engaging in these activities:

- Talk to both adoptive and nonadoptive parents of various races/ethnicities who are raising children of various races/ethnicities.
- Read memoirs by people of diverse races/ethnicities, including adopted people.
- Read authoritative sources about and first person accounts of transracial adoption.[5]
- Attend online and live workshops and trainings on transracial adoption.
- For White parents: Engage with communities of color while remaining cognizant of how you are approaching parents in these communities and the potential for White parents to burden parents of color with their questions and need for "education."

In addition to these activities, ask yourself the following questions (Adopt Connect, 2021; Goldberg, 2009b; Goldberg & Smith, 2009):

- How racially/ethnically diverse is my neighborhood and community?
  - What racial and ethnic groups are represented?
  - What services and supports are available that not only serve but center the experiences of such groups (e.g., after-school activities, health care, cultural and community centers)?

---

[5]The term *transracial adoption* generally refers to an adoption in which a child's race or ethnicity is different from one or both parents.

- To what extent are different racial/ethnic group(s) represented in the school community?
- Am I willing and able to move to a neighboring community that has greater representation of or is better able to serve different racial/ethnic group(s)?
- How and in what ways are my family and friend networks racially or ethnically diverse?
- How supportive would my family and friends be of me adopting a child of different racial/ethnic group(s)?
- How willing am I to cultivate new relationships and community connections that will benefit my child, especially if I am the only racial/ethnic outsider at a particular school, community event, or community resource center?
- How and in what ways am I committed to learning about how to parent and care for a child of different racial/ethnic group(s)? Am I willing to
  - learn a new language?
  - travel to new places?
  - learn how to care for a child of a different race's hair, skin, and so on?
- Am I committed to a life that embraces my child's race, ethnicity, and culture(s)?
- Am I ready and open to encounter questions and criticism about my child and my parenting of my child, such as from strangers, family members, friends, teachers, and so forth?

Such activities and questions are, of course, just the beginning. Embedded within these activities and questions should be exploration of one's own consciousness of and attitudes about race, personal experiences as someone of a dominant or minority race, and willingness and commitment to foster a strong racial and cultural identity in a child. All prospective adopters should also consider the possibility that they will face increased visibility as a multiracial LGBTQ parent household. Such families will face stresses associated with both heterosexism and racism, and the negative impact of negative attitudes will be especially potent if they come from within their family and friend networks (Goldberg & Gianino, 2012).

Interestingly, there is some evidence that, compared with White heterosexual couples, White same-gender couples are more likely to consider transracial adoption and also more likely to adopt transracially (Farr & Patterson, 2009; Gates et al., 2007; Goldberg, 2009b; Goldberg & Smith, 2009). One of the most common arguments against transracial adoption is that no matter how well-meaning, White families cannot teach Black children, in particular, how to cope in a society in which they are almost certain to encounter racism (Simon & Altstein, 2000). Thus, LGBTQ parents who adopt transracially may be vulnerable to stigma related to their status as LGBTQ as well as criticism related to their choice to adopt transracially.

A great deal of research suggests that although transracial adoption in and of itself does not create psychological and social problems in children, transracially adopted children and their families do face numerous challenges. The manner in which the parents cope with these challenges, therefore, is critical. Ideally, individuals and couples who choose to adopt transracially should be aware of their responsibility to create a new multiracial and multicultural identity as a family and to learn about their children's racial and ethnic heritage to foster a healthy self-image (Baden & Steward, 2000, 2007; Simon & Altstein, 2000). Indeed, parents' level of competence in this regard has a significant effect on their children's racial and ethnic identity and well-being. And yet, despite ample documentation of the need for specialized training for parents to help their children develop positive racial identities, we don't know much about how practitioners (e.g., adoption agency personnel, therapists) meet that need, especially for LGBTQ adoptive parents. Given the conflicting narratives within the professional literature as well as in the mass media regarding the appropriateness of transracial adoption, it is no wonder that prospective adoptive parents are confused about whether they can meet the needs of children of racial and cultural backgrounds that are different from their own. Indeed, the opening vignette demonstrates the complexities of this decision.

INDICATING RACIAL PREFERENCES

Historically, adoption agencies have allowed individuals to indicate the various races and racial combinations (e.g., biracial: White/Latinx) that they are open to. This practice has some problems. For example, consider a White individual who indicates an openness to adopting a biracial child (e.g., White/Black) but not a monoracial Black child. This seems to reflect, in part, societal constructions of race in which biracial and multiracial individuals are designated as "of color" yet are seen as distinct from monoracial (and particularly Black) individuals (Raleigh, 2016; Skinner et al., 2020) and, therefore, are presumed to require a different caliber of racial socialization experiences that perhaps seem easier to imagine and engineer.

Some adoption agencies recognize this as a problem and have changed their practices regarding how they assess prospective adopters' preferences and openness surrounding race. As opposed to listing every possible combination and permutation of racial/ethnic combinations and allowing prospective adopters to indicate which they are or are not open to, some agencies (e.g., Adoptions From the Heart) require that adopters who are open to adopting a biracial or multiracial child also be open to adopting a child who is monoracial and of color. Prospective adopters, then, can no longer indicate an openness to a biracial (Black/White) child but not a monoracial Black child. The perspective here is that prospective adopters should not go into parenting a child of color thinking that they can "relate to the White part"; they must understand that they are raising a child of color and be prepared (i.e., receive necessary education and training) for this reality (Goldberg, 2019). The reality is that many adoptive parents view multiracial children as distinct from Black children and may have incomplete knowledge of or inaccurate beliefs about the types of racialized experiences, including discrimination, that a multiracial child will or won't encounter (Khanna & Killian, 2015; Sweeney, 2013).

Gender and Age Preferences

Some individuals and couples have preferences related to the gender of the child they aim to adopt, but many do not. Gender preferences are especially relevant when considering LGBTQ adoption. GBQ men, in particular, may receive the message that they are not equipped to parent a girl child because children—and especially girls—need a "mommy." Amid the primacy placed on mothers in society and assumptions that girls need female role models, GBQ men may feel insecure about their ability to parent a girl, or they may worry about added scrutiny or criticism of their family from outsiders and thus indicate a preference to adopt a boy(s). Alternatively, some GBQ men appear to prefer adopting boys simply because they have male socialization and male body parts and anatomy, and they therefore feel more "equipped," or even excited, to parent a boy or boys (Berkowitz & Ryan, 2011; Goldberg, 2009a).

LGBQ women may experience some of the same types of pressures but to a lesser degree likely because women are often assumed to be capable of parenting children of any gender. They do not appear to experience doubts at the same frequency or degree regarding their ability to parent a boy—although they do experience concerns about role modeling, which they, like GBQ men, address through engagement of siblings, friends, pediatricians, and others who share their children's gender (Berkowitz & Ryan, 2011; Goldberg & Allen, 2007; see Chapter 7, this volume).

Age preferences are most relevant when considering adoption via the foster care system; indeed, interest in adopting a newborn is a factor that often drives the choice to adopt via private domestic adoption. Although older (e.g., school-aged) children are disproportionately represented in the child welfare system, prospective adopters tend to prefer infant and toddler-aged children. There are exceptions, of course, and some prospective adopters are exclusively interested in adopting older children—for example, because they are aware of older children's higher likelihood of never being adopted or because they have already raised children from birth and view this as a different type of parenting experience.

Openness to Prenatal Substance Exposure

Prospective adopters are asked to indicate their preferences, comfort level, and openness in relation to various other characteristics, such as prenatal drug and alcohol exposure, and mental and physical health needs and (dis)abilities. Regarding prenatal substance use, prospective adoptive parents should be familiar with the basics regarding how substance use affects fetal health and development. Currently in the United States, there are more opportunities to adopt newborns who have been exposed to opioids, such as codeine, oxycodone, morphine, or heroin, during pregnancy. In turn, infants who were prenatally exposed to opioids are at an elevated risk for preterm birth, poor fetal growth, and birth defects as well as developmental delays and speech/language impairments. It is important to know, however, that the postbirth (e.g., adoptive) environment can make a big difference in offsetting or minimizing long-term negative outcomes (Centers for Disease Control and Prevention, n.d.).

In deciding whether to adopt a substance-exposed baby, prospective adopters should discuss the issue with a variety of professionals, including pediatricians, neonatologists, and adoption professionals. When evaluating a particular expectant parent's specific experiences with drugs, it can be helpful to discuss the specific risks of their drug use, amount, and timing during the pregnancy. It is a great idea to have a physician lined up (especially one familiar with adoption medicine) to evaluate lab reports and provide input. While it is ideal to form a relationship with an expectant parent that is honest and trusting, it may not be possible to get a totally honest history from that parent regarding their past and present drug use.

If a child has already been born, it is a good idea to inquire about the baby's behavior—for example, how irritable or agitated versus calm and responsive they are. Before or soon after birth, it is a good idea to identify a local pediatrician who has some experience with prenatal substance exposure and adoption medicine in general, so that if and when challenges occur, you have a competent provider on hand to assist with responding to such issues, including early intervention and assessments, if necessary. Yet, at the same time, because it is ideal to prepare for the possibility of challenges, it is also useful to remember that no two situations are the same; the adoptive environment makes a significant difference, such that nurturing, stability, and stimulation can powerfully impact a child who was exposed to drugs or alcohol prenatally (Adoption Connection, n.d.-a, n.d.-b).

LEGAL ISSUES

Same-gender couples can now, in the era of federal marriage equality in the United States, petition to jointly adopt a child, whereas, in the past, some states did not allow same-gender couples to coadopt:

One partner had to adopt as a single parent, and then, in some cases, the other partner could complete a second-parent adoption and become the child's other legal parent. Couples may be required to be in a legally recognized relationship (e.g., married) to jointly adopt.

Notably, same-gender couples (and single LGBTQ people) who wish to adopt do continue to face legal challenges and hurdles in their quest to do so, depending on where they live. For example, a number of states are in the process of considering or trying to pass legislation to create broad "religious exemptions" that would enable, for example, religiously affiliated placement agencies to turn away same-gender couples and LGBTQ people seeking to adopt or foster (Moreau, 2019, para. 13). For more information about LGBTQ folks and second-parent adoptions, see HRC (n.d.-b). For more information about LGBTQ parenthood and legal issues, see the list of resources at the end of this chapter.

CONCLUSION

The decision to pursue adoption is just the first fork in the road. You must then decide on what type of adoption to pursue, what agency to work with, and what child characteristics (i.e., race, gender, age) to prioritize as you imagine your future life as a parent and as a family. Each of these subsequent decisions is complex and involves honest evaluation of your own, and perhaps your partner's, strengths and limitations as well as areas for potential growth and possibility.

As you move forward in your journey, it is important to remember that there is only so much that you can control in becoming a parent. Take a deep breath, assess your resources and needs, and then take the next step.

RESOURCES

Adopt Connect. (2021, April 14). *Questions to ask yourself when considering a transracial adoption.* https://adopt-connect.com/questions-to-ask-yourself-when-considering-a-transracial-adoption

Adoption Connection. (n.d.-b). *12 tips in adopting a drug-exposed baby.* https://adoptionconnection.jfcs.org/12-tips-when-considering-adopting-a-drug-exposed-baby/#

Bayless, K. (2018, November 5). Gay adoption: How to start the process. *Parents Magazine.* https://www.parents.com/parenting/adoption/facts/gay-adoption-how-to-start-the-process/

Child Welfare Information Gateway. (2013). *Supporting your LGBTQ youth: A guide for foster parents.* U.S. Department of Health and Human Services, Children's Bureau. https://www.childwelfare.gov/pubPDFs/LGBTQyouth.pdf

Child Welfare Information Gateway. (2016). *Frequently asked questions from lesbian, gay, bisexual, transgender, and questioning (LGBTQ) prospective foster and adoptive parents.* U.S. Department of Health and Human Services, Children's Bureau. https://www.childwelfare.gov/pubPDFs/faq_lgbt.pdf

Child Welfare Information Gateway. (2018). *Addressing the needs of young children in child welfare: Part C—Early intervention services.* U.S. Department of Health and Human Services, Children's Bureau. https://www.childwelfare.gov/pubPDFs/partc.pdf

Child Welfare Information Gateway. (2019). *Helping children and youth maintain relationships with birth families and caregivers.* U.S. Department of Health and Human Services, Administration for Children & Families, Children's Bureau. https://www.childwelfare.gov/pubPDFs/bulletins_maintainrelationships.pdf

Child Welfare Information Gateway. (2021a). *Parenting your adopted preschooler.* U.S. Department of Health and Human Services, Administration for Children & Families, Children's Bureau. https://www.childwelfare.gov/pubs/factsheets/preschool/

Child Welfare Information Gateway. (2021b). *Parenting your adopted school-age child.* U.S. Department of Health and Human Services, Administration for Children & Families, Children's Bureau. https://www.childwelfare.gov/pubs/factsheets/parent-school-age/

Child Welfare Information Gateway. (2021c). *Parenting your adopted teenager.* U.S. Department of Health and Human Services, Administration for Children & Families, Children's Bureau. https://www.childwelfare.gov/pubs/factsheets/parent-teenager/

Human Rights Campaign. (n.d.-a). *Adoption options overview.* https://www.hrc.org/resources/adoption-options-overview

LEGAL RESOURCES

For legal information and resources pertaining to LGBTQ parenthood, consult the following organizations' websites:

- American Civil Liberties Union, https://www.aclu.org
- Family Equality, https://www.familyequality.org
- Human Rights Campaign, https://www.hrc.org
- Lambda Legal, https://www.lambdalegal.org
- LGBTQ+ Bar Association, https://lgbtbar.org/gethelp
- Movement Advancement Project, https://www.lgbtmap.org
- National Center for Lesbian Rights, https://www.nclrights.org
- The Williams Institute, https://williamsinstitute.law.ucla.edu

CHAPTER 3

CONSIDERING AND CHOOSING DONOR INSEMINATION

Gwen, a Black, 35-year-old high school English teacher, and Sara, a White, 40-year-old manager for a large retail clothing store, were living together for just more than a year when they decided to pursue parenthood. Both identified as cisgender women and queer. As a child, Sara had cancer and had received treatments that negatively impacted her fertility and made it unlikely for her to become pregnant. This, in addition to her older age, made her a less obvious choice to carry a child. Gwen was never particularly interested in becoming pregnant.

After extensive discussions with Sara about their shared vision of becoming parents "as soon as humanly possible," however, Gwen felt that her becoming pregnant—as opposed to pursuing adoption—was the most expedient way to reach this goal. Furthermore, both women agreed that, in a White supremacist culture, it was of added importance and value for Gwen, who was Black, to be the gestational parent. Indeed, both women felt that it was not worth potentially extensive and costly fertility treatments to ensure that Sara, who was White, had a position of greater perceived relative power in relation to their future child. However, they did feel that it might be worth pursuing a White or biracial sperm donor so that their child would resemble both of them.

Gwen and Sara gave careful thought to their friend and family network as they considered potential sperm donors. They were not comfortable asking Sara's only brother, Jeff, because the siblings did not have a close relationship and Jeff had been "less than welcoming" of Gwen as Sara's significant other. Sara did not have any cousins she felt she knew well enough to approach about the possibility of being a sperm donor. They considered their friend network, which was notably diverse in terms of race/ethnicity, sexual orientation, and gender identity. They both got excited about Micah, a White cis gay friend in his mid-40s whom Gwen had worked with in her prior career as a set builder for theater. Micah was a hilarious, warm, and musically talented nonsmoker with no notable health issues—as far as Gwen knew.

They invited Micah to coffee to discuss the issue, and he expressed feeling flattered but needed time to decide. Both women assured him that was no problem. But, after 2 months, they worried that time was not on their side because Gwen was approaching her 36th birthday. After some gentle nudging, Micah confessed that he still wasn't sure. The couple took his hesitation as "not a great sign" and started to look into sperm banks.

They ultimately settled on an open-identity donor—the donor's identity is released if, after age 18, the donor-conceived offspring requests that information—whose mother was White and whose father was biracial (Black/White). The donor was also Jewish, a whiz at Scrabble, and enjoyed watching and playing competitive sports—all characteristics that Sara shared. The couple was also drawn to the donor because his baby picture resembled Sara's brother, Jeff. And both women had a strong positive response to the donor's audio interview: They loved his description of his curious and admittedly mischievous nature, and they were warmed by his description of a "very close" relationship with his mother. With an unremarkable (in a good way) health history and strong indicators of intelligence (e.g., based on grades, education level), this donor seemed like a great match. Indeed, when their son was born, both Sara and Gwen remarked at how much baby Marcus "looked and seemed like a perfect blend of both of us."

CHOOSING DONOR INSEMINATION OVER ADOPTION

In Chapter 2, we learned that lesbian, gay, bisexual, transgender (trans), and queer (LGBTQ) people are much more likely to adopt their children than cis heterosexual people. Still, many lesbian, gay, bisexual, and queer (LGBQ) women in particular do ultimately choose to pursue biological parenthood (i.e., donor insemination [DI]) instead of adoption. Various studies have found that at least half of LGBQ women considered adoption before pursuing DI—but far less (12% in one study) acknowledged actually taking steps toward adopting, including calling agencies and taking adoption classes (Chabot & Ames, 2004; Goldberg & Scheib, 2015; Wendland et al., 1996). Women who go "straight to DI" and do not seriously consider adoption as a possible pathway to parenthood generally emphasize their desire to be pregnant, give birth, breastfeed, or have a genetic link to one's child. They also cite various deterrents to pursuing adoption, such as perceived costliness, the unpredictable or grueling nature of the adoption process, and worries about a greater likelihood of emotional, behavioral, or health challenges in adopted children. Some also fear legal barriers and adoption agency stigma (Goldberg & Scheib, 2015). Indeed, folks with uteruses may also view DI (and pregnancy) as a simpler, easier route to parenthood, assuming that no fertility interventions are required (Bock,

2000). Also, even though it can be uncomfortable or awkward to acknowledge it, some people strongly prefer a racially matched child and see biological parenthood as the most promising route to achieving this (Daniels, 1994). Some folks may also wish to avoid what they perceive as "saddling" their children with multiple potential stigmas—for example, being a child of queer parents who is also adopted and of a different race than their parents (Ben-Ari & Weinburg-Kurnik, 2007).

It is important for you to be aware that financial resources are layered with decision making about and options for pursuing parenthood. LGBQ women and people with uteruses who strongly wish to parent a child from birth and who also have few financial resources may wish to seek pregnancy using DI over adoption. Private adoption—which yields the greater likelihood of adopting a newborn—is costly, and although adopting an infant via foster care is possible, most available children are older (i.e., are not infants; Downing et al., 2009). So, as you consider various routes to parenthood, be mindful of the different costs associated with each one.

MAKING DECISIONS ABOUT CONCEPTION

People may assume that a female couple—or a couple in which both partners have uteruses—will necessarily be overjoyed to have "two wombs to choose from." There is often an assumption that both partners in a given couple are equally interested in and willing to inseminate, carry a pregnancy, give birth, and nurse/chestfeed. Yet, in many couples, one partner has a greater desire to experience pregnancy and childbirth—and one partner may have no desire at all to do so (Goldberg, 2006). In fact, a Belgian study of 95 female couples who were undergoing DI at a clinic found that in only 14% of couples did both partners wish to become pregnant (Baetens et al., 2003), typically choosing the older partner to go first. And a study of 100 Dutch lesbian couples with children found that in just one third of families had both mothers given birth (Bos et al., 2003). In the LGBTQ Family Building Project (Goldberg, 2021), 45% of cis women and trans folks said their decision about who would carry was impacted by one partner's strong desire to be pregnant, give birth, or chestfeed; likewise, 41% said that the decision was affected by one partner's strong desire *not* to be pregnant, give birth, or chestfeed. Thus, equal desires for or enactment of biogenetic parenthood may be more the exception than the rule.[1]

Choosing Who Will Be the Gestational Parent

Sometimes the partner who will carry and bear the child is chosen "by default" because the other partner is regarded as too old to be successful in conceiving a child or they have already tried and have been unsuccessful. Indeed, in the LGBTQ Family Building Project, 11% of cis women and trans participants said that they or their partner had tried to conceive and were unsuccessful, which influenced who carried the child. Another 27% cited health and age considerations in who carried. Job flexibility and insurance can also play a role, as can extended family members' beliefs and attitudes. For example, couples may worry that one partner's extended family members will not be as supportive or embracing of a non-biologically related child, perhaps because of personal or cultural beliefs around family, and thus choose that partner to conceive and carry their child (Chabot & Ames, 2004; Goldberg, 2006, 2010a). Nonbinary and trans masculine individuals may also worry about stigma or hypervisibility. As one participant in the LGBTQ Family

---

[1]In some cases, both partners try to conceive at the same time or alternate who tries (i.e., trade off each cycle).

Building Project shared, decision making about who would carry was shaped by their "concern about social stigma of being a pregnant man [and] fears of discrimination from medical professionals."

Reciprocal in vitro fertilization (IVF) is an increasingly available possibility that some LGBTQ folks may explore. *Reciprocal IVF* refers to one partner in a couple providing the eggs and the other carrying the fetus. This practice enables the couple to conceive a child together (with the contribution of sperm) via a combined genetic and biological link, thereby minimizing asymmetry in biological/ genetic ties to the child and potential feelings of jealousy or insecurity on the part of one parent (Bos & Gartrell, 2020; Gilmour, 2018). In a sense, it is the closest thing to having a baby together. Reciprocal IVF may also be chosen because the partner who wishes to carry the child has difficulty getting pregnant, prompting the other partner to provide the eggs ("We put my partner's egg in me. She did not want to carry, and I did, but it hadn't worked to get me pregnant," said one participant in the LGBTQ Family Building Project). The total cost of reciprocal IVF varies, but estimates range from $5,000 to $30,000, on average, and it is typically not covered by insurance. (Indeed, insurance coverage for IVF,[2] in general, is not

---

[2]The average cost for a single regular (not reciprocal) IVF cycle is approximately $12,000, and this does not cover the cost of medications, which typically range from $1,500 to $3,000 per cycle. Insurance does not always cover IVF but may pay some expenses (e.g., the cost of monitoring, some portion of the medications). As Weigel et al. (2020) reported, fertility treatments are financially inaccessible for many people in the United States, a reality that particularly affects LGBTQ people, given that they frequently rely on fertility services to become parents.

More often than not, fertility services are not covered by private or public insurance; just 15 states require some private insurers to cover fertility services, and only one state Medicaid program covers fertility treatment.

mandated in most states, and, in those states that do require at least some coverage, insurance carriers often do not cover costs associated with reciprocal IVF unless there is a "medical necessity.") Thus, it is not an inexpensive endeavor and is simply not an option for some couples. In the LGBTQ Family Building Project, just 27 participants indicated that they had used reciprocal IVF in becoming parents, with 17 of them carrying the child, and 10 providing the eggs.

Evaluating Personal, Relational, and Social Factors

Assuming that reciprocal IVF is not used, couples must decide who will carry and give birth to the child. There is surprisingly little explicit formalized guidance for couples in which both partners possess uteruses regarding the process of making such a decision. In addition to considering each individual's health, reproductive capacity, and age as well as each partner's relative interest in being pregnant and giving birth, it may also be useful to consider several other key personal, relational, and social factors.

Even in states with coverage laws, many people are not eligible for fertility treatments (e.g., in Hawaii, patients are only eligible for IVF after 5 years of unexplained infertility; in New Jersey, you can only access these services if you are younger than 46 years old). Also, it is not always made clear if LGBTQ individuals meet eligibility criteria for these benefits in the absence of a diagnosis of infertility. Furthermore, many state laws regarding mandates for infertility treatment do contain stipulations that exclude LGBTQ people: For example, in Arkansas, Hawaii, and Texas, IVF services must use the couple's eggs and sperm, rather than a donor's, thus excluding same-sex couples. For more information about insurance coverage of fertility services in the United States, see Weigel et al. (2020).

Power, Privilege, and Visibility

Society tends to privilege biogenetic connections. In turn, you should consider with your partner various dimensions of power and privilege (e.g., race, ability) as you evaluate what it would be like for each of you to carry the child, be genetically related to the child, and be more easily recognizable as the child's parent. For example, if you are a White, able-bodied person who is also the gestational parent, and your partner is a Latinx, (dis)abled person who is the nongestational parent, how might this intensify existing differences in privilege and social capital, both within your relationship and in terms of how you are viewed by outsiders?

Personal Reactions to Differential Treatment

You should explore with your partner how each of you anticipates feeling and reacting to social invisibility—as well as, of course, strategies for counteracting such invisibility. Such strategies may include giving the child the nongestational parent's last name; having the child's sperm donor resemble the nongestational parent to the extent

---

Things to Consider in Deciding Which Partner Will Carry

- interest
- health
- age
- social support
- insurance
- job flexibility
- work hours
- privilege and power
- personal feelings and history (e.g., jealousy, grief)

---

possible; and having the nongestational parent take on an active, involved role in relation to the child. Likewise, you and your partner should explore, individually and together, how each of you might feel if the child more easily or quickly attached to the gestational parent as a result of pregnancy, chestfeeding, or time spent together during parental leave. One of you may have a much stronger negative reaction in anticipating such differential treatment, possibly because of greater investment in being seen and experienced as a mother or primary caregiving figure.

FAMILY SUPPORT

Sometimes family members may struggle to accept a child whom they perceive as "unrelated" to them. Depending on how close you are to each of your respective extended families and whether you anticipate depending on family for housing, practical assistance (e.g., child care, money), and emotional support, it may be important for you to consider how each set of families might respond to a child not genetically related to them. This may inform decision making related to who carries the child, whether adoption is a better option (e.g., this neutralizes the biological differential), or what conversations feel necessary to have with extended family members before pursuing parenthood.

For couples in which one partner tries unsuccessfully to get pregnant (Partner A), and the couple "lands" on the other partner (Partner B) as the person who will pursue pregnancy by "default," it is imperative that the couple explore the potential impact of the pregnancy and birth on both partners. If Partner A anticipates that they will experience deep grief and jealousy, the couple may wish to delay pursuing pregnancy with Partner B, pursue individual or couples therapy, or consider other family-building options like adoption. Likewise, if Partner B is highly reluctant to be pregnant or give birth, for example, because of gender identity concerns or worries related to the impact of a pregnancy on Partner A or their relationship, it is important for the couple to discuss these concerns and consider hitting pause on getting pregnant.

For couples in which both partners are healthy and wish to become pregnant,[3] several options are available. First, both partners may decide to get pregnant at approximately the same time, possibly using sperm from the same donor to enable the two children to have a genetic connection. Or, the couple may decide for one partner to inseminate first, with the goal of having the other partner (perhaps the younger one—the one with more time) get pregnant at a later point, thus spacing the two siblings apart.

Of course, because things often do not go as planned (e.g., one partner may get pregnant more quickly, one or both partners may experience miscarriage), it is important—if you go this route—to try to anticipate a variety of potential scenarios regarding pregnancy success and timing. The process of having both partners try to become pregnant at the same time, for example, may be exciting, but it may also lead to a more intense experience. Being pregnant "together" may be challenging at times because each partner is riding their own individual physical and emotional roller coaster of pregnancy alongside the other. (Notably, popular press accounts of lesbian couples in which both partners are pregnant

---

[3]It is helpful to remember that even healthy folks may not conceive right away. Even among cis heterosexual couples, pregnancy is rarely achieved on the "first try" (i.e., the first cycle); rather, it may take 4 to 6 months to conceive, or possibly longer. People with uteruses do become less fertile as they age, and it typically takes longer for individuals in their 30s to conceive than it does for individuals in their 20s—yet the majority of people in their 30s (i.e., more than three quarters) are indeed able to conceive within 2 years of trying.

at the same time tend to focus on the positive and unique nature of the experience, with limited attention given to the challenges and potential ups and downs of the process [Fitzpatrick, 2018; Marcoux, 2018].)

Keep in mind that choosing who will carry the child may feel like an easy decision for some couples and a very difficult decision for others. Furthermore, remember that what you prefer or hope for may not always happen—at least not right away. It is a good idea to imagine various scenarios and how you might feel if each of them were to play out. This process may alert you or your partner to the need for counseling or education before taking the first steps toward insemination and beyond.

CHOOSING A TYPE OF DONOR

A range of options are available for individuals and couples seeking a sperm donor. In the United States, many fertility clinics offer the option of using either the sperm of an anonymous or *closed-identity donor* who intends to remain anonymous permanently (i.e., an unknown donor) or the sperm of an *open-identity donor*, one whose identity is released if the donor-conceived offspring requests it after reaching the age of 18 (Scheib et al., 2000). Notably, some sperm banks, such as The Sperm Bank of California (TSBC), no longer offer an anonymous option. On their website, they have noted that "having only donors who agree to release their identity to donor-conceived adults is part of our [TSBC's] long-term commitment to the well-being of families and donors" (TSBC, n.d., para. 1).

Queer and trans folks who opt for unknown donors may be motivated by nervousness about outside interference, the potential for unpleasant or unhealthy boundaries on the part of a known donor, or role confusion (Goldberg, 2006). Indeed, more than half (54%) of participants in the LGBTQ Family Building Project who chose an

Why Choose an Unknown Donor or Open-Identity Donor Over a Known One?

Among the 296 cis and trans participants in the LGBTQ Family Building Project who used DI, 36% used an unknown donor for at least one child, 44% used an open-identity donor for at least one child, and 24% used a known donor for at least one child.

Among those who chose to use an unknown or open-identity donor, reasons for pursuing this route over a known donor included (from most to least common) the following:

- 60%: legal/paternity concerns
- 54%: boundary/role concerns
- 15%: tried a known donor, didn't work out (e.g., couldn't get pregnant, relationship with possible donor "got complicated")
- 12%: had someone in mind, but that person said no
- something else: problems with access to potential known donor's sperm (they lived out of state), participants wanted to "combine our ethnicities," friends' use of a known donor was a "nightmare," had specific genetic needs that warranted a specific type of donor

unknown or open-identity donor said that boundary- or role-related concerns discouraged them from pursuing insemination with a known donor. Individuals who choose unknown donors may experience relief about the absence of current or future interaction with a third party, but this may be accompanied by anxiety or worry that their children may experience psychological or identity challenges related to not knowing their donor's identity, especially in adolescence or adulthood (Gartrell et al., 1996).

Queer and trans folks who opt for open-identity donors over unknown donors may do so in part because the idea of a known donor seems too threatening or uncertain (or they simply do not have anyone to ask). At the same time, though, they believe that (a) offspring have a fundamental right to know their sperm donor's identity, (b) this knowledge will aid in identity development, or (c) this option may be important for medical or health-related reasons down the road. Thus, the open-identity option may seem to be a good "intermediary" between a known donor and an unknown donor, allowing the possibility of future contact and information exchange but avoiding much of the relational ambiguity or navigation that may characterize a known donor situation.

Individuals and couples who choose a known donor—that is, use sperm from a person they know—are often influenced by a strong belief that children deserve to know about their origins and will benefit from having a relationship with their other genetic half. In addition, they may be motivated by a desire to have easy access to health or medical information. They also may be reassured by the presence of a positive, trusting relationship with the donor such that they are not highly concerned about the possibility of fuzzy boundaries or an unwanted level of involvement by the donor (Goldberg, 2010a; Goldberg & Allen, 2013; Touroni & Coyle, 2002). In the LGBTQ Family Building Project, 70 participants (24%) used a known donor for at least one of their children. Two thirds (66%) of them chose a known donor because they wanted the child to be able to contact or know their other genetic contributor; 47% chose a known donor because someone they liked and trusted was willing to provide sperm; more than one third (36%) said it was less expensive than obtaining sperm from a sperm bank; and 13% said they wanted a genetic connection to both parents, so they used a male relative's sperm (i.e., a cousin or brother of the nongenetic parent). Some gave other reasons, such as discomfort with the lack of regulation surrounding sperm donation, a desire for fresh sperm to increase the chances of conception, and a wish to avoid medical intervention as much as possible.

In deciding whether to take steps toward pursuing a known donor (i.e., sperm from a friend or acquaintance) versus an unknown or open-identity donor (i.e., sperm from a sperm bank), it is important to consider your values and priorities in several arenas as well as your financial and social resources. Ask yourself the following questions (Family Equality Council, 2021b; Gurevich, 2020):

- How important is it that my child is related to someone whom I know personally?
- How important is it that my child (and I/our family) can contact a donor regarding medical or mental health issues that might arise for my child?
- How important is it that my child has some genetic relationship to both parents?
  This can be achieved via reciprocal IVF, as discussed, but also through having the sperm donor be a member of the nongestational parent's family, such as their brother or cousin.
- How important is it that my child have physical and background characteristics of both parents?
  It may be hard to find a known donor who shares valued characteristics with the nongestational parent, such as race, religion, or physical features. Sperm banks offer greater potential for such matching by virtue of the wide range of choices available. However, sperm banks are still significantly limited in certain domains: They do indeed have a "diversity problem" (Hatem, 2020; Perez, 2018), and sperm donors of certain racial/ethnic backgrounds are generally quite rare.
- How important is it that my child has an ongoing relationship with their donor?
- How much money am I able or willing to spend on sperm?
  Vials of sperm from a sperm bank cost between $400 and $1,000, on average, with most people buying multiple vials to accommodate multiple attempts before becoming pregnant. While sperm from a known donor may be "free" (assuming

that quarantining the sperm is unnecessary),[4] you must also consider the costs of legal fees associated with defining and delimiting the donor's rights vis-à-vis the child.[5]

- To what extent do I value or require a comprehensive medical and mental health background "check" of my donor? Interestingly, because of their extensive screening and data-gathering process, sperm banks tend to have more thorough and complete descriptions of sperm donors' medical and mental health backgrounds than the information you would typically obtain from a potential sperm-donor-friend.

  If interviewing potential known donors, be sure to gather information about drug, alcohol, and cigarette use, both past and present, including time period and frequency; health histories and causes of death of parents and grandparents; desires and intentions regarding relationship and contact with offspring that result from sperm donation; whether and how this might change in the future (e.g., if they marry or have or adopt children); if they would be willing to have their sperm tested before donation; and whether they would be willing to donate more sperm in the future (e.g., for potential additional children).

---

[4]As noted in Chapter 1, individuals who are pursuing IUI or IVF or otherwise inseminating with the assistance of medical providers (as opposed to inseminating at home) should be aware that if they are using sperm from a known donor, they are required to quarantine such sperm because federal regulations require quarantining of known donor sperm for 6 months to rule out the presence of infectious disease. Folks should also be aware of the costs associated with infectious disease testing (full panels typically cost more than $1,000).

[5]For details on why a written agreement between you and the sperm donor is important, see Law Office of Brian Esser (2014).

- Do I/my partner have anyone in our lives that we feel we could ask to be the donor?

  Here, you should be considering not just what people you know but whether they are honest (at a minimum), have good boundaries, are mentally and physically healthy, and possess other qualities you deem important (e.g., in terms of personality; intelligence; creativity; attractiveness; and racial, cultural, and religious background).

  If you strongly value having a known donor but don't have anyone in your inner circle whom you would ask, consider letting friends, family, and acquaintances know about your interest, and seek potential leads.

- How much concern or worry do I have related to fuzzy boundaries or expectations regarding a donor's role? How willing am I to engage in potentially challenging or tense conversations with the donor related to their role (e.g., whether they should be consulted in certain types of parenting decisions, their level of contact with the child)? How prepared and willing am I for the possibility of changes, tensions, and conflicts in my relationship with the donor?

- How important is it to pick the "ideal" or "dream" donor (i.e., to match the donor's physical, personality, and cultural/religious background to the nongestational parent; to optimize physical attractiveness or other physical features, such as race or height, and intelligence) versus picking a donor who is known and has a relationship with my child?

Of course, no matter what you choose, there is always the possibility that things will not turn out as you expect or hope. Indeed, consider Gwen and Sara in the opening vignette, who strongly desired a known donor, thought they had found the perfect match, but then ultimately ended up choosing an open-identity donor through a sperm bank. You may find a known donor you believe is perfect but who eventually ends up withdrawing emotionally or physically from your family and not playing any type of role in your child's life. You may choose an unknown or open-identity donor out of concerns related to boundary management but ultimately question your decision to prioritize boundary clarity when your child demonstrates a strong desire to know their donor. A lot will happen in the future that you cannot anticipate. That's okay. You are not alone. Consult with a therapist or family planning specialist, or talk with other families who have taken a variety of paths to parenthood, and try not to spin in the wheels of worry and indecision for too long. Consider setting a deadline for making a decision about what path to pursue, and work toward clarity with that goal in mind.

CHOOSING A DONOR

The process of selecting a sperm donor is a weighty one. Assuming you are selecting a donor from a sperm bank, know that most, if not all, sperm banks offer matching consultations such that professionals can help you narrow down your list of donors from an unwieldy number to a manageable set of possibilities.

Start by considering physical attributes as well as psychological characteristics (e.g., sense of humor, intelligence). You will be able to narrow those attributes further from, say, Latinx donors who are taller than 5'8" and have at least some athletic interests or background to those who meet these basic characteristics and also resonate in more intangible ways (e.g., their essay and survey questions regarding temperament, life experiences, and family history appeal to you; you feel connected to the donor after hearing their voice on an audio interview or looking at their baby pictures). You may also be interested in doing genetic matching (often offered by sperm banks), which aims to ensure that your unique genetic profile is well matched with a potential donor's.

Think carefully about the nongestational parent's physical and psychosocial profile. To what extent would you like their racial, religious, cultural, or physical characteristics to be approximated in the donor? (What would the child look like or be like if you and your partner could have a child together as a couple?)

Likewise, consider what medical or mental health issues are present in the gestational or genetically linked parent's history. Try to avoid "doubling up" on any of those issues by scanning for these in the donor's profile and avoiding any donors with similar negative features (e.g., a history of asthma, a history of brain cancer).

Figure out what is "very important" and what is "not so important but a plus." Aim to prioritize the most important attributes or features. Agencies may promise the "perfect match," but don't get stuck on finding perfection. Keep in mind that you may need to explore a few different sperm banks if you cannot find many potential matches on important characteristics, such as race. Indeed, most sperm donors are White, and some sperm banks have very few donors of color, especially Black donors.[6]

The Sperm Bank of California (n.d.)—which has been in operation since 1982, and was the first to offer services to lesbian couples and single women as well as to track and limit the number of births per donor—has suggested that it is important to not get "hung up" on a particular idea of what the sperm donor looks like, including their hair and eye color, height and weight, and race. Although such physical considerations make sense, it is important to consider all of the information that is available to you in modern sperm donor profiles, which can help to form a more complete portrait of the individual

---

[6]See, for example, Hatem (2020) and Vaughn (2021).

at hand—who they are as a person. Sperm donor profiles provide information about education level, occupation, career goals, marital status, ethnic origin, interests, and family medical history. Education level, career goals, and medical history in particular appear to be especially important to many contemporary intended parents seeking a sperm donor.

GOING DOWN THE DONOR INSEMINATION PATHWAY: ISSUES TO CONSIDER

If you are building your family via DI, there are a few unique issues for you to be mindful of as you proceed down this path.

The Reality of "Donor Siblings"

Over the past 5 years, mainstream media have published a number of articles detailing the experiences of young adults who discover that they have a large number (e.g., 20–35) of donor-linked siblings[7] (also referred to as same-donor offspring, genetic half-siblings, donor siblings, or "diblings"; Baden-Lasar, 2019; Otero-Amad, 2019). These numbers are meant to, and do, startle the average reader: How on earth is it possible that a single sperm donor has so many progeny? Indeed, some high-profile stories have featured individuals with 100 donor-linked siblings! For example, a 2011

---

[7]Some mental health professionals and some LGBTQ family members in particular highlight problems with the term "donor siblings," noting that the use of the term "sibling" implies a type of social relationship that may create potentially unrealistic expectations of connection; promote heteronormative ideas of family (based on genetic relatedness); and may, in turn, indirectly denigrate families built on social ties.

article in *The New York Times* was titled "One Sperm Donor, 150 Offspring" (Mroz, 2011). And, a 2019 contestant on the TV show *The Bachelorette* indicated that they were a "sperm donor with 114 kids" (Zhang, 2019).

Some countries, including Belgium and France, place a limit on the number of families a given sperm donor can donate to (six, in both cases). However, there is no federal law governing the number of donations or recipient families in a number of countries, including the United States. Most sperm banks, though, now limit the number of births that can be attributed to any one donor, with some using the actual number of births as their metric, and others using the number of family units. Fairfax Cryobank (n.d.) states the following on its website regarding donor sperm distribution:

> Fairfax Cryobank limits the total number of births for any donor based on the application of several criteria. Specifically, a donor's sales will cease when either of the following criteria is reached: (1) Maximum of 25–30 family units (children from the same donor living in one home) reported within the U.S.; OR (2) Total number of units sold reaches our designated limit (actual numbers are not disclosed). In addition, we also monitor the reported location of births and limit the geographic distribution of a donor. (para. 4)

When exploring DI, it is a good idea to determine the sperm bank's standards and guidelines regarding sperm distribution. Indeed, the ethical issues of allowing sperm donors to donate "three times a week, for five years" (Fauntleroy, 2017, para. 17), for example—as was the case for the donor whose sperm resulted in the birth of Wendy Kramer's son, Ryan—continue to be debated, with some experts advocating for federal regulation of sperm donation (Fauntleroy, 2017). The Kramers went on to establish The Donor Sibling Registry, a national registry (see https://donorsiblingregistry.com/)

that aims to connect, educate, and support donor-linked families. In the absence of any federal regulation, then, it is important for you, as the consumer, to ask about and know the sperm bank's rules and regulations.

It is also a good idea to investigate the bank's procedures for connecting families who have used the same donor. Some banks, such as the Seattle Sperm Bank (2021), provide opportunities for families with a mutual interest in connecting to do so with their assistance. Specifically, families who officially declare their interest to connect with other families who used the same sperm donor are connected to each other, which has the potential to "create community, compare parenting experiences, exchange medical information, and even meet in person should all parties choose to pursue this option" (Seattle Sperm Bank, 2021, para. 2). Even though it may not be your top concern when selecting a sperm bank, explore what options they have to connect with donor siblings' families.

As time goes on, children and parents may want to identify and possibly get to know genetic relatives of the child—simply out of curiosity, yes, but also for practical and emotional reasons (e.g., to gain information about shared characteristics, to get support surrounding a challenging diagnosis). There is growing awareness of the importance of enabling children to have access to information about people who connect them to their origins (Scheib et al., 2020), which is reflected in the practices and policies of both sperm banks and adoption agencies. Indeed, the practice of *open adoption*, whereby adoptive parents have some type of contact with the birth parents before or after the placement of the child (or both), has become increasingly common over the past several decades. These shifts reflect a larger movement toward greater transparency and openness in relation to children's origins (Cahn, 2013; Goldberg, 2019).

Discrimination in the Family-Building Process

It is helpful to know that although discrimination against LGBTQ people seeking to become pregnant has certainly declined in the past few decades, certain regions, hospitals, and providers continue to operate in ways that are explicitly or implicitly alienating to LGBTQ people and couples (Cacciatore & Raffo, 2011; Goldberg et al., 2009; Peel, 2010). Indeed, the medical system continues to be fairly heteronormative, which creates a variety of barriers for LGBTQ people who are building families.

Things to Look for in Evaluating Providers

- website, social media (images, language)
- physical office, waiting room (art, magazines)
- restrooms (single stall or gender inclusive)
- forms, paperwork
- formal policies
- provider training, education

"Pursuing IVF, we dealt with queer-phobia. We would have had to freeze our donor's sperm and have it tested after 6 months. We lied and said he was a sexual partner. We faced a lot of pushback and skepticism and polyphobia. [I also faced] a lot of fear about encountering the reproductive medicine world and providers during pregnancy as a trans/ nonbinary gestational parent post-top surgery."[8]

—PARTICIPANT IN THE LGBTQ FAMILY BUILDING PROJECT

---

[8]*Top surgery* refers to surgical procedures on the chest (e.g., removal of chest tissue, chest contouring).

For example, health professionals may ignore or fail to fully acknowledge the noncarrying partner in prenatal classes, or, in the case of miscarriage, they may minimize the noncarrying partner's grief and loss. Clinic forms may be inappropriate for LGBTQ people. For example, they may assume a mother–father family constellation or that all people with uteruses identify as women. Indeed, pregnant people who are masculine presenting are especially vulnerable to discrimination in the perinatal care environment. The sexual identities and histories of bisexual people are typically invisible in reproductive settings. Of note here is that while some bisexual people may not care if a provider assumes they are heterosexual or gay based on their partnership status, other individuals experience this as a form of erasure. Clinic forms that acknowledge the possibility of bisexuality are typically met with surprise and even delight by bisexual people (Goldberg, Ross, et al., 2017).

Depending on your resources and where you live, you may have access to a broad range of providers (e.g., ob-gyns, midwives, doulas) and systems (e.g., hospitals, sperm banks, and you may be able to actively assess and prioritize their LGBTQ inclusiveness in deciding on your family-building team of professionals. However, many LGBTQ people have few choices with regard to providers and thus may need to actively advocate for themselves in health care settings (e.g., pointing out where language, practices, and policies could be more inclusive). This may feel really challenging, especially if you are a person who does not like to "make waves" or does not wish to educate from the position/perspective of being oppressed. However, if it makes you feel better, you may be making things better for the next LGBTQ person or couple who walks through the doors of that hospital.

Following is a list of things to consider or advocate for, if they are important to you (see also Lai-Boyd, 2020):

- What images (people, families) and language appear on the provider's website? Are the images and language on the provider's website, social media, and so on LGBTQ inclusive or welcoming, or not? How do they make you feel?

For example: Are the featured images exclusively heteronormative (male–female couple with baby), or are other family constellations featured? Is the text gendered ("motherhood," "fatherhood," "breastfeeding"), or are there indicators of inclusivity (e.g., references to LGBTQ people, "parenthood," "chestfeeding")?

- Does the provider reference any LGBTQ-specific training or education—for example, among individual team members or staff in general?
- Does the physical waiting room contain materials and health information that is relevant to and inclusive of LGBTQ people? How does the waiting room make you feel?
- Does the facility have gender-inclusive/single-stall restrooms?
- Does the provider have, and emphasize the presence of, non-discriminatory policies?
- Does the provider/practice use forms that are inclusive of all prospective parents (e.g., referring to "parents" as opposed to "mothers")?

Notably, many LGBTQ people may find the process of searching for LGBTQ-inclusive providers, midwives, doulas, fertility specialists, and sperm banks to be quite emotionally taxing. Preparing to become pregnant and give birth are themselves part of an emotionally vulnerable process, especially for first-time parents. LGBTQ people may find that their sense of emotional and physical vulnerability is intensified inasmuch as they are also members of a community whose health care needs and experiences are often invisible or misunderstood. Interestingly, anecdotal evidence suggests that LGBTQ people may be especially likely to seek out midwifery care versus traditional care, perhaps, in part, because midwives (who are outside of the traditional hospital system) seem to find it easier to adapt to and use language that is inclusive of LGBTQ people. Journalist Lindsay King-Miller (2018), writing for *Rewire* magazine, for example, explained:

> When my genderqueer partner Charlie and I decided we wanted to have a baby, we realized quickly that much of the medical field surrounding conception, pregnancy, and birth was never intended to accommodate our family. The doctors who performed our intrauterine insemination [IUI] referred to Charlie [the gestational parent] as "mama," called our sperm donor "the dad" and didn't acknowledge me as a parent at all. We hired a home-birth midwife for many reasons, but one was so that our daughter's birth would be attended by someone who didn't need to be reminded that Charlie uses "he" pronouns while he was crowning. (para. 6)

Midwifery practices and associations have often been at the forefront of change and inclusive leadership regarding equitable treatment of LGBTQ individuals and couples, and they offer informational and educational materials to providers seeking to provide better care for LGBTQ-birthing people and their partners (Birth for Every Body, n.d.). Ultimately, you may wish to research the presence and accessibility of a range of provider types in your area before settling on one. Consider calling various providers with a set list of questions that are important to you. Ask friends about their experiences. Use social media to get a sense of what other LGBTQ people's experiences have been with various providers in your area.

THINKING ABOUT FERTILITY PRESERVATION, PREGNANCY, AND BEYOND: UNIQUE CONSIDERATIONS FOR TRANS FOLKS

If you or your partner is trans, this section is for you. Trans people who are interested in or have undergone gender-affirming treatments, including hormone therapy and surgery, face unique considerations with regard to family building. Trans people who think that they may want to be genetically related to a child or children may wish to explore fertility preservation options because gender-affirming interventions can impair or eliminate reproductive potential (Ainsworth et al., 2020; Hudson et al., 2018). Clinical options for fertility preservation in trans people depend, in part, on what gender-affirming medical or surgical interventions have already been pursued (as well as pubertal status, in young people).

Trans people assigned female at birth (AFAB) who have not pursued gender-affirming hormone therapy or surgery have a variety of fertility preservation options available to them, including oocyte (egg) cryopreservation, embryo cryopreservation, or ovarian tissue cryopreservation (Ainsworth et al., 2020). The first two of these require a controlled ovarian stimulation with subsequent transvaginal ultrasounds, which may be uncomfortable or downright distressing for trans folks. AFAB trans people who have already begun hormone therapy can still pursue oocyte or embryo cryopreservation but will need to discontinue therapy for at least 3 to 6 months before stimulation. Stopping testosterone hormone treatment can be a scary and uncertain process because this can lead to unwanted changes in body shape (Ellis et al., 2015). Oocytes obtained after stimulation can be cryopreserved or fertilized with sperm provided by a partner or donor. Embryos can be implanted into a gestational carrier (i.e., surrogacy) or in a partner. Ovarian tissue can be cryopreserved at any point but is ideally performed at the time of surgery. This is considered experimental in the United States, although it is an established option in Europe (The Practice Committee of the American Society for Reproductive Medicine, 2014).

Pregnancy itself can involve joy and happiness about having a child but also conflict between one's internal gender identity

"As an AFAB nonbinary person, I found some of the physical aspects of pregnancy—breast growth, body attention from others—tough. Breastfeeding was also just awful and intolerable."

"I did not want to carry, but my wife had health issues. I would not have agreed to try, but we found a lesbian midwife I felt comfortable with and respected my deal breakers—any internal exams, ultrasounds, Pap smears, et cetera. I was able to get pregnant with my wife and a small syringe. I wouldn't have been able to do it any other way. I only felt dysphoric the handful of times I had to see an ob-gyn and was pressured, not respected."

"Society views pregnancy as entirely a woman's domain, a feminine woman at that. Clothes were a particularly challenging obstacle, as I don't wear women's clothes and had very few options to feel remotely like myself."

—TRANS PARTICIPANTS IN THE LGBTQ FAMILY BUILDING PROJECT

and a society that perceives pregnant people as women. It also can involve loneliness because of a lack of support or resources for trans men and nonbinary people who are gestational parents. Most pregnancy clothing, for example, is highly feminized and thus inappropriate for many trans, masculine, and gender nonconforming parents-to-be. Such parents-to-be may, in turn, opt to seek out baggy "menswear" or explore gender-inclusive pregnancy wear options: In fact, there is a slowly growing, but often financially inaccessible, industry of gender-expansive pregnancy clothing (Meyers, 2015; Witte, n.d.). The birth itself can be especially uncomfortable for trans men and transmasculine folks because their bodies are on display in a medical setting, leading some to prefer planned or scheduled cesarean sections over vaginal births.[9] Trans men and transmasculine people may also be more likely than the general public to give birth at home (Ellis et al., 2015; Light et al., 2014). Notably, though, some trans people do experience a sense of deep comfort in and appreciation for their bodies during pregnancy and while chestfeeding: As one participant in the LGBTQ Family Building Project said, "Pregnancy was the most comfortable I felt with my gender."

Fertility preservation options are also available for trans people assigned male at birth (AMAB). For AMAB trans folks who have not received gender-affirming hormone therapy or surgery, options include cryopreservation of semen or testicular tissue, or embryo creation with the use of fresh sperm if pursuing pregnancy with a partner who can get pregnant or with the use of donor oocytes (i.e., eggs; Ainsworth et al., 2020). This semen can be obtained via ejaculated specimens or via testicular sperm extraction; semen from ejaculated specimens can be used for IUI or in IVF, whereas semen extracted from the testes can only be used for IVF. AMAB trans people who have already started gender-affirming hormone therapy and wish to pursue fertility preservation via sperm banking will need to discontinue medication before doing so. Research indicates that sperm counts in trans women who banked semen samples

---

[9]It is really okay to do whatever feels right for you—even if you're not trans. If labor is not for you, that is okay. The experience of having a provider, for example, check the dilation of the cervix during the lead-up to labor and delivery may be incredibly dysphoric because it involves the insertion of a finger into the cervix. You may wish to talk to your provider about alternate plans for delivery (e.g., at home, in a midwifery center) as you consider what this experience might be like for you. If you give birth in a hospital setting, you can include as part of your birth plan elements of what will make the birth experience more tolerable for you—for example, having members of the birth team stand closer to your head region rather than below the waist.

before hormonal treatments are greater than those who banked their semen 3 to 6 months after discontinuing hormone treatment, which are greater than the very low counts occurring in trans people who continue hormone treatment (Adeleye et al., 2019). AMAB trans people who have completed genital reconstruction do not have many fertility preservation options available to them.

CONCLUSION

Choices, choices, choices. Going down the road of DI as an LGBTQ person or couple can feel like entering a maze with dozens of doors. Remember that you can open a door, look around, and then close that door and keep moving if that is what makes sense for you. Of course, you may encounter various obstacles as you pursue this particular family-building route. Some doors may be barricaded with "Do Not Enter" signs. Others may be hard to open but ultimately give way with a little pushing. If you are pursuing DI with a partner, this process can be stressful but also illuminating because you are making these decisions together and hopefully learning and growing together in the process. Some of what you learn about yourself and each other (e.g., values and priorities, response to unexpected barriers and challenges) may ultimately be informative and helpful later on down the parenting road.

RESOURCES

Family Equality Council. (2021b). *Choosing between a known and unknown sperm donor.* https://www.familyequality.org/resources/choosing-between-a-known-and-unknown-sperm-donor/

Fitzpatrick, K. (2018, May 7). What it's like when your wife pregnant—at the same time as you. *Popsugar.* https://www.popsugar.com/news/Lesbian-Couple-Pregnant-Same-Time-43303404

Gurevich, R. (2020, January 30). *Understanding donor arrangements: Having a baby with third-party reproduction.* Verywell Family.

https://www.verywellfamily.com/understanding-donor-arrangements-4176290

Lai-Boyd, B. (2020, June 11). *Maternity care for LGBTQ+ people—How can we do better?* All 4 Maternity. https://www.all4maternity.com/maternity-care-for-lgbtq-people-how-can-we-do-better/

Meyers, D. (2015, April 17). *Designing maternity clothes for genderqueer parents.* The Cut. https://www.thecut.com/2015/04/maternity-clothes-for-genderqueer-parents.html

Perez, M. (2018, November 28). Where are all the sperm donors of color? *Rewire News Group.* https://rewirenewsgroup.com/article/2018/11/28/where-are-all-the-sperm-donors-of-color/

Sperm Bank, Inc., dba Fertility Center of California. (n.d.). *What should I look for in a sperm donor?* https://www.spermbankcalifornia.com/blog/what_should_i_look_sperm_donor.html

CHAPTER 4

SURROGACY AND OTHER FAMILY-BUILDING ROUTES

THIS CHAPTER COVERS:

> deciding on and seeking surrogacy
> taking steps in the surrogacy process
> managing genetic asymmetry
> pursuing other parenthood routes, beyond surrogacy

Brad is a White, 40-year-old cis man who is employed as a radiologist. His partner, Ryan, is a White, 36-year-old cis man who works as a literary agent. Both men identify as gay. The couple lives in a suburb of a major city on the East Coast, where they enjoy hiking, kayaking, and walking their dogs. After 10 years together, Brad and Ryan were ready to begin to pursue parenthood. Brad was especially excited about the possibility of pursuing surrogacy. An only child, he had lost both of his parents to cancer in his 20s. Brad had no living relatives, other than an uncle with whom he had a distant relationship. Thus, for Brad, the possibility of "bringing a child into the world, like heterosexual couples do all the time," who was genetically related to him, was profoundly significant, especially amid all of the losses that he had endured during his adulthood.

Ryan was deeply sympathetic to Brad but felt that he was "underselling" his ability to bond to a genetically unrelated child, pointing out to Brad that he had formed strong connections to the children of various friends. The couple had also taken in many rescue cats and dogs during their relationship, and Brad was always the "primary parent" to these creatures—attentive, loving, and ultimately beloved by them. Ryan fretted about the cost of surrogacy, noting that they would have to exhaust their savings and sell some valuables that Brad had inherited from his parents to "make it work." Brad relented, acknowledging the steep cost of surrogacy and the many sacrifices they would need to make to pay for it. He agreed to attend a few adoption and foster care webinars as well as an informational session at a local adoption agency. Yet, after several months of exploring adoption, Brad broke down, telling Ryan that it did not feel right and that he felt compelled to at least investigate surrogacy.

Thus began a 6-month tentative—and mostly online—exploration of surrogacy. The couple lived in a state that allowed surrogacy, which was a significant relief. In addition, consultation with a fertility doctor confirmed that Brad was a good candidate to provide sperm. However, overwhelmed by the legal and practical challenges associated with surrogacy, the couple decided to consult with an attorney specializing in surrogacy law before proceeding. With the attorney's support, they then researched various lesbian, gay, bisexual, transgender (trans), and queer (LGBTQ)–savvy surrogacy agencies and selected one after speaking with agency professionals and former clients.

The agency, Grow Your Family, was knowledgeable about LGBTQ-specific legal considerations and procedures, such as prebirth orders and second-parent adoptions. *Prebirth orders* are court proceedings that establish parental rights before the birth of the child and are available only in certain states. *Second-parent adoptions* permanently establish the nongenetic parent's rights to the child and are advisable even when pre- or postbirth orders are possible because adoptions are recognized nationwide, but not all states recognize parentage conferred via such orders (Circle Surrogacy, n.d.). The agency was also savvy regarding the unique nuances of both the egg and surrogate selection processes for same-gender couples.

Brad and Ryan ultimately prioritized an egg donor who would share certain characteristics with Ryan: brown-haired, tall, and talented in the language arts. They prioritized a surrogate with whom they felt a connection and who was, obviously, accepting of them as a gay couple. The couple ultimately matched with a surrogate, Emily, whom they liked very much. "She's like the little sister I never had," joked Brad. Brad and Ryan's surrogacy journey hit a roadblock when the first embryo transfer failed. After so many months of medical screening on the part of the egg donor and surrogate, legal paperwork, and excited anticipation, the couple felt this disappointment acutely. Ryan, in particular, found himself in a state of shock. However, consultation with Grow Your Family provided the reassurance that the couple needed to mentally prepare and ready themselves for the next embryo transfer. Thankfully, this second transfer was successful, and Emily became pregnant.

As the pregnancy unfolded, the couple confronted a difficult dynamic originating from Ryan's family. Ryan, who had never had a strong desire to be genetically related to a child, began to notice that his own parents seemed aloof whenever the subject of the couple's impending parenthood came up. After pushing his mother to explain, she acknowledged that she was upset that Brad was the genetic father and Ryan was not. "I just don't know how I feel about this," she confessed. Although frustrated, Ryan tried to be patient with his parents and told them that he hoped that they would support him and Brad and their growing family. Ryan also informed his mother that, according to his research, although nongenetically related relatives sometimes imagined that it would be hard to bond with hypothetical children, they typically had no difficulty doing so with actual children. And, in fact, that was exactly what happened: Ryan's parents were enamored of Brad and Ryan's daughter, Hannah, and Ryan's mother became Hannah's part-time caregiver.

Famous Gay Parents via Surrogacy

- Perez Hilton, celebrity blogger, is the parent of three children who were born with the help of surrogates and egg donors.
- Fashion designer Tom Ford and his partner, magazine editor Richard Buckley, are the parents of one child through surrogacy.
- Actor Neil Patrick Harris and his partner, David Burtka, are the parents of fraternal twins via gestational surrogate. Two embryos, each fertilized by one parent, were used. Thus, one child is biologically related to Harris, and one child is biologically related to Burtka.
- Singer Elton John and his partner, David Furnish, are parents to two children via surrogacy. Before pursuing surrogacy, they reportedly tried to adopt, but without success.
- Singer Ricky Martin is the parent of twins born via surrogate. When asked by one of his children, "Dad, was I in your belly?" he responded,

> You were in my heart and you are still in my heart. . . . There was a woman that I adore with all my heart that helped me bring you into this world. She lent me her belly so that you could come and when you were born she put you in my arms. (Moreno, 2014, paras. 4–5)

DECIDING ON AND SEEKING SURROGACY

Even though many prominent gay, bisexual, queer (GBQ) male celebrities have pursued surrogacy (e.g., Neil Patrick Harris, Ricky Martin, Anderson Cooper, Andy Cohen, Shaun T, Perez Hilton), leading to a societal conflation of "gay fatherhood" and "surrogacy," only a small number of LGBTQ people, mainly GBQ men, actually pursue surrogacy. Because of its high cost (more than $100,000 and often closer to $140,000—or $170,000 if egg donation is also used) and the fact that it is not legal in all U.S. states—or all countries (see Creative Family Connections, n.d.)—surrogacy is just not an option for many people. Research on GBQ male couples who pursue surrogacy[1] has documented high household incomes among these men, ranging from an average of $230,000 in one 2015 study to $370,000 in one 2017 study (Blake et al., 2017)—above the national average income for GBQ men who adopt their children (Gates et al., 2007). In the LGBTQ Family Building Project (Goldberg, 2021), half of the men who pursued surrogacy (11 of 23) had family incomes of more than $300,000, with just two reporting family incomes of $100,000 or less.

In addition to being quite affluent, GBQ men who pursue surrogacy are also disproportionately White compared with national data on GBQ adoptive parents (Gates et al., 2007). Thus, they tend to represent a fairly privileged group, especially when compared with GBQ fathers who formed their families in other ways—something that may create divisions within LGBTQ parenting communities (Carroll, 2018; Goldberg, Allen, & Carroll, 2020).

Maybe you have a powerful desire to be biologically connected to your future child. If this is the case, you have company: Among gay, bisexual, and queer (GBQ) men,[2] a strong desire to have a biological child can be a powerful motivator in pursuing surrogacy over adoption (Bergman et al., 2010; Berkowitz, 2020; Goldberg, 2012; Murphy, 2013). Indeed, you may wish to see yourself in your child(ren) and view biogenetic parenthood as "natural" much in the same way that heterosexual people often do (Murphy, 2013). For

---

[1]Some lesbian, gay, bisexual, queer cis women and trans/nonbinary folks also pursue surrogacy. However, within the LGBTQ community, most media and research attention has focused on GBQ cis men, so this section is written with that reality in mind.

[2]Existing work on surrogacy preferences and experiences within the LGBTQ community has largely focused on GBQ cis men, whose economic, racial, and gender privilege allows them more often than other groups to consider surrogacy as an option. Thus, the language in this chapter often reflects that focus (e.g., when referring to what we know about queer people's experiences of surrogacy).

some GBQ men, the possibility of having a genetically related child is a "dream come true," especially after coming out and believing that such an option would never be possible for them (K. O. Ward, 2020). Perceiving adoption as less desirable or less accessible, or as a process that offers little control (e.g., over the outcome, over one's treatment as GBQ men by adoption agencies and prospective birth parents), may also impact some men's choice to pursue surrogacy (Blake et al., 2017). In addition, GBQ men may worry that there are too many "unknowns" or uncontrollable factors in adoption (Berkowitz, 2020; Blake et al., 2017; Carone et al., 2017). In essence, GBQ men who desire surrogacy over adoption often do so because surrogacy seems to promise greater control; less uncertainty; and, ultimately, a genetic linkage to their children. In some cases, too, poor experiences with adoption may play a role. Some arrive at surrogacy because they have tried adoption and have been unsuccessful— for example, they experienced a failed match or placement, or they waited for months or years to be matched without success, leading them to "switch course." Some, too, experienced or anticipate discrimination from adoption agencies or the child welfare system. One participant in the LGBTQ Family Building Project said,

> We tried foster to adopt and adoption, but failed. We really thought we have such a great home that case workers should have been knocking at our door. Instead, most case managers ignored us, and some were offensive when refusing to consider us. We turned to surrogacy because adoption and foster to adopt were failing so badly and it was so disempowering and discouraging.

Another participant said,

> Our state does not prohibit discrimination by its Children's Services department in foster and adoptive services. We learned that the absence of a prohibition allowed any individual child

caseworker to choose to discriminate . . . without any consequence. We had foster children temporarily placed in our home by one case worker only to find that when the child reentered the system, they had a new case worker who would not return the child back to a previously successful placement. We are a gay couple. One of us is HIV positive (I would not disclose that in the home study if we had it to do over), and we are both middle-aged. We don't know precisely the reasons, but we know that many couples who trained with us got placements in the public system, when we did not.

Maybe you really want a child by surrogacy but cannot even begin to imagine how you might afford it. Perhaps then you jump onto the internet and discover something called "transnational surrogacy." Let's consider this option. GBQ men who are very interested in surrogacy but who have limited resources are sometimes tempted to pursue transnational compensated[3] surrogacy—hiring a surrogate from a different country, such as India—because it is less expensive. This process has also been referred to as *fertility tourism* or *reproductive outsourcing*—which hints at some of the moral critiques of this particular approach to family building. Namely, hiring a woman from a less-developed country to carry one's baby raises important ethical issues related to gender, labor, exploitation, and inequality (Berkowitz, 2020). For example, concerns have been raised over the exploitation and commodification of women and children, particularly in the context of stark socioeconomic disparities between prospective or intended parents and surrogates (Newson, 2016).

---

[3]*Compensated surrogacy* (also referred to as "commercial surrogacy") refers to a surrogacy arrangement in which the surrogate is compensated for her services beyond reimbursement of necessary medical expenses.

GBQ men who pursue family building via transnational surrogacy have been criticized for participating in and upholding racialized and heteronormative systems of kinship by virtue of (men) paying for (women) surrogates in less privileged nations (although, of note is that other folks offer an alternative perspective, suggesting that such men are "reworking" and creating new forms of kinship; Berkowitz, 2020). Ultimately, if you are interested in considering transnational surrogacy, you should be aware of, and ideally grapple with, the moral and ethical critiques that surround it and potentially seek consultation to facilitate a clear-eyed decision-making process. Furthermore, you should be advised that (a) you may incur additional costs if travel is required on multiple occasions to the country where the child is born, (b) you may need to stay in the country for as long as several weeks to obtain U.S. citizenship for the child as well as travel documents, and (c) a second-parent adoption may be required after you return home to establish parental rights for the genetically unrelated father.

Among those GBQ cis men (and trans people who produce sperm) who decide to move ahead with surrogacy, most will pursue *gestational surrogacy*, in which the surrogate is not the same person as the egg donor; that is, the donor eggs are fertilized by one person's sperm using in vitro fertilization (IVF), and the embryo that results is then transferred to the surrogate's uterus. This is often more appealing to GBQ men than *genetic (traditional) surrogacy* arrangements, in which the surrogate is also the egg donor, because this scenario is even more emotionally complex—but also less expensive because IVF is not involved. Surrogacy agencies that work with LGBTQ people typically recommend gestational surrogacy over genetic or traditional surrogacy arrangements because gestational surrogacy provides parents greater certainty over legal parentage—and perhaps less anxiety about the possibility that the surrogate will attach to the child (Berkowitz, 2020).

Genetic surrogacy is sometimes pursued with a female relative of the nongenetic parent (e.g., a sister) to enable both parents to have a genetic relationship to the child. However, although such a scenario may sound idyllic in theory, navigating the genetic, emotional, and legal dynamics that it presents is complex and warrants legal and therapeutic consultation.

TAKING STEPS IN THE SURROGACY PROCESS

LGBTQ people who pursue surrogacy should be aware that it can be a lengthy and complex process, consisting of several major steps (Tinker, 2019).

Deciding to Pursue Surrogacy

This is a major decision and may involve consideration of other parenthood avenues (e.g., foster care, adoption) and careful evaluation of one's finances. Furthermore, it involves the more specific decision of what type of surrogacy to pursue: gestational, genetic, or transnational (overseas) surrogacy.

Deciding on an Agency

This decision may occur after consultation with numerous agencies and exploration of their fees, practices, ethics, and treatment of LGBTQ clients specifically. It is highly advisable that surrogacy arrangements between a couple or individual and a surrogate be made with the assistance of an agency. Yes, you can independently manage such arrangements, but this process is logistically complicated, and the advice of a well-qualified lawyer throughout it is recommended (Berkowitz, 2020; May & Tenzek, 2016). A reputable surrogacy agency will have knowledge of surrogacy law and will be able to provide invaluable guidance and a sense of security. Indeed, the top considerations of GBQ men using surrogacy in the LGBTQ Family Building Project were (a) reputation as competent and effective and (b) a reputation as LGBTQ friendly, with 100% endorsing these considerations compared to just 26% who said that cost was a consideration and 16% who said that geographic factors affected their choice of an agency.

The good news is that there is an increasing number of LGBTQ-friendly surrogacy agencies. A 2018 analysis of 103 surrogacy agencies' websites showed that more than half (60 agencies) had language on their websites indicating that they provide services for gay men, with the majority featuring on their home pages their support for gay male clients (Jacobson, 2018). In the LGBTQ Family Building Project, 78% of GBQ men who had pursued surrogacy said that their agency was very LGBTQ friendly—which is notable given that fewer than half (48%) said that LGBTQ people were represented on the website of their agency. Thus, although website representation is a good index of awareness and inclusive practices, it may not be a definitive or singular marker of LGBTQ friendliness. LGBTQ client representation or staff members, for example, may be other useful initial markers of affirming practice. Try to "dig below" agencies' marketing materials to assess whether you will be treated fairly, equitably, and sensitively; indeed, savvy marketing does not necessarily mean that you will be offered culturally competent services.

Notably, in addition to considering the effectiveness and LGBTQ friendliness of an agency, you may wish to consider the degree to which the agency's business practices are ethical, transparent, and without conflicts of interest as well as align with your own moral/ethical compass. Ethical surrogacy agencies are, at a minimum, accountable to their clients, lawmakers, and the public, and they are fully transparent regarding their costs and programs. For example, as the Society for Ethics in Egg Donation and Surrogacy (n.d.) points out, agencies should not offer donors who are matched with other agencies a higher fee if they switch agencies, create a "bidding war" among prospective parents for the same egg donor as a means of determining who is willing to pay the most, or access to competitors' websites to obtain personal details about specific donors with the intention of reaching out to them regarding egg donation.

Matching With an Egg Donor and a Surrogate

After signing on with an agency, and, if relevant, matching with an egg donor,[4] you will be presented with possible surrogate match(es). If both you and the potential surrogate are interested in working together, you will be matched.

Both the surrogate and egg donor are screened heavily before being approved. Egg donors are screened for personal and medical history. Surrogates are subjected to a more extensive screening process, including pregnancy history, medical complications, and psychological evaluation. Surrogates should be at least 21 years old and should have already carried a pregnancy and given birth at least once so that they have a good understanding of the physical and emotional experience of pregnancy and delivery.

---

[4]Egg donors are typically anonymous in the United States, but some donor egg banks allow donors to choose if they want an "ID option" or "non-ID option" for intended parents. The ID option means that the egg donor agrees to release their identity and contact information to the egg donor–conceived child (not the recipient of the donor eggs), once the child reaches age 18—if they request such information.

Undergoing Medical Screenings

Once a match is made, the surrogate (gestational carrier) will be screened medically. Then medications and monitoring will begin.

Handling Legal Paperwork

You should work with a lawyer to draft a surrogacy contract while the surrogate works with their own lawyer. A surrogacy lawyer is an essential part of the surrogacy process: You cannot legally or ethically complete the process without one.

Being Involved in the Pregnancy

If the surrogate is being implanted with donor eggs, the surrogate will go to an IVF clinic for embryo transfer. If amenable to both parties, you or your partner, or both of you, as the intended parents, may be present for this important event. Assuming that the surrogate becomes pregnant, you as the intended parent(s) and the surrogate will be in touch during the pregnancy, with the surrogate sharing updates and ultrasounds. Many intended parents attend the 20-week ultrasound in particular.[5]

During the pregnancy, you also may wish to tour the hospital where your baby or babies will be born. At this stage, it is a good idea to explore the hospital's track record for working with LGBTQ people and those involved in surrogacy arrangements specifically.

---

[5]The 20-week ultrasound is typically one of the most detailed—and often longest—ultrasounds of the pregnancy. For more details on what you will learn at the 20-week ultrasound, see Daley (2019).

You should also work with your attorney(s) to discuss and establish parental rights.

Attending the Delivery

Your surrogacy contract—the contract you have with your surrogate—will address issues such as where the surrogate will be delivering the baby and who will be in attendance. In most cases, one or both intended parents are present in the delivery room. It is essential that you research the hospital or birthing center where your surrogate will give birth to get a sense of how experienced or familiar the facility is with your particular scenario. You may want to be prepared—with your partner and surrogate—for some uncomfortable moments with hospital staff and be ready to provide a simple and straightforward explanation of who you are. You may also wish to make signs for the hospital room door that denote the roles of all involved and how all parties wish to be referred to (e.g., the surrogate is not the mother; the intended parent(s) may wish to be referred to as "parent," "father," or something else). (Of note: Just 39% of GBQ men who pursued surrogacy in the LGBTQ Family Building Project said that the hospital where their surrogate delivered was very LGBTQ friendly, with the remainder indicating that the hospital was "neutral" or "somewhat" LGBTQ friendly.)

CONSIDERING OTHER ASPECTS OF SURROGACY

How to Decide on an Egg Donor?

Similar to the selection of sperm donors, LGBTQ prospective parents consider appearance, intelligence, and talents as well as whether the egg donor resembles one or both of their family members. Physical similarity with the nongenetic parent/partner may be a particularly important consideration. Evaluate whether these or other factors might be important in your decision making.

How to Decide Who Is the Genetic Parent?

You may decide to form embryos with both partners' sperm and see what happens.[6] Or you may desire two children—twins—with each child genetically connected to one parent. It is in fact possible to create embryos using the same egg donor and the biology from each parent, such that half of the eggs are fertilized with one person's sperm and the other half with the other person's sperm. Or, you may want two children eventually, but not at the same time, and thus pursue one pregnancy at a time, with each of you taking a turn providing the sperm. Or, perhaps, one of you may simply have a greater desire to be genetically related, making the decision somewhat simpler in terms of who provides the sperm.

Fertility and genetic consultation may impact this decision as well, such that each potential genetic parent's health, genetic profile, family medical history, and age (indeed, sperm quality declines with age) may come into play in deciding who is the best candidate to provide sperm. As one gay father in the LGBTQ Family Building Project shared, "I have a family history of cancer, depression, and anxiety. My partner does not have a family history of diseases with

---

[6]It is possible that both men may ultimately be related to a child or children, if multiple embryos are implanted, resulting in twins or multiples. The process of mixing sperm means that mature eggs are fertilized with sperm from both partners. The medical team assesses the quality of the embryos, and then, in coordination with the couple, a decision about which embryo or embryos to transfer is made. The couple may opt to have multiple embryos implanted, thereby increasing the likelihood of twins. Multiple embryo transfer and the possibility of twins are indeed often acceptable or even desirable to male couples (Sylvestre-Margolis et al., 2015).

high potential of being genetically transmitted." Another gay father explained, "We created embryos from both of our genetic material and asked the clinic to use the healthiest looking embryo without disclosing who the genetic link was to. We only found out the genetic link shortly prior to birth."

What Are the Key Legal Issues at Hand?

You should know and understand the laws of whatever state the surrogate delivers the baby in because the federal government does not regulate surrogacy. Thus, as long as the surrogate delivers in a state where surrogacy is legal, there will very likely be no custody issues (i.e., in which a gestational surrogate obtains legal rights to a child). It is essential, too, that you know the ins and outs of the legalities surrounding surrogacy by same-gender couples. Some states allow married same-gender couples to enter into surrogacy contracts (e.g., California; Connecticut; Washington, DC; Nevada; Texas) and allow prebirth parentage orders, enabling both partners to be named on the birth certificate and to establish legal parentage following the birth. Other states have vague or inconsistent laws surrounding surrogacy, which may make it challenging to obtain prebirth parentage orders. Because of the unsettled and inconsistent legal landscape, you should be certain that your surrogacy agency understands the unique issues for LGBTQ people, and you should pursue additional legal counsel if you have remaining concerns, doubts, or questions.

The typical timetable for becoming a parent via surrogacy is a bit over a year from start to finish. First, it generally takes a few months, maybe more, to find an appropriate surrogate. Then, you can expect up to a few months of waiting while the surrogate is cleared medically, psychologically, and legally, after which the surrogacy contract will be drafted for your review. After signing, it may take a few months to prepare the egg donor for retrieval and the IVF cycle (which could also happen during the time when the surrogate is being cleared medically). Then, it will take an average of 2 months to prepare the surrogate for the embryo transfer. Assuming all goes well, you then enter the 9-month waiting period (in a typical pregnancy). But various obstacles or roadblocks may delay or extend this process, including issues with the embryo transfer; unforeseen or disputed costs associated with the process (e.g., medical procedures); and events, such as the COVID-19 pandemic, which may slow or halt nonemergency medical procedures and appointments. Ultimately, it's best to be prepared that the process may take longer than expected because of various issues that may arise.

MANAGING GENETIC ASYMMETRY IN FAMILIES FORMED VIA SURROGACY

Surrogacy, like donor insemination, often involves *genetic asymmetry*, in which one partner is genetically related to the child and one partner is not, although it differs in that the experiences of pregnancy, birth, and chestfeeding are not relevant. Nevertheless, many of the same issues and considerations apply when contemplating who should provide the sperm or the possible implications of the inevitable genetic asymmetry that results (e.g., in terms of jealousy and bonding).

Health and age considerations (including who possesses "better genes"; Greenfeld & Seli, 2011, p. 277), as well as relative desire to be the genetic parent, appear to factor into GBQ men's decision making, with equivalent levels of desire sometimes leading couples to form embryos with both partners' sperm and see what happens. In a 2017 study of 74 GBQ fathers (Blake et al., 2017), the authors found that in half of respondents, both men provided sperm, leaving genetic fatherhood to chance. For almost one quarter, having a genetic tie to the child was more significant to one partner than the other, which influenced their decision making, and 12% planned to take turns in who would have a genetic tie to the child. Medical reasons affected the decision making of 4% of fathers. In addition to interest or desire in being the genetic parent as well as health or medical reasons, it may also be worthwhile to consider other dimensions of power and privilege. For example, consider each intended parent's race and (dis)ability status, because both will impact how the parents are regarded by the outside world and how their parenthood status will be evaluated (e.g., interrogated, respected).

It is important to initiate and maintain direct and open communication with your partner as you make, and anticipate the consequences of, this decision. For example, when a couple decides to form embryos with both partners' sperm because both have a desire to be genetically related to the child, it is helpful to anticipate that one partner may ultimately experience feelings of sadness or envy related to a lack of genetic relatedness. Therapy can help to facilitate dialogue surrounding the decision-making process regarding who will be the genetic parent as well as to guide open and honest communication about concerns related to genetic asymmetry. Therapy can also help you to anticipate and hopefully strategize ways to address challenges that may come into play (e.g., feelings of or societal perceptions of one parent as more of the "real" parent). It can also help you to think about how you will approach sharing information about genetic parenthood with individuals outside of your family. For example, will you share details of who is the genetic parent with immediate family? Friends? Extended family? How will you talk about this? What questions from outsiders are you willing or unwilling to answer, and how will you respond to people who ask intrusive or inappropriate questions?

Almost one quarter (22%) of the GBQ fathers who pursued surrogacy in the LGBTQ Family Building Project shared that they did not disclose who was the genetically related parent to anyone outside of their family. "We don't disclose who contributed the sperm even when asked," said one. "We don't tell anyone who the genetic parent is. It's none of their business," said another. It may be helpful to work with a therapist who is skilled in working with LGBTQ individuals and couples not only before but also after the family-building process as you adjust to parenthood, establish your parental roles and identities, and make decisions about what family-building related information you are comfortable sharing with outsiders.

PURSUING OTHER ROUTES TO PARENTHOOD: COPARENTING, CIS/HETERONORMATIVE SEX, STEPPARENTING

Beyond surrogacy (and adoption and donor insemination, already covered in Chapters 2 and 3, respectively), there are several other key routes to parenthood worth addressing. Namely, these are coparenting, cis/heteronormative sex, and stepparenting.

Coparenting Arrangements

Some LGBTQ individuals and couples pursue coparenting arrangements—for example, a cis male couple and a cis female couple might elect to become parents together, whereby one woman would be impregnated with the sperm from one of the men (Bos, 2010). Alternatively, some single GBQ men elect to conceive and raise children with single women, a decision sometimes informed by the belief that having two different-gender parents is the ideal setting in which to raise children as well as the desire to ensure a maternal influence (Erera & Segal-Engelchin, 2014). It is important that if you pursue this avenue, all issues of contact and responsibility for the child are clearly communicated before insemination. You should seek legal advice from someone with expertise in LGBTQ family-building and coparenting arrangements. You will need to make an agreement that outlines each party's level of parental responsibility, including financial contributions, living arrangements, and contact with the child.

Cis/Heteronormative Sex

Some LGBTQ people become parents via cis/heteronormative sex, either in the context of a different-gender romantic relationship (e.g., as in the case of a bisexual parent) or in the context of a prearranged sexual encounter for the explicit purpose of conceiving (e.g., a lesbian-identified woman might have sex with a male friend rather than insemination using his sperm as a means of enhancing the likelihood of conception). Bisexual and other nonmonosexual[7] individuals who are in different-gender relationships are often perceived as heterosexual—a reality that confers a certain degree of privilege (e.g., it protects them from discrimination) but can also lead to feelings of invisibility. One cis woman in the LGBTQ Family Building Project shared,

> I've often "passed" as straight even when married to a woman. Now I feel like I need to mention my previous marriage because I am in a heterosexual relationship. It's a very strange dynamic, and I do feel invisible—but now within the LBGTQ community.

Another cis woman said,

> Just having children makes people more convinced that I'm straight, both within the LGBTQ+ community and also from straight people. And both will literally argue to my face that I don't know my own sexuality because my partner is male and we have children.

Likewise, some trans parents become parents in the context of different-gender relationships before transitioning—for example, a trans man may have been previously married to a cis man and had a child in the context of that relationship. Some trans people have

---

[7]*Nonmonosexual* refers to people who are attracted to more than one gender (e.g., queer, bisexual, pansexual).

children after transitioning—for example, a trans man partnered with a cis man may elect to become pregnant using his partner's sperm. Although pregnancy itself may be experienced as gender incongruous or even traumatic, that parent can ultimately claim a parental identity and title that is consistent with their gender identity (e.g., dad; Haines et al., 2014; Pyne, 2012; Pyne et al., 2015).

Stepparenting

Other LGBTQ people become parents in the context of stepparenting—that is, by partnering with a person who already has children, sometimes from a prior heterosexual relationship or marriage. This scenario is believed to be fairly common. To many people's surprise, the majority of children under 18 who live in LGBTQ parent households entered them following a heterosexual relationship dissolution rather than via planned LGBTQ parent families using insemination, surrogacy, foster care, or adoption (Goldberg, Gartrell, & Gates, 2014; Tasker & Lavender-Stott, 2020).

Becoming an LGBTQ stepfamily can involve unique issues, including boundary and role ambiguity in regard to the queer stepparent's place in the family as well as stigma directed at both parents and children (Jenkins, 2013; Robitaille & Saint-Jacques, 2009). Becoming a stepparent is challenging on its own because there are not clear guidelines or expectations surrounding one's role, and each family member (children and parents) may be managing intense loss alongside trying to establish new relationships, routines, boundaries, and skills. Becoming a stepparent may be extra challenging as an LGBTQ person, given the lack of societal recognition and validation of same-gender relationships that persists despite advancements in LGBTQ rights (Acosta, 2021). Hostility or resentment from family members (e.g., the children's other parent) can add to challenging dynamics for the LGBTQ stepparent—for example, making it more challenging to form positive relationships with the children (Tasker &

Lavender-Stott, 2020). Reasons for the separation or divorce (e.g., violence, infidelity), time since the separation, whether the postseparation coparenting relationship is civil or strained, and physical and legal custody arrangements can all impact family dynamics as well as the degree of tension that the LGBTQ stepparent may encounter in relation to the children's other parents and the children themselves.

Counseling and connection with other members of the LGBTQ parenting community who have also navigated stepfamily formation dynamics may be helpful to you if you are an LGBTQ stepparent. Yet it can be hard to find folks who share one's experiences as a stepparent, much less an LGBTQ stepparent. Online resources and communities may be your best bet, especially if you live in a rural area or one without a visible and active LGBTQ community. The National Stepfamily Resource Center (https://www.stepfamilies.info/) is one major clearinghouse for general stepparenting information; there are also online (e.g., Facebook) groups for LGBTQ stepparents. Family therapy can also be enormously helpful to newly constituted stepfamilies.

CONCLUSION

Surrogacy is not an option for many members of the LGBTQ community because of its high cost. Most queer people who pursue surrogacy are affluent White cis men. As illustrated in the opening vignette, a variety of factors may inform the desire to pursue genetic parenthood, including reasons that are generally taken for granted or are readily accepted when they are espoused by cis heterosexual people (e.g., "I just wanted a genetic connection to my child"). Some folks may really, really want to pursue surrogacy but simply not have the ability to do it (e.g., an older gay man with a low sperm count, a trans woman who did not bank her sperm before transitioning, a single bisexual man with limited income).

If you are working through grief or a sense of loss surrounding an inability to have a genetic child via surrogacy, some of the infertility-related resources that are geared toward heterosexual couples may be of use to you. But, in addition, seeking out resources that are LGBTQ specific may be especially important. An LGBTQ-competent therapist who is also competent in reproductive loss might be particularly helpful. If you are unable to locate someone with such qualifications, it may be possible to get what you need from multiple sources (e.g., online resources and support groups for reproductive loss, online resources and support groups for LGBTQ parents-to-be and parents).

RESOURCES

Circle Surrogacy. (n.d.). *Surrogacy by state: Get the facts.* https://www.circlesurrogacy.com/surrogacy/surrogacy-by-state-surrogacy-laws

Craven, C. (2019). *Reproductive losses: Challenges to LGBTQ family-making.* Routledge. https://doi.org/10.4324/9780429431715

Kaufman, D. (2020, July 24). The fight for fertility equality. *The New York Times.* https://www.nytimes.com/2020/07/22/style/lgbtq-fertility-surrogacy-coverage.html

Men Having Babies, https://www.menhavingbabies.org

This international nonprofit organization offers guidance, advocacy, and financial assistance for current and future gay surrogacy parents.

National Stepfamily Resource Center, https://www.stepfamilies.info/

Society for Ethics in Egg Donation and Surrogacy (SEEDS), https://www.seedsethics.org/

SEEDS is a nonprofit group that seeks to define and uphold the highest ethical standards for egg donation and surrogacy programs in relation to clients, clinics, donors, surrogates, and others.

Tinker, B. (2019). *The top 10 questions about surrogacy for same-sex couples, answered.* CNN. https://www.cnn.com/2019/06/14/health/same-sex-surrogacy-faq/index.html

CHAPTER 5

CHOOSING LGBTQ-FRIENDLY ADOPTION AGENCIES AND HEALTH SERVICE PROVIDERS

THIS CHAPTER COVERS:

> choosing an adoption agency
> choosing reproductive health providers
> considering trans-specific factors

Nicky, a Black, nonbinary queer teacher and Jessica, a Black, cis queer computer programmer, were together for 5 years when they began to explore parenthood. They live in a suburb in the Midwest, approximately 30 minutes away from the nearest major city. The couple has several friends who adopted through the state's child welfare system, so they were familiar with adopting through foster care. They also were familiar with private domestic adoption because one of Nicky's coworkers had adopted a newborn using this route.

The couple was open to adopting a child younger than age 5 years, which led them to initially explore adoption via the child welfare system. They attended a 2-hour introductory session about the process of adopting through foster care, which covered topics like the requirements to become a foster parent in the state, required trainings and paperwork, and the home study. The other attendees were predominantly White, presumably heterosexual couples; two single adults were also in attendance.

When the facilitator, Bethany, asked them to go around and give their names, Nicky and Jessica both added their pronouns (they/them and she/hers, respectively). Bethany looked startled and quickly averted her eyes. Even though both Nicky and Jessica raised their hands at various points to answer questions that were posed, Bethany never called on them, and it seemed she was avoiding them. Furthermore, all of the examples Bethany provided throughout the training referenced seemingly heterosexual couples (e.g., "Jim and Mary are a White couple who aren't sure if their extended family will be accepting of a child of a different race," "Bill and Tonya are a couple with biological kids who are thinking of adopting"). As the session concluded, Nicky and Jessica got the distinct feeling that Bethany was talking to them when she said, "This path might not be right for all of you"; indeed, Bethany glanced in their direction as she said this.

Walking out to the car after the session, Nicky remarked wryly, "Well, that was interesting! It's hard to know which part of us she liked less. There are many to choose from." Jessica nodded, her head filled with questions: Was Bethany hostile to them? And, if so, was it because of their gender identity/ expression, sexual orientation, race, or something else? Would the other social workers and agency personnel that they would likely interface with in the future be similarly dismissive and cold toward them? Should they look into other options now or in the future? "Let's call Debbie and Maureen when we get home," said Jessica, referring to their friends who had adopted through the local child welfare system. "I want to get the lowdown from them in terms of what to expect—after all, they made it through the process and adopted two kids."

ADOPTION AGENCIES AND PROFESSIONALS

Nicky and Jessica experienced something that lesbian, gay, bisexual, transgender (trans), and queer (LGBTQ) individuals, particularly those with multiple marginalized identities, might encounter from adoption and foster care agencies and professionals: vague or subtle signs that they may not be welcomed and are even "undesirable" as potential applicants. Despite the change in attitudes toward LGBTQ parenting over the past few decades, some social service agency personnel still hold the belief that children need a mother and a father for normal development to occur or that LGBTQ parents will provide an inadequate or even harmful environment for children (Goldberg et al., 2007; Mallon, 2011). Such beliefs may also be held by people involved in the child welfare and legal systems, such as social workers and judges, and LGBTQ people may therefore encounter a variety of roadblocks that discourage or, in some cases, prevent them from becoming parents. Because of such challenges, people like Nicky and Jessica might give up on the possibility of fostering or adopting— a devastating outcome, not just for Nicky and Jessica but for the children who might have flourished in their care.

Even if they persevered in pursuing adoption or foster care despite the initially cold reception they encountered from social services, Nicky or Jessica might encounter obstacles at other stages of their journey. *Home studies*, which are formal evaluations of the prospective foster or adoptive parents' lives and their suitability for child placements,[1] may be written up by social workers who are biased against LGBTQ prospective adopters (Goldberg et al., 2007; Goldberg, Frost, et al., 2019: Goldberg, Tornello, et al., 2020; Mallon, 2011). In turn, home studies may be written in ways that highlight applicants' sexual orientation or gender identity such that

---

[1]Adoption home studies consist of a detailed written report and assessment of prospective adoptive parents' home and life. Regardless of the type of adoption or entity that assists families in the process (e.g., public agency, private agency, attorney), nearly all families must complete the home study process before proceeding with an adoptive placement.

they are unlikely to be seen as stable, appropriate potential parents (Goldberg, Frost, et al., 2019). As one trans queer prospective adoptive parent in a 2019 study said,

> I was asked invasive questions about my genitals during the homestudy interview and about what surgeries I have had. My whole interview/section of the homestudy report focused on my transition. . . . Social workers made comments to us and asked us if we were going to "make the kids trans." (Goldberg, Frost, et al., 2019, p. 6)

LGBTQ people may find that their applications to foster or adopt are rejected, or they may simply not receive calls for potential child placements (Goldberg, Downing, & Sauck, 2007; Goldberg, Frost, et al., 2019). Consistently being denied child placements or simply not hearing back from social workers and social service agencies about potential placements can create a vague sense of anxiety about the possibility of discrimination. But, a lack of direct evidence of such discrimination and fear of "rocking the boat" can cause some LGBTQ applicants to stay silent, worried that voicing their frustrations could cause further negative treatment.

LGBTQ applicants may also find that they are being held to a higher standard in terms of being considered a "legitimate" or acceptable fosterer or adopter (Wood, 2016). They may be coerced (e.g., by social workers) into presenting themselves in ways that downplay their sexuality or that highlight their "suitability" in distinct ways, such as detailing how they can provide "gender role models" for children (Hicks, 2008). Some LGBTQ applicants reported receiving the message that they will be successful in adopting or fostering only if they characterize themselves as gender normative, monogamous, nonpolitical, and middle-class, and without other "deficits" (besides their sexual orientation, that is), such as mental health or substance issues (Hicks, 2008; Riggs, 2011; Wood, 2016).

Some LGBTQ parents have even reported feeling pressured to take more challenging or hard-to-place children, the assumption being that because they themselves are less desirable applicants, they cannot afford to be choosy (Goldberg, 2012; Goldberg, Frost, et al., 2019). As one respondent in a 2019 study of LGBTQ foster and adoptive parents shared, "As white lesbians, we were told we could only adopt children of color or those with disabilities. This was very common amongst all our friends, those using county agencies as well as private agencies" (Goldberg, Frost, et al., 2019, p. 11).

Beyond child welfare and adoption workers, birth parents may also be biased against placement of children in LGBTQ-parent households (e.g., they may resist placement of their children with a same-gender couple; Goldberg, Frost, et al., 2019; S. Ryan & Whitlock, 2007). Said one lesbian woman in a 2019 study of LGBTQ foster and adoptive parents,

> Social services refused to terminate parental rights . . . because the birth parents didn't want the kids to be adopted by lesbians. The birth parents had horribly abused and neglected the children, so adoption was an appropriate action. Social service[s] threatened to look for another adoptive family if they terminated even though the children had been with us three years, and all professionals working with the kids advised that it was in the children's best interest to stay with us and be adopted by us. We had to take the social services to court to force them to terminate rights and allow us to adopt. (Goldberg, Frost, et al., 2019, p. 6)

As this quote reveals, discrimination across various systems (e.g., birth family, social services) may operate together to undermine child placement with LGBTQ people. Discrimination in the legal realm is yet another systemic barrier that queer and trans people may encounter. Although, currently, all states within the United States technically allow for adoption by same-gender couples, this is a fairly recent change, with some states having historically banned LGBTQ adoption and others having operated on de facto bans through the requirement that adoptive couples be married (Goldberg et al., 2013). With the 2015 U.S. Supreme Court marriage equality ruling (*Obergefell v. Hodges*, 2015) and the repeal of specific LGBTQ adoption bans (e.g., in Florida via *Florida Department of Children and Families v. IN RE: Adoption of X. X. G. and N. R. G., Appellees*, 2010), adoption is now theoretically broadly available to LGBTQ people in the United States. However, removing discriminatory legislation does not guarantee immediate change. The threat of discriminatory treatment often lingers in its aftermath, and legal and social service systems may act as "gatekeepers," thwarting LGBTQ adopters' efforts to become parents. Furthermore, during Donald J. Trump's presidency (2016–2020), a number of religious exemption bills were introduced in U.S. state legislatures, which, in some cases, became law, thus allowing private agencies contracting with child welfare departments to deny applications from LGBTQ people based on religious or moral convictions (Bewkes et al., 2018; Moreau, 2018). It goes without saying that where you live can have a powerful impact on your experience navigating the legal arm of adoption. As one lesbian woman in a 2019 study of LGBTQ foster and adoptive parents shared,

> We have had custody of the children for over five years. The parents have voluntarily terminated their rights, but the judge in our county refuses to grant our adoption by giving us the run around and saying we have to start all over. We've already invested $10,000 and we have yet to have a day in front of a judge. Lawyers around here don't want their practice to be hurt by representing us and they don't want to upset any of the judges they know personally. (Goldberg, Frost, et al., 2019, p. 6)

Limited Options, Restricted Choices

Your options regarding what adoption agency or professionals you work with may be limited based on a number of factors. First, you may be limited to working with your local child welfare agency because you are committed to adopting through foster care or because you have limited financial resources (recall that private adoption typically costs $15,000 or more; see Chapter 2). Even if you pursue adoption through a private agency, your options may be constrained based on where you live. Couples like Nicky and Jessica, who live outside of major metropolitan areas, likely face fewer options than those who live in cities, particularly progressive cities, such as Boston, Seattle, and San Francisco. LGBTQ prospective adoptive or foster parents sometimes choose to work with LGBTQ-friendly, but geographically distant, agencies—and while this choice may enable affirming services and representation, applicants may be forced to access support virtually as opposed to in person—for example, if a long drive or plane ride is required to physically meet with agency personnel (Kinkler & Goldberg, 2011).

The Center for American Progress conducted a 2018 analysis of LGBTQ prospective adopters' options regarding accessing LGBTQ-inclusive options in states that are generally inhospitable to LGBTQ adopters. The center highlighted Texas as a large state that nevertheless has few LGBTQ-inclusive adoption agencies, thus demonstrating the burden on LGBTQ people who seek to foster or adopt. In its report, the center stated:

> In three of the 10 most populous cities of Texas, there is no agency that is explicitly affirming of LGBTQ people within the greater metropolitan region. . . . A same-sex couple in El Paso might avoid the nearest agency one mile away for fear of being turned away, and instead drive 348 miles to an agency with an LGBTQ-inclusive nondiscrimination policy on their website.

Similarly, there are child-placing agencies within 30 miles of Corpus Christi and within four miles of Laredo, but the nearest agencies that explicitly welcome LGBTQ people by having an LGBTQ-inclusive nondiscrimination policy posted on their websites are 67 and 153 miles away, respectively. (Bewkes et al., 2018, paras. 9, 65)

Where you live matters in other ways, too. As noted, some states have religious exemption policies or laws that allow agencies to discriminate against LGBTQ applicants. Historically, discriminatory laws and policies related to who can adopt or foster children have resulted in some LGBTQ people's giving up on their parenting aspirations altogether or choosing alternative path to parenthood, such as surrogacy. One participant in the LGBTQ Family Building Project (Goldberg, 2021) who ultimately chose to pursue surrogacy said, "We weren't able to adopt in [Virginia], so surrogacy was the only/best option for us." Another participant who ended up pursuing surrogacy said, "Texas was trying to make it illegal for gay couples to adopt when we were starting our family." Indeed, in the LGBTQ Family Building Project, among the 174 participants (32% of the overall sample) who had adopted or fostered children, 35% said that fears or perceptions of discrimination by agencies and social workers had, at one point, been a barrier to, or reason for delaying initiation of, the family-building process.

Unique Forms of Discrimination

Depending on your unique identities and family situation, you might encounter additional forms of discrimination during the adoption process. Bisexual people sometimes face negative stereotypes specific to bisexuality, such as the assumption that bisexual people are overly sexual and polyamorous—characteristics that are assumed to negatively affect children (Moss, 2012). Such stereotypes of bisexual people may lead some adoption agency professionals to assume that bisexual people are less fit to parent (Ross & Dobinson, 2013).

People who are in consensually nonmonogamous relationships may also face discrimination if seeking to build their families through adoption or other means (Pallotta-Chiarolli et al., 2020). Of note, there are currently few formal policies on polyamorous people seeking to adopt. If you are a member of a polyamorous relationship and pursuing adoption, you should interview multiple adoption agencies and also consult with an attorney who practices family law in your jurisdiction to determine your options. Several states currently allow for three parents on a birth certificate, and some states allow for three-parent adoptions. In turn, it is possible that one could do a second- or third-parent adoption of the child after the initial placement is finalized (Family Equality Council, 2021a). Family Equality, The National LGBTQ+ Bar Association, and other national LGBTQ organizations offer support and resources for parents and prospective parents in polyamorous relationships.

Trans, nonbinary, and gender nonconforming (i.e., trans) applicants face challenges as well (Goldberg, Frost, et al., 2019). Again, it is important to interview agencies with an eye toward whether they are trans inclusive specifically. If you are a trans prospective adoptive or foster parent, attend carefully to the ways in which agencies do or do not acknowledge you in recruitment and training materials, physical environment, and visual cues. A list of specific questions to ask yourself as you evaluate potential agencies appears in the next section.

LGBTQ-Affirming Adoption Agencies

The Human Rights Campaign's All Children–All Families project has partnered with child welfare agencies around the country to improve the services it provides to the LGBTQ community. In a 2020 report, it highlighted 100 of those agencies, which were selected because of their commitment to implementing the All Children–All Families' "Benchmarks of LGBTQ Inclusion" and because of their excellent efforts to becoming LGBTQ welcoming and affirming. This report, and the list of both private and public agencies, can be found online (see Human Rights Campaign, 2020a).

Even if none of the agencies listed is accessible to you, don't despair. Many agencies simply did not take part in this initiative but are nevertheless LGBTQ affirming. In searching for an LGBTQ-friendly agency, you can ask a number of questions to evaluate each agency's commitment to LGBTQ inclusion. Some of these questions can be answered by looking at a given agency's website or materials, but some may require a phone call or further investigation. And, of course, it is important to assess for and inquire about their competence more generally as well as to get a sense of their reputation among community members and adoptive parents more broadly. In the LGBTQ Family Building Project, 72% of adoptive or foster parents considered the LGBTQ friendliness of adoption agencies when choosing an agency, whereas 50% considered the agency's reputation as effective and competent. Thus, both LGBTQ friendliness and general reputation may be important to the extent that it is possible to prioritize these agency qualities. Indeed, 12% of participants said that they chose their agency because it was their local child welfare agency (i.e., they had few choices), and another 24% said that cost was an important consideration in choosing an agency. Other considerations, such as location and ease of completing the necessary paperwork and programming, as well as agency philosophy and ethics (e.g., do they have options counseling for expectant parents? Do they offer lifelong counseling to birth parents?), may also be important in selecting an agency.

Questions to Ask Yourself in Evaluating Potential Adoption Agencies

The following questions were informed by the Human Rights Campaign (2020a) and Child Welfare Information Gateway (2016):

- Does the agency have written policies to protect LGBTQ clients from discrimination?
  - Is this policy inclusive of sexual orientation, gender identity, and gender expression?
  - Is this policy clearly communicated to clients?
- Are agency staff trained on LGBTQ competence and inclusion?
  - For example, do they receive training on creating an LGBTQ-inclusive training experience? Do they receive guidance on conducting LGBTQ-affirming home studies?
  - Does the agency indicate if they have any LGBTQ staff members? Are LGBTQ staff members diverse with respect to race and ethnicity and gender identity and expression?
- Does the agency take an explicitly welcoming stance of LGBTQ prospective parents? Consider the following:
  - *Agency forms and paperwork.* Do these use inclusive language—for example, "Parent A," "Parent B" versus "mother," "father"? Is there an option to indicate other genders besides male and female? Is there an option to indicate a name other than one's legal name? Is there an option to indicate one's pronouns, such as she/her, he/him, they/them?
  - *Visuals and images in social media, website, brochures, physical agency (e.g., waiting rooms, offices).* Are these inclusive of diverse relationship types (e.g., same-sex couples), gender presentations, and so forth?
  - *External communications (website, social media, ads, printed materials).* Do they express a commitment to working with,

supporting, and welcoming LGBTQ clients? Do they actively reach out to and seek to recruit LGBTQ applicants (e.g., using ads featuring same-sex couples or trans parents, attending LGBTQ events)?

- *LGBTQ-specific content and supports.* Does training include LGBTQ-specific content? Is that content delivered via skillful means? Are LGBTQ-specific resources (e.g., legal) for outside supports and services provided? Are the providers of such resources vetted to ensure that they are LGBTQ competent?

It may be useful to call or visit adoption agencies to get a sense of whether they are genuinely affirming. You can also ask about the agency's experience with LGBTQ applicants: what number of LGBTQ clients the agency serves per year, the LGBTQ percentage of their total client base, whether you can contact past LGBTQ clients, how the agency presents LGBTQ prospective parents to expectant parents who are considering adoption, and how long LGBTQ prospective parents typically wait for a match. You may want to ask other LGBTQ parents in your community, including

---

Spotlight on LGBTQ-Inclusive Adoption Agencies

One of the agencies that achieved the highest benchmark ("innovative inclusion") established by HRC's (2020a) All Children–All Families initiative is the private adoption agency, Adoptions Together, in Calverton, Maryland. Check out their website (https://www.adoptionstogether.org/) to see an example of thoughtful inclusion of LGBTQ prospective clients and adopters.

Adoptions Together specifically mentions that it welcomes trans and bisexual applicants. The agency's website contains a list of frequently asked questions relevant to LGBTQ applicants.

friends and friends of friends, about their experiences and whether they have recommendations for agencies to use or to avoid. If you live in a state or jurisdiction with laws restricting LGBTQ foster and adoptive parents, inquire about how the agency has historically navigated such challenges (Child Welfare Information Gateway, 2016).

Trans-Specific Questions to Ask Yourself

In addition to evaluating the items (e.g., inclusive gender options on agency website and written materials) mentioned earlier, if you or your partner(s) are trans, it is also worth asking yourself these questions (Perry, 2017):

- Are trans people mentioned (e.g., as in LGBTQ)?
  - If so, is this mention accompanied by attention to their unique circumstances—for example, privacy and disclosure concerns in the adoption process and home study, and unique strengths, such as trans people's empathy toward, and willingness to adopt, children with challenging backgrounds?
  - Are trans people encompassed or acknowledged in paperwork as well as in images or visual cues on the website?
- Are any staff members designated as trans-competent or having received special training in supporting or completing home studies for trans applicants?
- Are there any staff members who are openly trans-identified?
- Does the agency have established relationships with trans organizations or trans resource centers?
- Are trans resource lists comprehensive, up-to-date, and regularly maintained (e.g., those appearing on the agency's website)?

- In open houses, informational sessions, and so on, do staff include pronouns on their nametags or in their verbal introductions?
- Does the physical agency have gender-inclusive or single-stall restrooms, with clear signage indicating them (e.g., "All Gender Restroom")?

ADOPTION ATTORNEYS AND INDEPENDENT ADOPTIONS

In all adoptions, attorneys must be involved. In agency adoptions, consultation with an attorney will be facilitated along with all other adoption services, including matching with birth parents, counseling, support, and so on. In an independent adoption, the prospective adoptive parent(s) is working directly with an attorney only—no agency. Adoption agencies offer a lot of assistance and services, whereas attorneys in independent adoptions offer minimal assistance. For example, attorneys in independent adoptions rarely provide matching or screening services, so families who seek to pursue a private adoption independently have typically already matched with an expectant parent; this is also the option that families may choose if they are pursuing adoption of a relative's child. Some families are drawn to independent adoptions because they are lower cost, involve fewer people, and may perceived as less intrusive. The downside, though, is that they are more "DIY" [do it yourself] and do not involve the same level of support and guidance as those facilitated by agencies, generally speaking.[2]

---

[2]For more details on the distinctions between independent and agency adoptions—and the pros and cons of each—see Adoption Agencies (n.d.), Pact (n.d.), and American Adoptions (n.d.).

Many of the same questions that you would ask of adoption agencies can be asked of adoption attorneys in terms of finding a good match. In addition, be sure to ask questions about the extensiveness of their adoption expertise, including

- knowledge of your state's laws regarding adoption;
- level of preparation for all potential scenarios that might arise in your adoption journey;
- track record (e.g., how many nonrelative adoptions have they completed this year? In the past 5 years?);
- how much of their practice is devoted to adoption;
- experiences with, handling of, and perspective on open adoption; and
- experience with LGBTQ adoptions specifically.

In addition, be thoughtful about your personal connection to a potential attorney. You will be working intensively with this person. Do you like them? Do they seem honest and empathic? Will they relate to expectant parents in a way that feels good to you (e.g., how do they talk about expectant parents? What is their perspective on and knowledge of open adoption?)?

And, of course, ask questions about attorney fees and costs (e.g., Are rates hourly? Will you be billed for the attorney's work only or by work performed by legal/office staff?). Also, ensure that you have a "full picture" of what to expect in this area. For a comprehensive list of potential questions to ask, see Caughman and Motley (n.d.-b).

REPRODUCTIVE HEALTH CARE

Although awareness and acceptance of LGBTQ family building is growing, stigma and discrimination surrounding LGBTQ people's use of reproductive technologies to become parents remain. Some

LGBTQ individuals, for example, may encounter fertility clinics[3] that seem disinclined to work with them—for example, because they do not necessarily possess a medical infertility diagnosis (an assumption of "need" based on a heteronormative model of family building, whereby only heterosexual couples should need the support of fertility services; Corbett et al., 2013). Clinics may also be resistant to perform cycle monitoring, intrauterine insemination (IUI), and other services when they discover that the person seeking sperm donor insemination is doing so as a single person or in the context of a relationship that is not heterosexual (or monogamous, or both) in nature (Corbett et al., 2013).

For LGBTQ people who are seeking assistance through a fertility center, their first exposure to a given clinic is usually the center's website. Fertility clinic websites typically provide education that familiarizes patients with the different assisted reproductive technology procedures available in general and through their center specifically (e.g., IUI, intracervical insemination, in vitro fertilization

---

[3]LGBTQ people may seek the assistance of fertility centers rather than do insemination (or have cis/heteronormative sex) on their own, for a variety of reasons. In a 2020 study of Australian lesbian, bisexual, and queer women's motivations for and experiences with using fertility services, the authors found that among the top reasons for using fertility services—endorsed by 40% or more of participants—were: concerns regarding establishing legal recognition of parenting relationships; needing donor sperm or eggs, or surrogacy services; ensuring that the child(ren) would have access to the identity of the sperm/egg donor; having access to deidentified sperm or eggs; believing that it would be more successful than self-insemination or heterosexual sex; contracting a sexually transmitted infection/HIV through unscreened sperm; knowing about a fertility problem requiring intervention; and gaining access to counseling services (Power et al., 2020).

[IVF]).[4] Yet, many websites do not include content that addresses the unique family-building circumstances of LGBTQ people (e.g., IUI and IVF with donor sperm, surrogacy, oocyte cryopreservation for postpubertal trans men, cryopreservation of sperm for postpubertal trans women). A 2016 study of 389 fertility clinics' websites found that in 2014, just 31% of websites contained LGBTQ-specific information; this number increased to 45.5% in 2015 (Jin & Dasgupta, 2016). A 2017 study (Wu et al., 2017) of 379 fertility clinics' websites similarly found that 53% featured LGBTQ inclusive content. Such content was more common among larger practices and practices in the Northeast and on the West Coast of the United States; only 39% of practices in both the Midwest and South featured inclusive content. Regarding language, lesbians were the most frequently mentioned (72%); followed by lesbian, gay, bisexual, and transgender (trans)/LGBTQ (69%); and gay (68%). More rarely used terms were trans/transgender (32%) and bisexual (15%).

That study (Wu et al., 2017) is important because it shows how LGBTQ people living in certain regions, and certain LGBTQ subgroups, may find it more challenging to locate practices that seem, at least based on their websites, LGBTQ inclusive. This could cause LGBTQ people to give up on or delay family building, or it

---

[4]As noted in Chapter 1, *IVF* is a procedure in which the egg and sperm meet outside of the body in a petri dish. The fertilized egg is then placed into the uterus by a health care provider. *IUI* occurs when the sperm is placed into the uterus via a small tube that is passed up the cervix and into the uterus by a health care provider. *Intracervical insemination* is when the sperm is placed into the cervix via a small tube. It can be done by a health care provider or at home using a specially designed syringe. *Intravaginal insemination* (IVI) occurs when the sperm is placed into the vagina with a syringe and is often done at home by the individual or with the help of partner(s).

could cost them "extra" in terms of traveling or even moving to access inclusive services. Interestingly, some clinics and centers do provide services to LGBTQ people but do not advertise this on their website (Corbett et al., 2013). Similarly, some fertility clinics accept single women as clients but make no mention of them on their websites (Johnson, 2012). These omissions may function to "gatekeep" who accesses services by upholding a heteronormative (partnered and heterosexual) framework of reproduction.

Research on LGBTQ couples pursuing parenthood has documented other challenges that they may encounter when searching for and interacting with ob-gyns and other perinatal health providers, for example. Heterosexist assumptions and beliefs can pervade patient–provider interactions, paperwork, and the physical office environment (Gregg, 2018). Health assessments related to pregnancy planning or prenatal care often inquire about sexual history—for example, to assess risk for sexually transmitted infections and how conception was or will be achieved. Such assessments may be heteronormative, assuming an exclusively heterosexual sexual history or a cis/heteronormative sex as the mode of conception—or both (Goldberg, Ross, et al., 2017). Clinics also routinely assume that clients are coming to them because of fertility difficulties (i.e., trouble conceiving through cis/heteronormative sex), and their questioning (e.g., "How long have you and your husband been trying to conceive?") and associated recommendations may reflect this assumption.

In the LGBTQ couple context, the nonbirthing parent-to-be is especially vulnerable to exclusion and poor treatment. Their "role" as a future parent is not always readily understood or acknowledged by perinatal health providers (Goldberg, 2010a; Gregg, 2018). Some providers may explicitly ignore or exclude the nonbirthing parent, whereas others may refer to them as a "friend" or question where the "father" is. Providers also frequently make assumptions about gender identity—for example, they assume that the pregnant person identifies as female (Gregg, 2018; Malmquist & Nelson, 2014). Being ignored, misunderstood, and invalidated in the perinatal context can amplify the stigma and invisibility that LGBTQ people face in the broader society. For example, while biological lesbian, gay, bisexual, and queer (LGBQ) mothers are treated as real parents by default, nonbiological LGBQ mothers must prove themselves as parents. Likewise, trans men who are pregnant are often misgendered and may experience intense invalidation (e.g., that they are not "real" men; Hoffkling et al., 2017).

LGBTQ people seeking pregnancy and birth services may prefer midwifery care over traditional ob-gyns because it is less medicalized and can offer a more person-centered, holistic model of care (King-Miller, 2018; Light et al., 2014). The midwifery model may be especially appealing to trans people because it gives them greater control over their birthing experience (Besse et al., 2020; Light et al., 2014). Indeed, midwifery spaces are often less likely to cater to, or focus predominantly on, cis heterosexual women—and this is reflected in their literature, brochures, restrooms, and the like (Besse et al., 2020). Midwives may also be more likely to approach queer cis women as presumably fertile, rather than medicalize their situation (i.e., presuming that they are infertile and in need of intervention; Priddle, 2015).

Regardless of what type of provider(s) you choose, it is important to know about the different options. Ob-gyns typically work out of hospitals or clinical settings. Midwives may attend births in hospitals, work out of birthing centers, help clients deliver at home, or all three. Doulas are another option that you may wish to explore regardless of whether you decide to work with an ob-gyn or midwife (but be aware that doulas are typically not covered by insurance). Doulas provide additional support to the birthing parent regardless of where they give birth. If you have a high-risk pregnancy or particular medical conditions, you may wish to seek hospital-based

---

Spotlight on MAIA Midwifery

MAIA Midwifery & Fertility Services (https://maiamidwifery.com/) is a great example of a practice that centers on LGBTQ people. Founded by Stephanie Brill, it is now owned and run by Kristin Kali, a licensed midwife.

MAIA offers both online and in-person services (e.g., family-building consultations, semen analysis and review) in the Seattle area. The organization is explicitly inclusive of trans and queer prospective parents, different family constellations (e.g., LGBTQ coparenting arrangements, including those involving a known sperm donor, polyamorous families, single-parent families). In addition, MAIA offers a variety of support groups for queer/trans people that are focused on topics and experiences ranging from insemination to pregnancy to early parenthood.

---

care. Be aware that if you choose to work with hospital-based midwives and ob-gyn, you will interface with the entire hospital system. In turn, you should be knowledgeable about the hospital's policies and practices vis-à-vis LGBTQ folks.

It is important to be aware that finances as well as insurance coverage may impact the options you have available to you, including what reproductive technologies are accessible (e.g., IVF is quite costly) as well as your choice of health care providers. LGBTQ people with more financial resources can also prioritize LGBTQ friendliness in their provider search to a greater degree than LGBTQ people of limited financial means—and they have greater choice and flexibility to explore other options if they encounter discrimination in a particular health care environment.

LGBTQ-Affirming Services and Providers

In addition to being limited by their financial resources, LGBTQ folks who are pursuing parenthood using reproductive technologies (including fertility centers, sperm banks, donor egg banks, surrogacy agencies, ob-gyns, and midwives) may be constrained by location. Although it may be possible to conduct a national search for, say, a sperm bank, you will be geographically limited when determining your support team for your pregnancy and birth journey. Thus, practical factors (e.g., finances, location) are inevitably balanced against a desire to work with LGBTQ-affirming services and providers.

Some fertility centers, such as those in major metropolitan areas, provide many services to LGBTQ folks—for example, IUI with donor sperm; IVF with donor eggs, donor sperm, or a gestational surrogate, or a combination of all three; and reciprocal IVF (covered in Chapter 3)—and are well-versed in the legal elements of LGBTQ family building. For example, Boston IVF (see http://www.gayivf.com/) provides all of these services, and the center's website features personal testimonials from diverse individuals and couples regarding their parenthood journeys.

Questions to Ask Fertility Centers

Many of the same questions that you might ask adoption agencies (e.g., regarding inclusive paperwork, gender-inclusive restrooms, staff training on LGBTQ inclusivity, nondiscrimination policies) are relevant to evaluating fertility centers. Some additional, more specific questions you might ask are these (Leondires, n.d.):

- Are there providers who are board-certified reproductive endocrinologists? This designation implies a high level of training, and, in turn, the ability to recommend evaluations, advanced treatments, and medications.
- How are fertility issues discussed on the website and in materials? Is there an implication that all fertility "problems" involve issues concerning heterosexual couples (e.g., low sperm count,

inability to conceive via cis/heteronormative sex after a speci-
fied period)? Is there an acknowledgment that what LGBTQ
people are dealing with is arguably best described as "social
infertility"?[5]

- Does the office and website include LGBTQ-inclusive art and
visuals (e.g., pregnant woman and female partner), or do they
solely feature ostensibly different-gender or heterosexual couples?
- How are LGBTQ people's experiences centered? For example,
are there queer/trans support groups related to navigating pregnancy, birth, and the postpartum period?
- Is the nongestational or nonbirthing partner acknowledged as a
parent-to-be and included in all relevant procedures and appointments? Are there resources (e.g., support groups) that acknowledge and center their unique experience and vantage point?

Asking these questions and others of fertility centers can help you
get a sense of whether and to what extent they truly embody LGBTQ
inclusiveness in a meaningful and holistic way—beyond glossy
marketing materials that may promise inclusion but fail to deliver.
Other questions, of course, will also be important to ask—such as
those related to experience (e.g., How long have the providers been
working there? What is the turnover rate like? How long has the
center been around?); effectiveness (What is their delivery/live birth
rate?); ethicality (e.g., Does the center have age limits in terms of
who they will provide treatments to?); and services and procedures
offered, insurance coverage, and costs.[6]

---

[5]For more details on this discussion (i.e., the notion of "social infertility"),
see Kaufman (2020).

[6]For other questions to ask (e.g., those related to specific procedures, risks,
outcomes), see Family Equality (n.d.) and Cherney and Frost (2020; see the
section "What Is the Success Rate of Fertility Treatments?").

Prenatal Care and Education

Prenatal care and childbirth education classes have the capacity to be affirming or alienating. LGBTQ people report feeling more comfortable when all parents-to-be are recognized and acknowledged as (future) parents; language (e.g., in in-person interactions and forms) is inclusive of diverse relationship configurations; and, in general, a heteronormative man–woman family-building model is not assumed (Brennan & Sell, 2014; Malmquist & Nelson, 2014; Priddle, 2015). Research suggests that inclusion of the non-birthing partner is especially salient to LGBTQ couples. As one participant in a study of LGBQ nonbiological mothers stated, "Our prenatal class instructor was excellent because she never used pronouns in the class, just the word coach" (Brennan & Sell, 2014, p. 535). Inclusive language in the context of prenatal education classes (e.g., using terms like "partner" or "coach") can go a long way in helping

---

Valued Resources: Perspectives of Trans and Nonbinary Participants in the LGBTQ Family Building Project

Asked about their most useful family-building resources (Goldberg, 2021), 77 trans and nonbinary participants shared these:

- Facebook groups (e.g., geared toward fertility tracking, birthing/ chestfeeding, transmasculine parents, queer fertility)
- specific LGBTQ fertility centers and donor insemination programs (e.g., Fenway Health, a community health center; California Cryobank; Sperm Bank of California)
- LGBTQ parenting organizations (e.g., Rainbow Families) and conferences
- LGBTQ/trans parents support groups
- attorneys
- midwives
- fertility doctors/staff
- friends (especially LGBTQ parents)

---

individuals with diverse gender, sexual, and relational configurations feel comfortable and welcomed (Brennan & Sell, 2014; Goldberg, 2006, 2010a).

Significantly, pregnant bisexual and queer cis women who are partnered or married to cis men (or to people whom providers perceive as cis men) are also vulnerable to assumptions about their sexuality and sexual history. Rarely are bisexual women acknowledged in perinatal environments. And, although some bisexual women feel that their sexuality is not relevant to the care that they receive, others desire some acknowledgment and validation (e.g., in the form of resources specifically for bisexual people) or, at the very least, evidence that the health care service is LGBTQ friendly more broadly, as demonstrated by triangles, rainbow decals, and other symbols of LGBTQ affirmation in the office and on the website (Goldberg, Ross, et al., 2017).

Currently, many organizations offer in-person and online LGBTQ-centered childbirth education. The Queer Birth Project (https://www.queerbirthproject.org/) and MAIA Midwifery (http://maiamidwifery.com/), for example, offer LGBTQ-centered childbirth education as well as support groups for gestational and nongestational parents.

Trans People's Experiences in the Health Care Environment

The experience of trying to conceive, being pregnant, and giving birth as a trans, nonbinary, or gender nonconforming person can be fraught with tension—tension that can be amplified or mitigated, depending on institutional and provider practices. Research with trans men and nonbinary people who were or had been pregnant highlights certain provider practices that are especially unwelcomed and some that are particularly appreciated. Knowledge of this research may be helpful to you as you try to anticipate—and circumvent—challenges during the family-building process, thus informing what questions to ask and what warning signs to look out for (Greenfield & Darwin, 2021; Hoffkling et al., 2017).

Trans and nonbinary people's primary challenges in the perinatal environment tend to be rooted in trans erasure or transphobia. For example, trans men and nonbinary people encounter providers who (a) treat them as strange or "unintelligible" as a pregnant man, (b) lack basic biomedical education regarding trans people and reproduction (e.g., effects of testosterone on reproductive organs, ease of conception, pregnancy outcomes, lactation), and (c) lack cultural competency (e.g., call them by the wrong name or pronoun, presume to know their genitals by their name or face, ignore intake forms documenting their gender). Some trans men and nonbinary people have described overt instances of transphobia, such as being laughed at or having nurses refuse to see them. Significantly, some trans people conceal their trans identity to avoid barriers at sperm banks, having heard that banks may deny sperm to clients who fail to meet their expectations for prospective parents. This type of scenario reflects how cisnormative beliefs about reproduction

---

Finding an LGBTQ-Friendly Provider

The *Healthcare Equality Index*: A Valuable Resource

The Human Rights Campaign's (2020b) *Healthcare Equality Index 2020* (HEI) surveyed more than 700 medical facilities in the United States about the degree to which they provided LGBTQ-inclusive care (HRC, 2020b). The survey evaluated staff training and nondiscrimination policies, among other areas. This can be a great starting point for finding an LGBTQ-competent provider because the *Healthcare Equality Index* provides a rating for each facility.

can create unique pregnancy- and birth-related challenges for trans people, particularly those with masculine gender expressions (Besse et al., 2020; Greenfield & Darwin, 2021). Trans men and nonbinary people generally share these wishes: that providers avoid making assumptions about them and that they try to consider how their language and physical setting may appear to cater exclusively to cis women giving birth.

The research further suggests that trans and nonbinary people value being seen and treated according to their gender identity by perinatal providers, as demonstrated by consistent and correct use of their names and pronouns throughout the process of reproductive planning, conception, pregnancy, and delivery. They also appreciate when providers not only affirm but normalize their gender. They appreciate when providers show respect for their privacy. Such practices can be profoundly important in helping trans people to feel safe during the vulnerable experience of pregnancy and birth. Participants also appreciate when providers know about reproductive options and biomedical issues related to trans people and their care—or, at the very least, seek to educate themselves or provide appropriate referrals, when necessary. Participants especially appreciate guidance regarding reproductive and fertility options and education about the effects (e.g., on their mood) of stopping hormone treatment (Hoffkling et al., 2017). Indeed, trans people need and deserve timely education and support in navigating the parenthood options available to them. A lack of knowledge about, and financial barriers to, fertility preservation can represent key obstacles to parenthood for trans people.

It is profoundly important that providers approach trans prospective parents and pregnant parents within a framework of compassionate care. As a trans person, you deserve care that is respectful and affirming—that may involve taking a trauma-informed approach to genital exams (e.g., detailed description of what is happening every step of the way, request for your consent at each stage); planning for a nonvaginal delivery; using nongendered terms to refer to body parts (or asking you what terms you use or prefer); and navigating the possibility of chestfeeding, if you haven't had top surgery that prevents it (Armuand et al., 2017; Besse et al., 2020).

You are also entitled to affirming psychotherapy or counseling—or both—before, during, and after you embark on your family-building journey. Receiving guidance and support from a therapist who has training and experience with trans people and parents specifically can be important in helping you to clarify fears, goals, challenges, and strengths related to family building. For example, one participant in the LGBTQ Family Building Project shared that the therapist they initially saw during the family building process was "unhelpful . . . [and] would chronically misgender me when talking about me being the gestational parent. I use they/them pronouns." However, this participant ultimately "switched therapists to someone who has provided space for me to process dysphoria and decisions about whether to chestfeed." For some folks, therapy can be significant in facilitating awareness of one's internalized transphobia or homophobia as hindering one's readiness to or confidence about becoming a parent. One trans participant shared, "I had so much internalized queer-phobia. . . . I had to come to terms with my queerness before I had the space to be a parent." Another trans participant felt that therapy provided helpful reassurance and affirmation that they would be a "good parent" and that they "[were] making the right decisions. [It was] especially helpful when navigating discrimination when trying to adopt." Recognizing—with or without the guidance of a therapist—your unique strengths and assets as a future parent, and your true deservingness to become a parent, can be enormously helpful. Indeed, confidence in your ability and right to parent may help you to stay on the path toward parenthood when you face obstacles and challenges along the way.

CONCLUSION

In searching for agencies, services, and providers to support your journey toward parenthood, remember this: You deserve affirming and competent care. Yet, you very well may not be able to find an agency or provider that checks all of your boxes. If you feel comfortable and safe doing so, you may wish to provide an agency or provider with feedback about what they could do differently to create a more inclusive and affirming environment for you and others like you. Some providers may not be well informed and experienced with LGBTQ clients but are happy to receive and incorporate feedback.

In other cases, however, you may be making trade-offs—for example, you may choose an adoption agency that is well-matched to your morals and values but has limited experience with LGBTQ folks over an agency that has extensive experience with LGBTQ adopters but is grounded in practices or ideals that you find questionable or problematic. Ultimately, however, it is important to remember that you have value as a person and deserve to be treated as such. To the extent possible, try to find providers who recognize your humanity and reflect this back at you.

RESOURCES

Birth for Every Body. (n.d.). *About gender.* http://www.birthforeverybody.org/what-we-do

Child Welfare Information Gateway. (2016). *Frequently asked questions from lesbian, gay, bisexual, transgender, and questioning (LGBTQ) prospective foster and adoptive parents.* U.S. Department of Health and Human Services, Children's Bureau. https://www.childwelfare.gov/pubPDFs/faq_lgbt.pdf

dminerva. (2019, July 11). Trans and pregnant: How to find competent, gender-affirming healthcare. *Healthline.* https://www.healthline.com/health/mental-health/trans-pregnancy-provider

Perry, J. R. (2017). *Promising practices for serving transgender & non-binary foster and adoptive parents.* The Human Rights Campaign Foundation. https://assets2.hrc.org/files/assets/resources/HRC_ACAF_Promising_Practices_Serving_Transgender_Non-Binary_Parents.pdf

CHAPTER 6

TRANSITIONING TO PARENTHOOD

THIS CHAPTER COVERS:

> mental health across the transition to parenthood
> signs of postpartum depression
> division of labor (e.g., housework, child care, paid work)
> social support across the transition to parenthood
> intersection of identities and the transition to parenthood

Jon and David are a male couple who live in Chicago. Jon, a high school math teacher, is multiracial (Black, Latinx, White) and cis. He also identifies as bisexual but tends to disclose that information only to close friends because he finds that it is easier to just allow others to see him as a gay man, given his long-term relationship with David. David is a White cis man who identifies as gay and is employed as the head of human resources at a midsized company. After 7 years together, David and Jon decided to get married, in part because both men wanted to be parents (it was one of the things that drew them together when they first met). The couple also felt that being married would help outsiders take their relationship seriously and perhaps mitigate some of the discrimination they might otherwise face in the family-building process.

After exploring their options, they decided to pursue a private domestic adoption. Both men really wanted to be parents to a child from birth. Although initially anxious about the prospect of openness in adoption (mainly because they feared they would never be chosen by prospective birth parents), they ultimately came to embrace it after learning more about an acquaintance's open adoption. The couple waited for almost 8 months before they were matched with a prospective birth mother, a 23-year-old multiracial woman named Amy. She loved how fun-loving the couple was and, as a bisexual woman herself, felt strongly that she wanted to place her child with a queer couple who might otherwise face barriers in becoming parents.

Amy and Jon connected over the bisexual erasure that they had each experienced throughout their lives as well as their multiracial identities. David and Jon both struggled with some of Amy's decisions during the pregnancy (e.g., she was a frequent fast-food eater and scoffed at their suggestions to take prenatal vitamins), but they did not feel that they could or should overstep certain boundaries. Amy embraced the couple and wanted them to be at her side when she gave birth—a scenario that took some explaining at the small county hospital where she would deliver. After a lengthy labor and delivery, Amy delivered a baby whom David and Jon named Annabelle. The couple had an open adoption and agreed that once Amy felt ready—maybe in a month or two—she would come visit Annabelle.

David and Jon took Annabelle home to their two-bedroom city apartment, ecstatic that they were finally parents. Both had pored over baby books in advance of becoming parents, pumped their parent friends for information—pacifiers: yes or no? Swaddling: yes or no?—and excitedly prepared their home for their child's arrival. Yet, adjusting to parenthood in a small apartment with a baby who cried constantly, especially after eating (an issue that was eventually diagnosed as a milk allergy), was a challenge, particularly for Jon. A self-described "neat freak," he found himself becoming preoccupied with the messy state of their apartment. He felt claustrophobic and panicky much of the time, and, feeling on edge and exhausted, snapped at David quite frequently—a behavior that David found startling and out of character. After one particularly tense exchange, David said to Jon, "I'm worried about you. You're not acting like yourself." Jon then tearfully acknowledged that he was consumed with anxiety and fear about something happening to Annabelle—for example, before her milk allergy diagnosis, he was convinced that she had something terribly wrong with her.

With a bit of prodding from David, Jon went to see a psychiatrist. Although reluctant to take medication, Jon agreed that simply talking to someone might be helpful. Yet, his initial encounter with the psychiatrist, Dr. Reed, was not validating. Despite completing paperwork online before the appointment in which he explained that he was married to a man, Dr. Reed asked Jon what his "wife thought about how things were going." On being corrected, Dr. Reed said, "Oh, sorry. I did not realize you were gay." Exhausted and frustrated, Jon did not bother explaining that he was bisexual. Jon also spent a lot of time answering Dr. Reed's questions about open adoption, about which the psychiatrist seemed aghast—"The mother is coming to visit you soon?!" Furthermore, Jon was not reassured when Dr. Reed said, "Well, you obviously didn't give birth, so we can't really call this postpartum anxiety."

Jon ended the appointment feeling as though his identity and experiences were not really seen or understood. At home, he went online and found plenty of research suggesting that, yes, postadoption anxiety and depression is a "thing." After investigating various providers located in his urban area, Jon was fortunate to find another psychiatrist who listed themselves as "adoption competent." This provider, Dr. Greene—who also demonstrated lesbian, gay, bisexual, transgender (trans), and queer (LGBTQ) competence in the form of open-ended questions, lack of assumptions, and inclusive paperwork—agreed with Jon that he was suffering from postadoption anxiety.

Dr. Greene helped Jon to recognize that after such an intense period of waiting and anticipation, becoming a parent can be really challenging, filled with unexpected stressors and unmet expectations. Furthermore, Jon was dealing with more than just some of the more typical stressors associated with the transition to parenthood: fatigue, lack of time alone, and child health concerns. Through discussing the months leading up to the adoption of Annabelle, Jon realized that he had been experiencing an intense sense of lack of control: first with regard to Amy's prenatal decisions and then the fear that she would change her mind and decide to parent. When she did decide to place the child with Jon and David, Jon's anxieties turned to worry that Amy would be "okay." He also became consumed with worry about Annabelle's health, in part because he did not feel intimately connected to or knowledgeable about her medical history. Jon acknowledged, too, that he was initially reluctant to seek treatment because of deeply hidden fears that he would be perceived as doubly unfit to care for his child in that he was both bisexual and having mental health challenges. He acknowledged that, although it was unrealistic, he nevertheless feared that the authorities might try to take Annabelle away.

Dr. Greene recommended a therapist, Dr. Simpson, who worked with Jon to process his anxieties and fears and also supported him in developing techniques (i.e., through cognitive behavior therapy) to manage them. David attended some of these sessions so that he could be present for and support Jon in his treatment. In addition, therapy with Dr. Simpson was important in helping the couple to explore and address some of the less healthy dynamics in their relationship that seemed to be exacerbated by Annabelle's arrival and, in turn, were related to Jon's anxiety. Namely, David often took on the role of caretaker to Jon when Jon became stressed, yet reacted with hurt feelings and withdrawal if and when Jon did not want his help.

Over time, Jon developed a greater sense of competence as a parent, which eased his anxieties. In addition, the couple worked on developing tools for respectful and empathic communication and strengthened their identity as a collaborative "team." They also sought outside help in the form of babysitting help from David's 16-year-old niece who lived nearby.

And, when Annabelle was about 6 months old, they sought consultation with their adoption agency to help them to strategize how to move forward with their open adoption. Indeed, even after 6 months, Amy was not yet ready to spend time with Annabelle or their family.

BIG CHANGES AHEAD: ROLES, RELATIONSHIPS, AND RESPONSIBILITIES

Becoming a parent is a life-changing transition. It is often a time of great joy and excitement, and it marks the welcome beginning of a different stage of one's life journey. Becoming a parent is also marked by disequilibrium, adjustment, and renegotiation in terms of one's identity, roles, and relationships. Many studies have examined the transition to parenthood, but they have tended to focus on heterosexual couples who have genetically related children (Kohn et al., 2012; Mckenzie & Carter, 2013; Mitnick et al., 2009).

Regardless of gender, sexual orientation, and parenthood route (e.g., cis/heteronormative sex, donor insemination [DI], adoption), all parents must incorporate the role and identity of "parent" into their current repertoire or roles and identities—and this inevitably creates shifts in other identities and roles (e.g., partner, professional). All parents must also navigate the demands of child care and the increased workload that accompanies parenthood—work that is likely to be greater if, for example, you become a parent to twins, or adopt siblings, or have a medically challenged child. The extra work demands that you (re)negotiate the division of unpaid and paid labor with your partner(s), and may prompt you to consider if and how you will engage outside help, such as paid child care, a decision that is especially salient for single parents.

Managing your changed relationship with your partner(s), your job/career role and responsibilities, and your new role as parent is inevitably made more complex against the backdrop of personal,

> ### Typical Challenges During the First Few Weeks of Parenthood
>
> - Recovering from birth: This may be stressful, especially if the delivery was difficult or different than expected, or you faced hostility or lack of understanding because of being LGBTQ.
> - Chestfeeding and bottle-feeding: Feeding may not come easily and may prompt feelings of inadequacy or frustration.
> - Fatigue: A lack of sleep can affect your mood, energy, patience, memory, and thinking.
> - Attachment: You may not immediately bond to your child. This can be distressing.
> - Body image: Bodies look different postbirth. Body image issues may be especially salient for trans and gender nonconforming folks.
> - Intimacy: Your physical and emotional relationship with your partner is changing as you both adjust to the role of parent.
> - Outsider influence: Friends, family, and social media all have ideas about how to "do" parenthood. These ideas may feel "off" to you because of values, sexual orientation, gender identity, and so on. It can be challenging to figure out your own parental identity.
> - Feeling overwhelmed: Becoming a parent involves *a lot* of changes. It is easy to feel overwhelmed by the sudden, 24–7 responsibility for a human.

family, friend, community, religious, societal, and cultural expectations. To nurse or chestfeed or not, and for how long? To send your child to day care or not, and when? To take the maximum amount of parental leave allotted, or not? If you are fortunate to be able to make these decisions, as opposed to having them made for you—as is the case for many new parents—you may struggle with what is the "right" thing to do for yourself and your family without being unduly influenced by the expectations and judgment of those around you. This can be a challenge for all parents but especially for LGBTQ parents, who navigate parenthood against a predominantly heterosexual backdrop of parenting arrangements and decisions.

A number of other significant changes may also occur during the transition to parenthood. These include adjusting to less sleep; managing feelings of loneliness; learning to juggle work and family; balancing increased financial obligations and pressures; and dealing with feelings of incompetence, imperfection, and not quite measuring up in multiple domains (e.g., parenting, relationships, work). Some new parents also struggle with general feelings of overwhelm and lack of control—feelings that are likely to be more intense for single parents and parents who are under significant financial pressure.

MENTAL HEALTH AND RELATIONSHIP QUALITY

Given all of these changes, it should come as no huge surprise that most new parents experience changes to their mental health across the transition to parenthood. That is, many new parents experience at least temporary increases in symptoms of anxiety, such as fearfulness and restlessness, or increases in symptoms of depression, such as sleep or appetite disturbances, lack of motivation, and feelings of helplessness. These changes are more pronounced for parents who lack sufficient emotional support (e.g., people to talk to) and practical support (e.g., help with child care from one's partner or others, or both) as well as parents who are experiencing conflict, strain, or violence in their intimate partner relationships (Faisal-Cury et al., 2021; Logsdon & McBride, 1994). New parents who perceive their children as especially challenging in their behavior or temperament also tend to experience worse mental health (Goldberg & Smith, 2008). Financial stress, unemployment, and a history of mental health difficulties are also associated with greater mental health struggles across the transition to parenthood (Katon et al., 2014).

Signs of Postpartum Depression

- depressed mood, mood swings
- frequent crying
- lack of interest in your child
- withdrawal from family or friends
- lack of appetite or eating much more than usual
- weight loss or weight gain
- sleep issues (e.g., insomnia, sleeping much more than usual)
- severe fatigue or lack of energy
- lack of interest in activities you used to enjoy
- intense irritability or anger
- feelings of worthlessness, helplessness, shame, guilt, or inadequacy
- reduced ability to concentrate, think, and make decisions
- memory issues
- anxiety or panic attacks
- thoughts of harming yourself or your child, or thoughts of death or suicide

Note. Postpartum depression can happen to adoptive parents and people of all genders.

Likewise, many new parents report declines in intimate relationship quality, including less satisfaction with the relationship or increased conflict. Lower income, financial worries, unplanned pregnancy, dissatisfaction with the division of labor, and poor communication or conflict management skills are often associated with poorer relationship quality (Adamsons, 2013; Doss et al., 2009; Lawrence et al., 2010).

The limited research that has explored the transition to parenthood for people in same-gender relationships has found that, like people in different-gender relationships, they experience declines in their mental health and relationship quality across the transition to parenthood (Goldberg et al., 2010; Goldberg & Smith, 2011). Some predictors of lesbian, gay, bisexual, and

Signs of Postpartum Anxiety

- constant or pervasive worry
- persistent feeling of dread or sense of danger
- persistent feeling of being "on edge," as if preparing for something to go wrong
- insomnia or difficulty falling or staying asleep
- overwhelming sense of stress about being a good parent
- racing thoughts
- fatigue
- heart palpitations, rapid breathing, or chest pain
- hyperventilation or sweating
- nausea or vomiting
- shakiness, jitteriness, or agitation
- dizziness
- in the form of obsessive–compulsive disorder: obsessions presenting as persistent, intrusive, and upsetting thoughts that involve the child; compulsions (e.g., cleaning, counting, checking) performed repeatedly to neutralize fears; parental recognition that their fears and thoughts are bizarre but feelings of shame or discomfort about revealing them to others

Note. Postpartum anxiety can happen to adoptive parents and people of all genders.

queer (LGBQ) people's mental health and relationship quality are similar to predictors for heterosexual people. For example, higher levels of support from one's family, friends, and workplace have been linked to better mental health among LGBQ women during the transition to parenthood (Goldberg & Smith, 2008, 2011). Likewise, healthier and more adaptive coping skills are associated with better relationship quality among LGBQ people across the transition to parenthood (Goldberg et al., 2010). Personal well-being (e.g., fewer symptoms of depression and anxiety) and greater preparation for parenthood also have been linked to relationship quality among LGBQ people across the transition to parenthood (Goldberg et al., 2010).

But the process of becoming a parent and navigating the transition to parenthood is indeed different for LGBTQ folks. It can be complicated by societal obstacles to parenthood (e.g., prejudice encountered in the family-building process); nuances of the particular family building route (e.g., adoption, foster care, DI, surrogacy); lack of LGBTQ parent role models or supports; lack of support from friends and family; and stigma within one's neighborhood, community, workplace, or place of religious worship. For many LGBTQ parents, too, becoming a parent is a lengthy and highly intentional process that may involve many months and years of work and waiting. In turn, when the highly anticipated goal of parenthood is reached, the reality may be more challenging than expected, which may create feelings of sadness, guilt, or ambivalence.

In some cases, too, parents differ in their genetic relationship to the child and, in turn, their social recognition as a parent in that genetic/gestational parenthood is generally given more weight or is seen as more "real" than social parenthood (Cao et al., 2016; Goldberg & Perry-Jenkins, 2007). Also, historically, many LGBTQ parents have faced barriers in terms of their legal relationship to their child, such that, in many families, only one parent was legally recognized as the child's parent: the genetic parent in families formed with the use of reproductive technologies or in families built through adoption or the parent who legally adopted as a single parent if coparent or joint adoption was not permitted.[1] Such differences in

---

[1]Laws and policies surrounding coparent or joint adoption by same-gender couples have changed drastically in many states over the past decade. Before 2017, states varied widely in their adoption laws, with some granting full adoption rights to same-gender couples (i.e., allowing couples to jointly adopt their children); others allowing only second-parent adoptions (e.g.,

genetic, legal, and social recognition within couples can create friction, especially if the nongenetic/nongestational or nonlegal parent feels less recognized as a parent, or the genetic/gestational or legal parent feels entitled to more recognition or rights as a parent. (For LGBTQ parents in more complex arrangements, such as those in consensually nonmonogamous [CNM] relationships, lack of recognition for one or more partners may be especially significant.)

Couples who adopt—who have also been found to experience declines in mental health and relationship quality (Goldberg et al., 2010; Goldberg & Smith, 2011; South et al., 2019)—experience unique stressors that may affect their mental health. Parents who become foster parents with the intention to adopt may face a lengthy period during which they are not yet legal parents—and may never be, depending on the outcome of the placement (e.g., if the child or children return to their birth parents). Parenting in legal limbo can be uniquely stressful as parents anxiously await confirmation that they can fully embrace the identity, role, and title of "parent" (Goldberg et al., 2011; Goldberg, Moyer, et al., 2012). Parents who adopt via domestic private adoption may be navigating early relationships with their children's birth parents and anticipating what

---

a nongestational mother could adopt the child her partner birthed); and others banning adoption by LGBTQ folks. Same-gender couples who adopted from abroad almost uniformly had one parent adopt as a single parent because coparent adoptions by same-gender couples were generally not permitted.

In 2016, a federal district court struck down the last of the gay adoption bans—in Mississippi (*Campaign for Southern Equality v. Mississippi Department of Services, et al.*, 2016). In 2017, the U.S. Supreme Court ruled that all states must treat same-gender couples equally to heterosexual couples in the issuing of birth certificates (*Marisa N. Pavan, et al. v. Nathaniel Smith*, 2017). These court rulings, taken together, have made adoption by same-gender couples legal in all 50 states.

these relationships might look like in the future. Adoptive parents, including LGBTQ parents, may also be dealing with lingering feelings of loss, disappointment, or anger regarding their inability to conceive or have a biological child (Goldberg, 2010b; Goldberg et al., 2009). The transition to adoptive parenthood is also unique in that the timing of it is often uncertain; there is no predictable timetable (e.g., 9 months) during which to prepare for impending parenthood (Goldberg, 2010b). In turn, it is possible to become parents "overnight"—with little warning—for example, a birth parent might deliver a child in the hospital and make an adoption plan (Goldberg, 2019).

LGBTQ folks who adopt—who, as we learned in previous chapters, are often more open to adopting children with special needs, older children, and siblings than cis heterosexual folks—may face a variety of both expected and unexpected stressors during the early weeks and months of parenthood related to their children's abuse, neglect, or trauma history; attachment or behavioral challenges; health care needs, or a combination of these factors. All of these issues—legal uncertainty, new relationships with birth family, loss surrounding infertility, unexpected timing of parenthood, and child-specific challenges—may impact new adoptive parents' mental health, thus amplifying stress, uncertainty, and feelings of parenting incompetence that, if not offset by access to supports and services, could contribute to depression and anxiety.

Couples who adopt may experience unique stressors to their intimate relationships as well. One study of 84 individuals in same-gender and different-gender relationships who were placed with a child via foster care 3 months earlier found that, just like heterosexual biological parents, some participants described the loss of their partner's undivided attention as stressful to the relationship (Goldberg, Kinkler, et al., 2014; Goldberg, Moyer, et al., 2012). Adoption-specific stressors were also identified, including the need to find state-approved child care to facilitate "couple time" and the legal insecurity of foster-to-adopt placements. And, some members of same-gender couples cited experiences with stigma (e.g., homophobic birth parents or social workers) as a stressor impacting their relationships (Goldberg, Kinkler, et al., 2014; Goldberg, Moyer, et al., 2012).

Other research suggests that a history of infertility may have lingering effects on adoptive couples' relationships (Goldberg, 2010b; M. Ward, 1998). And, not surprising, couples who adopt older children or siblings described additional strains to their intimate partner relationships that often were related to differing approaches to children's adjustment or behavioral issues (R. L. Frost & Goldberg, 2020; M. Ward, 1998). Notably, however, couples who make it through the challenging and complex process of adoption (and sometimes infertility) often show significant relationship strengths and resilience and may even experience increased closeness across the transition to parenthood (Timm et al., 2011).

Not All Parents . . .

Not all parents experience mental health and relationship declines, and there are things that individuals and couples can do to mitigate these declines. Early researchers of the transition to parenthood pointed out, quite rightly, that we generally tend to focus on averages— that is, on average parents' mental health declines (Belsky, 1990; Belsky & Rovine, 1984). But there are subgroups of parents who decline and then improve, or who improve overall, or who show no change at all.

For example, in the LGBTQ Family Building Project (Goldberg, 2021), just 37% of parents said that their mental health declined across the first year of parenthood, with another 12% reporting decline followed by improvement (see the pie chart on mental health

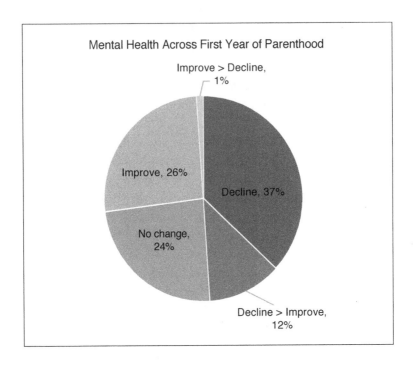

in the first year of parenthood). Another 24% reported no change, 26% reported improvement, and just 1% reported improvement followed by decline. Indeed, *most* parents—72%—said that their life satisfaction increased during the first year of parenthood. Thus, although almost half of parents described some decline in mental health, almost three quarters reported increased life satisfaction, highlighting the importance of considering multiple domains of "what makes life good" when it comes to exploring the impact of new parenthood.

Similarly, just more than half—52%—of parents said that their intimate relationship quality declined during the first year of parenthood, with another 7% saying it declined and then improved (see the pie chart on changes in the quality of the relationship in

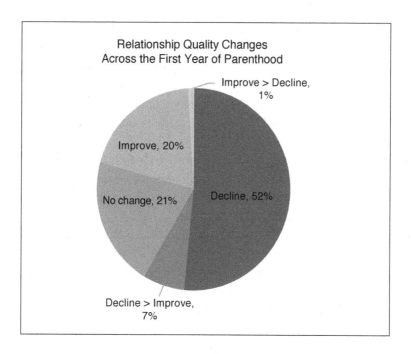

Relationship Quality Changes
Across the First Year of Parenthood

Improve > Decline, 1%

Improve, 20%

No change, 21%

Decline, 52%

Decline > Improve, 7%

the first year of parenthood). Sexual intimacy, however, declined for almost three quarters (71%) of parents.

Help and Support

LGBTQ parents face numerous obstacles to receiving mental health and relationship support during the transition to parenthood and beyond. LGBTQ parents may be fearful of disclosing mental health symptoms to health care providers out of fear of being judged—for example, confirming stereotypes that queer people are mentally unfit to raise children—and even having their children removed from their homes (Alang & Fomotar, 2015). These fears are rooted in historical data: Lesbian mothers in the 1970s and 1980s were known to lose custody of their children in the context of ending heterosexual marriages; their ex-husbands would argue that women's sexual orientation (often a reason for the marriage ending) rendered them unfit to parent (Tasker & Lavender-Stott, 2020). LGBTQ parents may also lack access to LGBTQ-competent providers, particularly if they are living in politically conservative regions or have limited financial resources.

LGBTQ parents may find support from friends as well as online (Alang & Fomotar, 2015). For example, they may search out LGBTQ parents, especially those with similar parenting philosophies or those who share certain key characteristics (e.g., family-building route, age of child), via specialized online support forums, such as those found on BabyCenter (see https://community.babycenter.com/) and Facebook (see https://www.facebook.com/; Blackwell et al., 2016). Such online support can be important in offering LGBTQ parents support and validation. But like all new parents, they may need—and certainly deserve—affirming, knowledgeable providers who are aware of the societal pressures that impinge on LGBTQ parents as well as the varied and often complex paths that they take to parenthood, and the impact of these paths on the challenges they may face during their parenthood journeys.

Finding an LGBTQ-friendly and affirming therapist is made easier by online sources, such as *Psychology Today*, which offer searchable directories of therapists (e.g., you can search by location, insurance, and key areas of expertise, including sexual orientation or gender identity). In the event that you cannot find a therapist in your area, teletherapy (e.g., therapy via videoconferencing or phone) is often available and may be more accessible for some LGBTQ folks (e.g., those with disabilities, those in rural areas) as well as more affordable. Pay attention to how therapists represent themselves and what type of information they put online (e.g., images, language), and notice any strong reactions you have, positive or negative.

> *"Like every couple who becomes a parent, there are learning curves. With each stage our child passes through, we have new things to learn. As a couple we have had times where intimacy and time as a couple is hard because jobs and child-raising take front and center. But we are always big on checking in, expressing feelings, and listening. So, we always seem to work through and find the balance.*
>
> *When it comes to child care, we are very much in it together. . . . It's more the other household stuff. Sometimes the day-to-day chores become one sided. But, again, we talk it out. . . . We have always had good mechanisms for discussing it, communicating, and rebalancing."*
>
> —PARTICIPANT IN THE LGBTQ PARENTING PROJECT

Consider arranging a 10- to 20-minute brief phone consultation to help determine whether it is a good fit. You can ask them about their qualifications, experience, and approach during that call as well as just get a "feel" for whether it is a possible match.

Couples Therapy Can Help, Too . . .

Couples therapy or relationship-focused counseling may also help during the transition to parenthood. Such counseling can aid new parents in anticipating and coping with various challenges, including unexpected disagreements and difficulties in communicating, grief and loss issues (e.g., related to infertility or pregnancy loss), and problem-solving around the division of chores and parenting responsibilities. Even couples who feel that their relationships are relatively strong may benefit from relationship-focused counseling during the transition to parenthood and beyond because parenthood can amplify issues that were previously manageable but now take on new meaning or urgency (e.g., different ways of spending money, challenging relationships with in-laws).

Regardless of whether you seek out relationship-focused counseling, research suggests a couple of key practices that can support your relationship during the transition to parenthood (Belsky & Kelly, 1994; Price et al., 2016):

- Check in regularly: New parents should regularly check in with their partner(s) about how they are doing, including how they are feeling about parenthood and their relationship. These check-ins should ideally occur during downtime (e.g., when the child is sleeping).
- Discuss how to handle new issues: New parenthood involves a lot of new issues and challenges, including negotiating "who does what," financial obligations, and so on—and often on little sleep and with little alone time. Address one issue at a time, perhaps at a designated time. Focus on solutions and remain flexible (e.g., what worked in the past may not work now).
- Make time: New parents often don't have time to get away for long periods of alone time together. Even if it's just 15 to 30 minutes of time sitting on the porch enjoying an iced tea, taking a walk, or snuggling on the couch, making time for each other on a daily or at least weekly basis can help to maintain closeness and connection.
- Get support: Develop a roster of individuals (e.g., family, friends, babysitters) who can be counted on for regular and occasional child care. If you don't have family and friends who can help with child care, consider asking for child care referrals from friends or enlist a babysitting or child care service.
- Be flexible: It may be necessary to try out new ways of handling conflict, finding time together, getting time alone, and connecting with one another. Remain open to the possibility that you may need to shift your outlook or approach.

- Prioritize intimacy: It is easy to become overwhelmed with fatigue and stress and ignore intimacy and sex. Physical changes (e.g., associated with pregnancy) may also be a barrier. Seek opportunities to touch and cuddle as well as to communicate. Your sexual life may change but should not be put on the back burner indefinitely.
- Value each other: Acknowledge your partner's contributions and express appreciation. Remind yourself that you have chosen to be on this journey together and that you have each other for support.

Worth noting here is that in the LGBTQ Family Building Project, partnered participants (who had children of varying ages) were asked about sources of tension in their relationship with their partner. The top five issues endorsed were sexual intimacy issues (45%), parenting disagreements (36%), communication issues (34%), division of labor (32%), and financial issues (25%). This gives a sense of the kind of issues that are likely to be salient not just during the transition to parenthood but possibly beyond.

THE DIVISION OF LABOR: DISHES, DIAPERS, AND DUSTING

One area that emerges as salient for many same-gender couples during the transition to parenthood is the division of labor. Overall, same-gender couples tend to share paid and unpaid labor (e.g., child care, housework) more equally than heterosexual couples, both in general and when they become parents specifically (Chan et al., 1998; Goldberg, Smith, & Perry-Jenkins, 2012; Patterson et al., 2004; Prickett et al., 2015). But when differences in contributions to paid and unpaid labor do occur, they can cause tension in part because same-gender couples may have higher expectations for equality— or at least equity—in the division of labor. Women and trans folks in particular seem sensitive to inequities in the division of labor,

---

Division of Labor in the LGBTQ Family Building Project

Parents were asked to rate on a scale from 0 (*none of it*) to 100 (*all of it*) what percentage they did in terms of child care, housework, and paid work as well as what they preferred.

- Regarding child care: They said they did 59%, on average, and they preferred to do 53.5%, on average (a 5.5% difference).
- Regarding housework: They said they did 55%, on average, and they preferred to do 48%, on average (a 7% difference).
- Regarding paid work: They said they did 57%, on average, and they preferred to do 53%, on average (a 4% difference).

The following were endorsed as the biggest barriers to dividing labor more equally:

- 44%: differences in earning capacity
- 43%: different levels of interest in tasks
- 41%: different personal standards (e.g., for cleanliness)
- 39%: differences in energy or emotional resources
- 36%: differences in work hours
- 23%: different abilities or competence
- 21%: child preferences for one parent
- 16%: differences in ability or health
- 8%: gender role expectations

---

even when it favors them, perhaps partly reflecting their socialization as individuals on the lower rungs of gender and power hierarchies (Goldberg, 2013). And large discrepancies between the actual division of labor (e.g., how chores are divided, who does what) and ideal or preferred division of labor are related to poorer mental health and relationship quality among parents (Tornello et al., 2015).

Discrepancies in the division of labor may occur along the lines of biology. That is, among female couples who became parents via DI, gestational mothers tend to perform more unpaid work and nongestational mothers tend to perform more paid work as a result, in part, of the early demands of breastfeeding and greater access to parental leave for the gestational mother (Goldberg & Perry-Jenkins, 2007). Likewise, research on lesbian stepparent families has found that biological mothers perform more housework than stepmothers, which was associated with greater power over other aspects of the household, such as household decision making (Moore, 2008). Beyond biological or genetic factors, relative work hours and financial contributions also seem to affect the division of labor. Within same-gender couples who are parents, partners who work fewer hours or earn less of the household income tend to do more housework and child care (Goldberg, Smith, & Perry-Jenkins, 2012). And, it perhaps goes without saying that having more income often enables couples to divide chores more equally—and may minimize conflict related to the division of labor. For example, when couples can "buy out" of certain tasks (e.g., through the use of housecleaners, nannies, laundry services, car washes, restaurant takeout), this reduces their overall workload and makes it easier to share (Goldberg, 2013; Goldberg, Smith, & Perry-Jenkins, 2012).

Importantly, differences in contributions to unpaid and paid labor do not necessarily lead to tension or conflict. Although the dominant mantra is that (a) same-gender couples divide labor more equally than heterosexual couples and (b) equality (or equity) is desired by and ideal for all (Goldberg, 2013), some people in queer relationships have work–family arrangements that do not conform to a perfect 50–50 split but are actually working well for them. If one partner loves their career, and one partner wants to stay home with young children, then this is probably a better arrangement than having both partners work outside the home and contribute equally to child care. (See the TV series *Modern Family* [Levitan et al.,

---

Modern Family: Season 1, Episode 20: "Benched"

Modern Family (Levitan et al., 2009–2020) is a show that in part features a gay couple, Mitchell and Cameron, raising their adopted daughter, Lily. Early on, Cameron stays home with Lily, and Mitchell works. However, in this episode (Levitan, Lloyd, Zuker, & Koch, 2010), Mitchell (played by Jesse Tyler Ferguson) is unemployed and thus stays home with Lily while Cameron (played by Eric Stonestreet) takes a job with a greeting card company.

Neither partner is happy with this arrangement—Mitchell misses work, and Cameron misses his primary caregiver role—even though both pretend to be fine with it. By the end of the episode, both admit they are unhappy and want things to return to the way they were.

2009–2020] for a good illustration of this point!) As one participant in the LGBTQ Family Building Project said,

> I am happy with the way we arranged our division of labor. I chose to work halftime because I wanted to spend more time with the boys and be very involved with their schools and activities. We took a big income hit, but I don't regret our choices. I appreciate her sacrifices in commuting and working full time. She appreciates my contributions, and we both recognize that each of us work hard, whether the labor is paid or uncompensated.

Beyond personal preferences, work- and income-related constraints may also affect how unpaid labor is divided. For example, one partner may have a more flexible work schedule or lower pay than the other, exerting pressure on the couple to divide up labor unevenly (Downing & Goldberg, 2011; Goldberg, 2012; Goldberg, Smith, & Perry-Jenkins, 2012). Lengthy commutes and working nontraditional hours (e.g., the night shift) may also affect the division of unpaid labor. As one parent in the LGBTQ Family Building Project explained, "I have a 1½-hour commute. My wife works right next to the kids' school. That structures a lot of the differences in family roles."

> *"As far as gender role expectations go, it's not the same as straight couples. But I tend to be more of a nurturing and empathic person. And I usually do certain things because I see what it gives to my family: joy, happiness, pleasure. So, I take on certain roles that may be viewed as traditional female or a woman's. And I am comfortable with that."*
>
> *"It's more that, over time, it's assumed I will always take care of things, and sometimes when I don't, instead of accepting responsibility, it is on me. So, there is more pressure sometimes for me to get everything done while also working full time and making family time."*
>
> *"I also have higher standards for cleanliness and how things should be done. Accepting that some of this is my own issue, I assume the role of handling things like laundry and cleaning."*
>
> —PARTICIPANTS IN THE LGBTQ FAMILY BUILDING PROJECT

Regardless of exactly how unpaid and paid labor is divided, it is important to consider the following:

- Child care isn't housework, and housework isn't child care. One partner may prefer to do more of the child care (which involves a human or humans with whom one has a relationship) but not housework (which is often repetitive, dull, and unappreciated).
- Certain household tasks (often those that are the most time consuming and least valued, e.g., doing dishes) have been "feminized" through their historical association with women. Likewise, certain tasks have historically been associated with and thus relegated to men (e.g., making home repairs). A helpful exercise for couples may be to discuss what meanings and associations each partner has with child care and household tasks to ensure that, for example, performing most or all of the domestic labor will not be experienced as oppressive or gender

incongruent. This discussion can also involve critiquing and disentangling chores from their gendered associations.

- The ultimate goal of this exercise is to move beyond exploring personal and societal meanings attached to domestic labor and paid employment to figuring out long-term strategies that work.

- The division of housework and child care may need to be renegotiated. The birth or adoption of additional children, employment changes (e.g., a new job or schedule changes), and other life changes may prompt a renegotiation of tasks. Alternatively, it may be important to revisit the division of tasks if one or both partners would like a break from a chore or chores that they have taken primary responsibility for (e.g., cleaning the litter box, paying bills), or if they feel that a chore that was once divided approximately equally has gradually become one partner's responsibility (e.g., cooking, children's bedtime routine). One parent in the LGBTQ Family Building Project shared,

> My partner works in construction and so sometimes works a ton of hours, and, other times, is unemployed. That makes it hard to shift responsibilities around, as one person gets used to and develops some competency in their areas. We have tried to assign her bigger but less frequent tasks to balance that out.

- Showing your partner(s) grace, compassion, and appreciation goes a long way. Each partner's load may wax and wane a bit, depending on a variety of factors, including work stress, mental health, and physical health. If your partner is under extreme work stress and you are dealing with fewer demands at the moment, you might offer to take the kids to their haircuts while your partner takes a breather. Alternatively, maybe you prefer the solitude of chopping vegetables for dinner after work while your partner occupies the children. If so, communicate that preference as well as gratitude for your partner's ability and willingness to give you a little space. Over time, this dynamic of picking up each other's slack will hopefully become a way that you show care to each other. As one parent in the LGBTQ Family Building Project said, "We have a very fair division of labor. Fair isn't always equal, and we don't count hairs. We each have our responsibilities, and we share some and help with the other person's responsibilities when needed."

All in all, it is important to communicate about household and child care chores. Creating and discussing a chore chart (more on this in a moment) can be a great way to ensure that everyone is aware of all of the chores that need to be done regularly versus intermittently and develop a shared sense of "who does what." Creating this chart and evaluating who does the most frequently performed chores, for example, may reveal inequities that might go unnoticed if everyone were to continue on autopilot. This exercise might prompt important and useful discussions about the most disliked tasks in the house—for example, whether it is possible to match these to the partner who dislikes them less or at least ensure that one person is not doing all of the most despised chores. As one parent in the LGBTQ Family Building Project said, "I think our division is pretty 'equal,' though I tend to do more of the cleaning because I dislike it less, and she tends to manage the kids during that time."

It is also generally a good idea to talk about "standards." How often should certain chores (e.g., laundry, dishes, deep cleaning) be done? What does a "clean bathroom" look like to each partner? It can be useful to acknowledge openly where you and your partner(s) differ in your priorities regarding housework, cleanliness, and order.

This may help you and your partner(s) to realize where you each need to adjust your expectations and behaviors to reach some common ground—for example, one of you may need to relax your standards (e.g., in terms of when tasks get done, or how well), and one of you may need to do more than you think is absolutely necessary to maintain relationship harmony.

Likewise, you may need to discuss the issue of *when* things get done. For some couples, a key source of strain is that one partner might agree to do a task but ultimately does not perform it within the time window that the other partner imagined or prefers. This can result in frustration for both partners: The partner who agreed to do it, Partner A, feels micromanaged, whereas the other partner, Partner B, is annoyed that the task is not done. Ultimately, the partners need to agree to trust each other. Partner B must release their own sense of control or responsibility over that task, with the knowledge that it "will get done"—perhaps within some mutually agreed on time window that may be outside of what they prefer but is realistic for Partner A.[2]

Creating a Chore Chart

Creating a chore chart can be a useful exercise. With your partner(s), create a comprehensive list of all of the household tasks that need to be done. This list should include personal chores and communal or shared chores. You can organize this list in many ways: by room, type of task, or most beloved to most hated. However, the most productive way is often to organize by frequency—that is, how often the chores need to be done: daily, weekly, monthly, or yearly. Consider too how much time each chore typically takes.

---

[2]For more on the division of chores, see Maltby's (2018) *Real Simple* article "How to Split Household Chores So Everyone Shares the Work."

Daily chores, including child care tasks, might be as follows:

- cooking, preparing meals (including making lunches and brewing coffee)
- washing dishes, including loading and unloading the dishwasher, if relevant
- straightening up, putting things away
- cleaning up routine messes (e.g., wiping down countertops in kitchen and bathroom)
- caring for animals, including cleaning litter boxes, feeding animals, and walking dogs
- dressing and feeding children (child care tasks)
- driving children to and from day care, school, lessons, practices (child care task)
- overseeing homework, evening routines (e.g., bathing), and bedtime (child care tasks)

Less frequent (e.g., every few days or weekly) chores might be

- taking the garbage out, bringing the trash bins back in
- vacuuming
- cleaning the bathroom, including toilets
- cleaning the kitchen, including wiping down countertops, cooking range, and refrigerator
- changing the bedsheets
- doing laundry, including folding clothes and putting them away
- going grocery shopping, including making the list and putting groceries away
- sorting the mail
- doing lawn and yard work
- running errands (e.g., post office, bank)

Even less frequent tasks (e.g., every 2 weeks or every month) might be

- cleaning out the fridge
- cleaning the inside of the microwave
- dusting
- paying bills, managing finances
- planning and executing social activities for children (including buying birthday gifts); arranging for babysitters (child care tasks)

Even less frequent tasks (e.g., every few months) might be

- organizing or reorganizing closets, pantry, and cupboards
- taking care of car maintenance
- doing home repairs
- cleaning baseboards, radiators
- washing windows
- doing holiday planning (e.g., birthdays, vacations)
- signing children up for camps, making appointments for children (child care tasks)

Cultivating Attachment and Bonding

Another significant area related to the transition to parenthood is one's relationship to one's child. Despite the pressures to immediately bond to one's child, the reality is that not all new parents experience an immediate attachment. Nongestational LGBQ mothers in particular have described the challenges of feeling attached to the child that their partner is carrying or has carried for 9 months (Wojnar & Katzenmeyer, 2014). Some women, in turn, purposefully engage in activities that can help to foster attachment, even during the prenatal period, such as reading books about pregnancy, attending prenatal appointments, and calling their future child by a special name.

Once the baby is born, nongestational mothers describe engaging in a variety of activities and strategies to both promote bonding and otherwise counterbalance the "leg up" that their partner has via genetic connection, pregnancy, birth, or nursing (Goldberg & Perry-Jenkins, 2007; Wojnar & Katzenmeyer, 2014). These behavioral strategies may help to enhance parental confidence and competence as well as support closeness and attachment to the child. (They may also be valuable strategies for adoptive parents, too.) Consider using these strategies if you are a nongestational parent:

- rocking the child, changing diapers, and performing other physically close activities
- being the primary caregiver or simply participating in parenting and child care equally
- developing special child care routines, such as being the "bedtime parent" or "bath time parent"
- taking time off at a different time than one's partner (e.g., back-to-back parental leave)
- making work changes (e.g., reducing hours, changing schedule) to allow for more time home
- bottle-feeding
- nursing or chestfeeding through lactation stimulation[3]

---

[3]The La Leche League provides guidance and support to individuals who wish to stimulate lactation:

It is possible to establish milk production for an adopted baby or baby born via gestational surrogate, even if you have never been pregnant or given birth. The amount of milk you may produce depends on many factors. Most people are able to produce at least a little milk. You might be able to induce lactation (start to produce

If you are a gestational parent, consider how you can facilitate your partner's equivalent role. Actively support them as they seek to engage with the child, possibly "backing off" or doing other household chores during times of one-on-one contact. Consider alternating chestfeeding with bottle-feeding to enable your partner the opportunity to participate in the intimate experience of feeding. (You can use formula or use a pump to expel milk.)

A variety of symbolic, linguistic, legal, and reproductive strategies may also help to promote the nongestational parent's role:

- giving the child the nongestational parent's last name or using a family hyphenated name
- having the nongestational parent choose what they wish to be called (e.g., Mama)

---

milk), and then build up your milk supply by putting your baby to your breast often and/or expressing frequently.

Some adoptive and nongestational parents stimulate milk production by using a breast pump every 2–3 hours, before the baby comes. It can take anything from a few days to a few weeks to start to produce drops of milk. The more stimulation your breasts get, the more milk you will produce. If you produce any milk before your baby comes you can store it to use later.

Even if your baby does not breastfeed, you can still hold them for all their feedings (and lots of holding in between!) and foster the same kind of attachment that nurturing through breastfeeding brings. (La Leche League, 2020, paras. 1–3 in the "Induced Lactation" section)

Be advised that the issue of chestfeeding by adoptive parents is not without debate within the adoption community (i.e., some adopted people, and some birth parents, find the practice questionable and/or offensive); see, for example, Creating a Family (n.d.), The Adopted Ones Blog (2013), and Musings of a Birthmom (2015). If you are a prospective adoptive parent who hopes to chestfeed, consider discussing this with your adoption agency/ support professionals, and expectant parents.

- ensuring that the nongestational parent completes a second-parent adoption[4]
- using reciprocal in vitro fertilization in which one partner carries the child using the other partner's egg

Sometimes parents want to know: What types of relationships do children have with their genetic/gestational and nongenetic/nongestational parents? How equivalent or different are these relationships? In a longitudinal study of lesbian-parent families formed via DI, researchers found that when children were 3½ to 4 years old, women described a range of patterns of parental preferences

---

[4]Second-parent or "stepparent" adoptions are, in the legal sense, a means of "confirming" parental rights. *Adoption* is usually defined as creating a legal parental relationship in which there was none before. In turn, these terms can feel inappropriate, and, as such, these adoptions can also be referred to as *confirmatory adoptions*, which more adequately captures the process by which a nongenetic or nongestational parent can confirm parental rights to their child. This will involve paperwork, typically a court hearing, and possibly a home study, depending on the state.

Married same-gender couples can pursue these adoptions in every state, but not all do, in part because many assume that having both the gestational and nongestational parent on a child's birth certificate establishes their parental rights. However, birth certificates are a form of record; they are not a determinant of legal parentage. In addition, some parents believe (e.g., based on where they live) that their parental rights will never be questioned.

The time and cost of a confirmatory adoption may discourage some people from pursuing them. Yet this adoption is important because it protects parents' rights (i.e., the nongenetic or nongestational parent's rights) in the event of a custody dispute, or if their parental rights are challenged, and it can help to ensure that their children have access to important benefits and resources (e.g., inheritance rights). In some states, a judgment of parentage is available to confirm parental rights by court order without the need for an adoption. This is a suitable alternative when it is available. See Nayak (n.d.) for more information.

on the part of their children (Goldberg et al., 2008). Many women described an initial preference for the genetic/gestational parent, which they often attributed to pregnancy, breastfeeding, or the "biological bond," followed by an "evening out" of such preferences, such that children preferred their moms equally or for different things (e.g., roughhousing and play, security and comfort), or, their preferences changed day to day or week to week. More rarely, parents described a stable preference for the gestational mother. When parents had multiple children, these children were sometimes described as having different preferred parents. Other research suggests that nongestational mothers may experience jealousy, at least early on, surrounding their partner's ability to be pregnant, give birth, or breastfeed, or their initially closer relationship with the child (Pelka, 2009). Such dynamics often dissipate over time but may become activated in certain settings or circumstances (e.g., when a nongenetic/nongestational parent's role or parental legitimacy is questioned or ignored; Goldberg et al., 2008).

For new adoptive parents—and especially those who adopt older children, who have experiences, memories, and attachments to prior caregivers—a delayed or gradual attachment may be especially common. In turn, it is useful for prospective adoptive parents to be aware of the diversity in initial attachment experiences. In a study of 90 LGBQ and heterosexual parents who were interviewed 2 years postadoption, more than one half of participants described a strong and stable bond to their child beginning at the time of placement, which they attributed to a variety of factors, such as the child's young age at placement as well as their own personality and strong desire to parent. Many parents, however, detailed a slow initial bond to their child, which they attributed to the shock of becoming parents overnight, not feeling entirely entitled to parent, and legal insecurities. This initially tentative bond gradually strengthened over time.

In turn, it is important for you to know, especially if you are considering adoptive parenthood, that you may not immediately bond to your child. It may help, however, to talk with a therapist before adopting about feelings of insecurity or a lack of a sense of entitlement to parent as well as any legal worries or concerns you may have—and what you can do, if anything, to address them.

BEYOND THE IMMEDIATE FAMILY: CHANGES IN SOCIAL SUPPORT NETWORKS

So far, this chapter has predominantly addressed what happens within the immediate family in terms of mental health, relationship issues, the division of labor, and the parent–child relationship. Yet, changes may also occur in new parents' relationships with folks outside of their immediate family during the transition to parenthood. Specifically, research suggests that, overall, LGBTQ parents often perceive less support from members of their family of origin than do heterosexual parents, but, at the same time, they tend to report greater support from family members than LGBTQ nonparents (DeMino et al., 2007; Goldberg, 2012).

It seems, too, that family members may become more supportive once a child enters the picture (Gartrell et al., 1999; Goldberg, 2006): For example, one study of lesbian new moms found that women's perceptions of support from their own and their partners' families increased across the transition to parenthood (Goldberg, 2006). Thus, some family members may push their feelings about nonheterosexuality or same-gender relationships aside and seek to repair problematic or damaged relationships in the interest of developing a relationship with a new grandchild or niece or nephew (Gartrell et al., 1999; Goldberg, 2012). In some cases, family ties may be strengthened by the arrival of a child such that, for example, LGBTQ parents feel closer to their parents after becoming parents themselves (Gartrell et al., 1999, 2006; Goldberg, 2012; Titlestad & Robinson, 2019). Also, there is evidence that regardless of parenthood status, LGBTQ people may experience increasing support from their families over time as families adjust to and come to accept their identities and relationship (Greif et al., 2019). As one parent in the LGBTQ Family Building Project said, "Initially, my mother-in-law didn't support me being an equal parent. This is 100% resolved now."

Of course, not all family members become more supportive and involved across the transition to parenthood. On announcing their intention to parent, some LGBTQ parents confront reduced support from their families. For example, family members may express opposition to this decision to parent on moral or religious grounds or because they believe that life as a member of an LGBTQ parent family will be too difficult—particularly for children. They may also oppose the LGBTQ person's route to parenthood (e.g., adoption in general or transracial adoption specifically) or feel less invested in children's lives if they are not genetically related to them (Gartrell et al., 1996; Goldberg, 2012; Patterson et al., 1998). In LGBTQ couples in which one partner gives birth, this decision may have implications for family-of-origin support, such that family members who lack a genetic relationship to the child may be less excited about the child's arrival and ultimately less involved in that child's life (Nordqvist, 2015; Patterson et al., 1998).

Relationships with friends may also shift across the transition to parenthood. LGBTQ parents may find that they drift apart from nonparent LGBTQ friends, while they become closer to cis heterosexual parents in their circle and community based on the shared experience of raising children. For many, "parent" or "queer parent" becomes one of their most salient identities (Forenza et al., 2021). Gay and bisexual men, in particular, have reported a lack of support and even outright rejection from childless gay friends and the LGBTQ community at large, sometimes noting that they are cast as assimilating to heteronormative ideals (e.g., the "package deal" of marriage, parenthood) and conformist values (Goldberg, 2012; Lewin, 2009). LGBTQ parents may also lose touch with their LGBTQ friends because children are not welcome in certain spaces or their friends do not want to spend time with children. Some LGBTQ parents do maintain friendships with nonparent LGBTQ friends but may also spend less time socializing together or may broaden their networks to include other parents (Bergman et al., 2010; Goldberg, 2012). Feelings of exclusion or nonsupport from the broader LGBTQ community may be more salient or significant for certain folks, such as bisexual parents, parents of color, and working-class parents because of additional issues of biphobia, racism, and classism, respectively, that they must deal with (Carroll, 2018; Goldberg, 2012; Goldberg, Frost, et al., 2018). Trans people, in particular, may find that becoming a parent drives a wedge between themselves and nonparent trans people, and trans parents may feel excluded from queer communities of parents as a result of transphobia within the queer community (Ellis et al., 2015; M. Ryan, 2009).

Support from family and friends is important for LGBTQ parents insomuch as it is linked to better well-being. For some LGBTQ parents, maintaining a relationship to the LGBTQ community at large may also be of great value because a sustained sense of connectedness and "sense of belonging" to the community may enhance their well-being (Manley, Goldberg, & Ross, 2018).

Interacting With Communities, Neighborhoods, Day Cares, and Beyond

LGBTQ parents interface with a variety of important and interrelated contexts during the transition to parenthood and beyond.

Where LGBTQ folks live has a significant impact on the ease or difficulty of navigating day-to-day interactions as well as access to resources that reflect and meet their families' needs. LGBTQ parent families in which one or both partners are men, trans, of color, disabled, or some combination of those identities, will face extra scrutiny because of the ways in which these identities do not figure into dominant ideas about "ideal" parenthood.

Living in an LGBTQ-unfriendly area can actually be bad for your health. Specifically, living in a state or community with anti-LGBTQ laws or policies has been linked to poorer mental health among LGBTQ parents (Goldberg & Smith, 2011; Goldberg, Smith, et al., 2019). Likewise, LGBTQ parents who live in less gay-friendly areas have been found to perceive more discrimination from their children's day cares and preschools than those in gay-friendly areas; perception of discrimination, in turn, creates stress (Goldberg & Smith, 2014). Although "moving" might seem to be a reasonable solution to this issue, geographic mobility is simply not an option—or necessarily desirable—for many LGBTQ parents. Financial constraints, job commitments, family obligations, or a love of and connection to rural life or a particular region may keep LGBTQ parent families rooted in regions that are hostile to their sexual, gender, and family identities (Goldberg et al., 2013; Goldberg, Weber, et al., 2014). Thus, it is essential that families do what they can to protect themselves—for example, through obtaining wills, powers of attorney, legal adoptions, and other legal safeguards.[5] The National LGBTQ+ Bar Association is a first

---

[5]See Elizabeth Schwartz's (2016) book *Before I Do: A Legal Guide to Marriage, Gay and Otherwise*. See also the Movement Advancement Project (https://www.lgbtmap.org/) and American Civil Liberties Union (https://www.aclu.org/) for more information about the necessity of and ways of obtaining legal safeguards.

stop in finding an LGBTQ-competent attorney for consultation in this regard.

Seeking Early Childhood Education

LGBTQ parents who are seeking day care or early childhood educational environments for their children should evaluate programs with questions in mind. (Some of this information can be gleaned from online or web-based materials, whereas other information is most easily and accurately obtained through speaking with a school or program administrator, or by visiting the site itself.) Questions include the following:

- Is the paperwork inclusive of different family forms, family building routes, gender identities, and relational configurations?
- Do teachers, materials, and web-based content refer to "parents" and "guardians" (vs. "mothers" and "fathers") or acknowledge the potential for caregiving situations that go beyond the heterosexual, two-parent family form?
- Do photos, images, children's books, art, toys, dolls, and music depict and promote inclusion of diverse family forms in terms of number of parents, parent gender/gender expression, family-building route, and racial makeup?
- Are holidays, celebrations, and assignments inclusive of a diverse range of families and family-building routes? For example, how is Mother's Day or Father's Day handled? Alternatively, is there a "Parents' Day"? How are adopted children's unique circumstances accounted for in birthday celebrations, if at all?
- Do teachers make an effort to use language and examples that reflect all kinds of families? Do they address hurtful or insensitive language choices or name-calling by children (Goldberg, Black, et al., 2017; Goldberg & Smith, 2014)?

OTHER IDENTITIES

A variety of other identities can intersect with one's LGBTQ status to shape and nuance their experience of the transition to parenthood. Here, just a few of them are identified so that interested folks can further ponder and explore these issues on their own.

Male Parents

Gay, bisexual, and queer (GBQ) cis men may experience additional scrutiny of their parenting abilities because women are often assumed to possess superior and more "natural" abilities as parents, and GBQ men parenting with other men presumably "lack" some fundamental ingredient in the parenting equation. Like most parents, however, GBQ men do not parent in a vacuum: Their children have access to birth mothers, female teachers and doctors, aunts and grandmothers, family friends, babysitters, and a variety of other female caregivers and role models. But the assumption that children "need" a caregiver of a particular gender is by itself problematic: Much research suggests that the quality of caregiving is far more important than the caregiver's assigned sex or gender. Nevertheless, all LGBTQ parents are vulnerable to scrutiny regarding their children's gender identity and gender expression and may therefore experience gender anxieties related to their children's having "normative" gendered interests, behaviors, expression, and so on (Averett, 2016; Goldberg, 2009a).

Trans and Gender Nonconforming Parents

Many LGBTQ folks will experience pregnancy, birth, and new parenthood in ways that differ from the dominant cis/heteronormative model that is so often assumed by parenting resources (e.g., books, blogs), therapists, and health care providers. Trans, nonbinary, and gender nonconforming folks, in particular, may experience scrutiny of their parenting identities and behaviors because of the ways in which they challenge cis/heteronormative assumptions. For example, they may carve out parental identities for themselves that differ from the gendered stereotypes of a mother or a father that are so frequently highlighted as the "only" way to be. In turn, they may meet resistance in trying to get outsiders to see, refer to, and accept them simply as a parent, for example—as opposed to a mother or father. Fortunately, an increasing number and range of parenting resources have emerged, especially online, that are explicitly encompassing of parents with a range of gender identities. Trans and gender nonconforming parents can find each other in these online spaces and share and bear witness to each other's evolving parenthood and gender journeys.

Consensually Nonmonogamous Parents

Some LGBTQ parents are in consensually nonmonogamous relationships or arrangements, which in many ways defy central assumptions around families and parenthood—namely, that people (and especially parents) don't have relationships with more than one person and that children have no more than two parents. LGBTQ parents in CNM relationships may have casual or more serious relationships with multiple individuals. In addition, they may reside with more than one partner. Transitioning to parenthood often means a "pause" on one's engagement in consensual nonmonogamy related to a lack of time, new roles, and new responsibilities (Manley, Legge, et al., 2018). Closing relationships temporarily early on during the transition to parenthood is one strategy for maintaining one's sanity during a stressful time (Manley, Legge, et al., 2018). It may be helpful for parents to anticipate such changes and to discuss them with partners or develop a plan for whether, when, and how to see partners on the transition to parenthood and beyond.

Bisexual Parents

Bisexual, pansexual, and queer parents may experience particular erasure during the transition to parenthood because, even more than ever, their sexual identity is interpreted through their relational configuration (as we saw in the opening vignette). Bisexual parents, at least women, may not feel welcomed or included in either dominant heteronormative parenting communities or LGBTQ communities, which can cause loneliness and strain (Manley, Goldberg, & Ross, 2018; Ross et al., 2010). It may be helpful, again, to identify other bisexual or queer parents in online groups or forums to find connection and support during a time when one may feel that one's identities on multiple fronts are invisible.

Stepparents

This chapter focuses largely on LGBTQ folks who are intentionally becoming parents. Stepparents become (step)parents through partnering with someone who already has children. This transition is uniquely different from the transition to intended parenthood because of the lack of shared experience with one's partner; the frequently older age of the children involved; and often the existence of a nonresidential parent who has legal and emotional claim to the children (e.g., "My partner came in after kids were born and rules/routines were established . . ., [and we are also] dealing with my ex-wife and her lack of parenting and mental instability and financial issues"; "We each spent many years as single parents, and coming together as a family has been difficult with 'two bosses' "). These differences lead to unique dynamics that intersect with one's LGBTQ status. LGBTQ stepparents may face particularly heightened levels of invisibility and stigma in society because of both their sexuality/ gender identity and stepparent role, particularly when interfacing

with schools and pediatricians. They may also face unique challenges in bonding with children and interacting with their partners' former partners, especially if their partner was previously in a
heterosexual relationship, and this represents their first "queer" relationship (Lynch, 2004a, 2004b; Tasker & Lavender-Stott, 2020).

Parents of Color

LGBTQ parents of color inevitably face certain unique issues as a
result of their own and their children's intersecting family and racial
identities. LGBTQ parents of color and their children are more likely
to be poor and to lack health insurance than White LGBTQ parents
and their children. In turn, they may face greater challenges accessing
high-quality, family–child supports and services (e.g., therapy) as well
as, specifically, accessing LGBTQ-friendly providers, not to mention
racially conscious providers. Furthermore, relatively LGBTQ-affirming
communities are not necessarily racially diverse; in turn, LGBTQ
parents of color may face difficult decisions about where to live,
balancing various competing considerations related to racial diversity and LGBTQ friendliness as well as cost of living, proximity to
job and extended family, school quality, and so on. LGBTQ parents
of color may face stigma related to their race as well as their gender,
sexual orientation, and family identities, such that their parenting
is doubly scrutinized by outsiders, including health care providers
and school officials. They may also encounter racial discrimination
within the larger LGBTQ community (Brainer et al., 2020).

CONCLUSION

The transition to parenthood is a monumental life transition.
LGBTQ parents face a variety of potentially unique stressors
related to their family-building route, stigma in the outside world,

and other intersecting identities. However, they may also bring certain resources to parenthood, such as an orientation toward equity (in terms of dividing up tasks) and a connection to the larger LGBTQ community, which can serve a source of strength and support.

As you transition to parenthood, seek support and advice. The internet can be a great place to start your journey and may offer a lot of wonderful ideas and inspiration, but hopefully you also have friends and family members who can support you as you make your way. Likewise, you may need professional support like the parents in the opening vignette. Parenthood is the ultimate marathon. You need sustenance, support, and a lot of patience with yourself as you make the journey.

RESOURCES

There are a lot of big questions to think about on your own and to discuss with your partner before the transition to parenthood, including things that you want to repeat from your own childhood and things you do not want to repeat (e.g., based on your parents' approach to parenting); how you envision and what worries you about the division of paid and unpaid labor; and your values or preferences regarding chestfeeding, circumcision, pacifiers, vaccinations, religion, discipline, day care, extracurriculars (e.g., sports, playing an instrument), and who should take parental leave and for how long. See, for example, these resources:

Boone, K. (n.d.). *35 talking topics for expectant parents!* https://www.balancingtheboones.com/home/2018/12/17/35-talking-topics-for-expectant-parents

The Danish Way of Parenting. (n.d.). *10 life changing questions for new parents.* http://thedanishway.com/10-life-changing-questions-for-new-parents/

OTHER RESOURCES

A number of books and podcasts address different aspects of LGBTQ parenting and the transition to parenthood specifically.

Books

Aizley, H. (Ed.). (2006). *Confessions of the other mother: Nonbiological lesbian moms tell all*. Beacon Press.

Ehrensaft, D. (2005). *Mommies, daddies, donors, surrogates: Answering tough questions and building strong families*. Guilford Press.

Kelton, J., & Hopkins, R. (2020). *If these ovaries could talk: The things we've learned about making an LGBTQ family*. Lit Riot Press.

MacDonald, T. (2016). *Where's the mother? Stories from a transgender dad*. Trans Canada Press.

LGBTQ Parenting Podcasts

Family Equality. (2019, December 26). *Our 10 favorite LGBTQ+ family podcasts of 2019*. https://www.familyequality.org/2019/12/26/our-10-favorite-lgbtq-family-podcasts-of-2019/

Lott, E. (2020, September 30). *7 best LGBTQ family & fertility podcasts you should be listening to*. Gay Parents to Be. https://www.gayparentstobe.com/gay-parenting-blog/best-lgbtq-family-fertility-podcasts-you-should-be-listening-to/

CHAPTER 7

PARENTING IN THE EARLY YEARS

THIS CHAPTER COVERS:

> choosing a school or day care
> preparing young children for heterosexist bias
> finding ways to counter and prevent heterosexist bias
> navigating gender normativity pressures in society
> tackling other parenting challenges in early parenthood

Tess is a Latinx, cis, queer-identified, single mom of 4-year-old Max. Max was conceived using sperm from a known donor, Ben, who is a college friend of Tess's and is White, cis, and gay. The conception occurred in the context of a committed relationship with Carr, Tess's former partner, who is a multiracial trans man. Tess and Carr split up when Max was 2 years old partly because Carr wanted to move out of the area and pursue acting full time, whereas Tess was unwilling to leave the small Midwest community where she was born and raised.

Max spends at least one long weekend a month with Carr and one month every summer. Tess and Carr's split is amicable, although there was a difficult adjustment period early on during which Tess resented Carr for leaving the family, and Carr resented Tess for her unwillingness to make a life change for him.

During the summer, Tess toured several potential preschools for Max. She has a flexible job as a project manager and also works part time as a consultant. Tess works mostly from home but requires reliable full-time day care so that she can put in the 40-plus hours that her work requires. In selecting a preschool, her primary concerns were hours (i.e., she needed an afternoon program; pickup at 3 p.m. was not feasible for her), a decent teacher–child ratio, a physically appealing and stimulating environment, affordability, and proximity to home.

With few options within a 15- to 20-minute radius, she ultimately chose Bright Futures, a preschool suggested by her former home day care provider. Clean and aesthetically appealing, affordable, just 7 minutes away, and with a sizable number of Latinx families, Tess felt good about her decision. When completing the paperwork for Bright Futures, however, she found herself hesitating over several questions, which seemed to presume marriage and a mother–father parenthood unit. Should she explain that Max's other parent was a trans man, who did not identify as a "dad" but rather as Max's "other parent"? Should she explain that Max also had a sperm donor, Ben, whom he saw regularly? Should she explain that she was not married to Max's other parent but that they nevertheless had worked out a custody arrangement involving occasional absences from school so Max could travel to see Carr? Tess wavered because she figured that, as a single parent, she would likely be the only one engaging with the school. Ultimately, she chose to just write, "I am a single parent. Max sees his other parent occasionally."

For a few weeks, things seemed to go great. Max made new friends and seemed to like his teachers. Tess was warmly met by Max's teachers at drop-off and pickup. In late September, Tess received a notification that, for Max's birthday celebration— which was coming up in a few days—he should bring in pictures of his family as well as something that was important to him (e.g., a book, a piece of clothing) to help tell his "story." Tess realized that it might be a good idea to prepare the teachers for Max's photos and "story"—after all, he identified both Carr and Ben as members of his family, and he called Carr "Doo-da" and Ben "Uncle Ben."

Sensing the potential for confusion and possibly a level of probing that Max would be unprepared for, she called Bright Futures. She explained a bit more about Max's family's background to the head of school, who seemed overwhelmed by all of the details but said she was "writing it all down." Tess asked that the information be conveyed to Max's teachers so they could facilitate the celebration with sensitivity. Tess made a mental note to check in with Max's teachers at drop-off the next day, well in advance of the birthday celebration. She also checked in with Max. Specifically, Tess asked him what photos he wanted to bring in ("One with all of us!" he said, choosing a photo of Max, Tess, Carr, and Ben at Max's last birthday party). In addition, Tess reminded Max that "some people might get confused about all of your amazing parents because they assume that kids just have two parents, a mom and a dad," at which Max laughed and said, "Well that's not true!" and subsequently referenced the origin stories of several of his favorite superheroes.

At drop-off the next day, Tess pulled one of Max's teachers aside and explained the basics of who Carr and Ben were. The teacher seemed a bit startled, having not yet been briefed by the head of school, but promised, "[I'll] try my best to keep it all straight!" Tess stifled the urge to roll her eyes and thanked the teacher.

Max's celebration was a few days later. At the end of the day, she picked him up, nervous but excited to hear how it had gone. "Good!" Max said. Max's retelling of the celebration primarily focused on the cupcakes he had brought in. "Did people like the photos?" she asked. "Did they ask any interesting questions?" Max pondered the questions, then said, "Madison asked if Doo-da was my dad, and I said, 'No, I have a Doo-da, not a dad.' I also said that Uncle Ben helped make me, and Jonah said that wasn't true. But then we had cupcakes." Tess wasn't ready to give up that easily. "How did Miss Carly [one of Max's teachers] handle those questions?" she asked. "Did she help out at all?" Max smiled a little. "Miss Carly did okay," he said. "She said that sometimes parents get help from other people to make a baby." Tess breathed a sigh of relief, silently thanking Miss Carly but also realizing that she probably needed to meet with Miss Carly and Max's other teachers to debrief and discuss how to handle such situations going forward. She also realized that it was probably important to spend some time talking with Max to more thoroughly prepare him for these kinds of experiences in the future. "We got lucky," she muttered to herself. She decided that it was time to talk to Bright Futures about their paperwork and offer some suggestions about how to help parents like her feel more seen and included.

SCHOOL DECISION MAKING

Many parents have little choice in terms of where their children attend school. They accept that their children will attend public school in the community where they live, and that's that. Some parents, however, have some choice over where their children attend school. These are often middle-class parents with geographic mobility who can choose to live in certain communities with an eye toward securing access to a "good" school system. Middle-class parents may also have access to multiple school options, including private school. In turn, parents with some degree of choice may seek out schools that have a good academic reputation but may also prioritize other factors, such as a strong athletic program, an arts emphasis, a racially diverse student body, or a bilingual education program. Typically, the ability to exert some choice over the school decision-making process is reflective of social class, which is intertwined with social and cultural capital (Ball et al., 1996; Reinoso, 2008).

Most parents send their children to the local public school (National Center for Education Statistics, 2021). Some parents may entertain alternatives to their neighborhood public school, such as through school choice, charter schools, and magnet schools.

Although typically cost free, these options are not accessible to all parents. For example, parents who live in communities that do not provide busing for students attending from out of the school district may be unable to entertain a school choice option because they cannot drive their children to school (e.g., given their work schedule, transportation issues). A minority of parents send their children to private schools, which vary greatly in cost (e.g., as low as $5,000 and as high as $30,000 or more per year, depending on the state and the specific school; Private School Review, 2021).

Research on lesbian, gay, bisexual, transgender (trans), and queer (LGBTQ) parents suggests that they often consider and weigh a variety of factors when evaluating potential day care, preschool, and elementary school options (Goldberg, Allen, et al., 2018; Goldberg & Smith, 2014), such as

- whether the school seems LGBTQ friendly (e.g., based on reputation, presence of LGBTQ parent families, how their family is treated on tours or in interviews);
- the racial and ethnic makeup and diversity of the school, particularly if they are a multiracial family and especially if their children are of color;
- the presence of other adoptive families, if their family is formed via adoption;
- academic reputation (e.g., based on test scores, teacher–student ratio);
- physical location and safety;
- academic, social, artistic, linguistic, and athletic resources and opportunities;
- specialized accommodations or resources (e.g., if children have special needs);
- cost; and
- proximity to home.

When evaluating different school options, LGBTQ parents often feel that they are juggling competing considerations, such that, ultimately, there is no "perfect school." Parents who are constrained by practical factors, such as cost (e.g., they cannot afford private school) and location (e.g., they live in a rural area and cannot spend a half hour driving to a school in a different community), as well as their children's special needs (e.g., their child needs to be in a school with certain accommodations), often have fewer choices and may need to sacrifice LGBTQ friendliness, racial diversity, academic reputation, and other factors to meet their "bottom line." Some parents may find that the school characteristics they value the most are in competition with one another, whereby, for example, choosing one (e.g., academically rigorous, dual-language program) means sacrificing another (e.g., racially/ethnically diverse, close to home).

Lesbian, gay, bisexual, and queer (LGBQ) parents with adopted children of color have sometimes been found to weigh academic rigor against racial/ethnic diversity, wondering whether it is more important for their child to be in a "top school"—that is, a school known for its good teachers and high test scores—or to be surrounded by people of the same racial/ethnic background. This work suggests that more privileged adoptive LGBQ parents tend to sacrifice racial diversity for academic rigor, believing that this is more important in ensuring a positive academic trajectory for their children (Goldberg, Allen, et al., 2018). White, wealthy, gay male parents, in particular, tend to prioritize academic excellence over other factors in choosing schools for their children (Goldberg, Allen, et al., 2018). Yet other research suggests that immersion in racially/ethnically diverse communities and schools should be prioritized for adopted children of color to offset the impact of living in a White family (if relevant) and in a White supremacist society. Indeed, White parents of adopted children of color must be aware of the potential costs of sacrificing racial diversity for other factors—for example, their child may struggle to establish a healthy racial identity and racial pride if they are the only Black child in a sea of Whiteness (Adoptive Families, n.d.-a; Valby, 2020). Adopted children of color who live in racially diverse neighborhoods and attend racially diverse schools often have a stronger sense of racial pride than adopted children who live among and attend a school with mostly White children (Fong & McRoy, 2016).

Again, many LGBTQ parents have little choice in terms of where their children attend school or where they live. Many live in areas not particularly LGBTQ friendly or that do not have many LGBTQ residents. LGBTQ parents may prefer rural life, have job- or commute-related constraints, or choose to live near extended family, thus leading them to live outside of urban centers or progressive enclaves in which LGBTQ parent families are more visible and accepted. In turn, to the extent that day cares and schools reflect the family makeup or values of their communities, LGBTQ families may face stigma in such settings. Likewise, their children who attend these day cares and schools may face mistreatment or invisibility.

PREPARATION IN EARLY CHILDHOOD TO DEAL WITH HETERONORMATIVITY

We live in a heteronormative society. All children, including those with LGBTQ parents, are likely exposed to media, including TV and children's books, that disproportionately represent mother–father families. In turn, as children develop, they become increasingly aware of how their families differ from those most commonly depicted in the media as well those that surround them in their schools and communities. Significantly, the dominant family that pervades societal depictions of family is not only male–female headed but is characterized by gender normativity, genetic relatedness, and racial sameness. In turn, children gradually develop a sense of whether and how their family deviates from the dominant norm in other ways, such as with regard to racial makeup and gender expression.

By preschool age, children begin to notice differences across families. As parents, you should focus on a couple of primary messages during this stage: family diversity (i.e., families come in all different shapes and sizes), love (i.e., your child is loved; love is an important part of what makes a family), and values (i.e., all families are valid; no one type of family is better than others). Beyond that, try to do the following (Kashef, 2019):

- Establish the basic story of your family and build in the details as your child gets older and can grasp their meaning. A preschooler will not understand the legal intricacies of adoption, nor will they understand the specifics of reproductive technologies. However, you can still share the basic narrative that another person was involved in helping your family come to be.

    As your child develops, you can share more details. Diane Ehrensaft's (2005) book *Mommies, Daddies, Donors, Surrogates: Answering Tough Questions and Building Strong Families* is a great resource to help you prepare for and think about these conversations. For children, Cory Silverberg's (2013) *What Makes a Baby* and Keiko Kasza's (1992) *A Mother for Choco* are useful starting points for talking about donor insemination and adoption, respectively.

- Tell the truth—always—but keep it simple. If your child is adopted, you can and should talk about their birth parents. However, you do not need to explain in detail the circumstances that led to your child's adoption until they are able to comprehend and absorb such information. At the preschool stage and earlier, you might share that your child's birth mother did not have a place to live at the time that they were born, but you do not need to provide details about her drug addiction, for example. A young child can probably understand the importance of having a home to raise a baby, but they cannot understand substance use or addiction.

- Look for natural openings to talk about and normalize the idea of "all types of families" as well as your particular family-building story. Books, TV shows, and movies are great jumping-off places for such conversations. You can use these to highlight your own family (e.g., "Oh, look! [Character] has two moms, too!") as well as other types of families (e.g., single-parent, grandparent-headed, adoptive) to underscore family diversity. A great book for starting this type of conversation is Todd Parr's (2003) *The Family Book*.

- Listen to the question that is asked and keep your response simple and straightforward. For example, a question like, "Why don't I have a dad?" warrants a response—but one that is fairly basic. You can "level up" the complexity as your child develops and matures. Try not to let your anxiety get the best of you, and remember that there is no need to explain the details of human reproduction to a 3-year-old.

- Allow children to enact fantasies and roles. If your child has two dads and they insist on a mom doll for their dollhouse, or your child plays "house" with a mother and a father, do not try to correct their play or explain that they have "two dads, no mom." Allowing your child the freedom of exploring different family types, roles, and identities is good for their development. Perhaps your child's play is a way of processing experiences and feelings, or maybe it is simply creative experimentation. Or, perhaps your child is imitating what they see in their friends' families or in the dominant media. You can always ask questions (e.g., "Tell me about the mom in this family. What's she like?"), but try to do so without an "agenda."

As children develop, they will not only notice how their family differs from a lot of the families around them but may also come into contact with people, including teachers and classmates, who challenge their ideas about their family's value and legitimacy. In the LGBTQ Family Building Project (Goldberg, 2021), many parents highlighted situations in which their young children encountered peers who questioned or doubted their family's formation or origin story (e.g., their peers asked what a donor was or wondered how a child could simply not have a dad) as well as peers who used the word "gay" in a negative way.

In some cases, children were teased by their peers, whereas in others, they were simply excluded (e.g., they were not invited to a birthday party if a peer's parents knew that they had LGBTQ parents). Some young children were described as coming into contact with teachers, camp counselors, and other adults who invalidated their families in some way—for example, failing to acknowledge their particular type of family in curricula, holiday celebrations, and storytelling, and, occasionally, challenging them or silencing them when they shared details of their families.

At the preschool or early elementary school age, peers might reveal their ignorance or lack of understanding about LGBTQ parent families through asking questions or making statements like the following:

- "Why don't you have a [dad/mom]?"
- "You don't have two dads. I don't believe you."
- "That's so gay."
- "I thought that other lady was your mom . . .?"
- "You have two dads? That's so [weird/gross]."
- "Your parents are gay, right? Are you gay, too?"
- "You're adopted? Wow. Where did they get you from?"
- "Why didn't your parents [want you/raise you/keep you]?"

LGBTQ Inclusiveness of Day Cares and Elementary Schools

Participants in the LGBTQ Family Building Project (Goldberg, 2021) were asked about aspects of LGBTQ inclusiveness and representation in their children's day cares and elementary schools. Here's what the data showed:

- Of the participants surveyed, 19% said their day cares had LGBTQ staff members (27% for elementary schools).
- Of the parents, 29% said their day cares had other LGBTQ parent families (also 29% for elementary schools).
- Just 12% said that LGBTQ families were mentioned or featured on day cares' websites or materials (15% for elementary schools).
- Of the participants, 24% said that day care paperwork was inclusive of diverse sexual orientations (also 24% for elementary schools).
- Just 13% said that day care paperwork was inclusive of diverse gender identities (15% for elementary schools).
- Many parents described "crossing out" mother–father options on paperwork to accurately represent their family or making suggestions about replacing those with more expansive options (e.g., Parent or Caregiver 1, 2, 3, and so on).
- Some parents living in religious or politically conservative communities mentioned that they had few day care or school choices. Thus, they were cautious about making waves by requesting greater inclusion, fearing backlash against them or their children.

- "Is that your mom or your dad? I can't tell. They don't look like a woman or a man."
- "Why does your mom have such a deep voice?"

Hopefully, your child or children will have a strong foundation of empowerment and support within their family so that by the time they encounter this type of interaction, they will have absorbed the truth that their family is valid and that they are loved.

Strategies for Minimizing and Managing LGBTQ Bias at School

As parents, you can do a number of things to prepare for and then deal with your children's experiences of invalidation, rejection, and teasing, if and when such experiences come to pass.

TALK TO THE SCHOOL PREEMPTIVELY

Consider having a conversation with teachers or administrators before the beginning of the school year. Explain the basic details of

---

Strategies to Prepare Children for Homophobia and Transphobia

Parents in the LGBTQ Family Building Project provided a variety of examples and scenarios to illustrate how they had sought to prepare their children for potential bias at school in extracurricular activities:

- "Most people have a mommy and a daddy. Some people have two mommies. You have two daddies. Some people think having two daddies is weird, but it's probably just because they haven't met a family like ours. We think it makes us cooler."
- "We talk about how his friends are raised by their grandparents or separated parents. We talk about how families are different."
- "We sought out and joined a family pride group and participated in play groups and outings with other LGBT [lesbian, gay, bisexual, and transgender (trans)] families with young children so that our kids wouldn't think or feel like they were the only ones with same-sex parents. I wanted to normalize it for them beyond their own home."
- "My children are still young, but they do get questions, such as, 'How were you born if you don't have a mom?' 'What happened to your mom?' . . . We have discussed the specialness of our family and the uniqueness of every family. They're prepared to answer, but, honestly, sometimes they don't want to be different than everyone else. They don't want to answer all the questions they get. . . . I tell my kids to say what they feel comfortable answering but not to lie."

---

your family, including what your child calls each parent and what they call other important adults in their life (e.g., the donor, the birth parents). Ask the staff if they have any questions. Use a matter-of-fact, straightforward tone because, after all, you are just sharing the basics of your family. There is nothing to be shy, awkward, or secretive about. Establish a sense of how LGBTQ affirming and savvy your child's teachers are, and go from there. If they seem welcoming and comfortable, you may be able to "relax" a little more. If they seem uncertain or acknowledge that you are their "first" LGBTQ parent family, consider asking if the teachers would like you to suggest resources or check in regularly about how things are going and if they have questions. As one parent said,

> [We have] always been very up front that we are a family with two moms. If the entity—pediatrician, day care, after-school program, et cetera—was going to have an issue, we wanted to get the vibe early, so we could find an alternative so our child didn't have to suffer due to their closed-mindedness.

Another parent shared,

> I always tell the teachers in advance that I am a transgender gestational parent, so they don't think my kids are lying when they say their father gave birth to them. I also ask that they do not use gender as a way to separate the kids or give them ideas of what to do/play with.[1]

GET INVOLVED

Get involved in your child's school, if you can. Join the Parent–Teacher Association or diversity committee, or attend their meetings

---

[1]It is appropriate to "pull back" on the amount and number of details you share with the school as your children grow older. However, at the preschool stage, such details are often important and helpful.

and, if possible, gradually seek out leadership positions. Volunteer. Be present. Donate materials. Being involved earns you visibility and also social capital. If and when something "comes up," you will be a known entity. It is harder to dismiss the concerns of an actively involved parent—one who has donated their energy and time to a school—than one who is a complete stranger.

Likewise, through entering leadership positions in the school, you have more power to create change from the inside (e.g., more inclusive curriculum, policies, paperwork). "We bought books for the class library about different kinds of families and arranged for PFLAG and local LGBTQ groups to present to staff at our kids' schools," said one parent in the LGBTQ Family Building Project. "I have read books with my child to their classes," said another. One parent who was very involved and served on a school committee said, "My presence in these spaces is a constant reminder to the staff that there is [a gay parent] in the room. I am always mentioning my spouse as my husband." One parent put it this way:

> I mostly just try and be really present and involved. I figure if I chaperone and bring enough cupcakes, everyone knows me, and that helps. The other kids are mostly surprised that I'm White, so being gay after that is less of a big deal. Speaking Spanish gives me some credibility with them.

Being an involved parent can also help if other issues, beyond LGBTQ-inclusiveness, need addressing. Parents who are involved in their children's schools may experience a more positive reception and faster "action" if issues arise around their children's learning needs, emotional/behavioral challenges, or adoption or race.

Of course, it is simply not always possible to be involved, much less highly involved, at school. In situations in which it is impossible to manage volunteering or leadership experiences, say, on top of work and family responsibilities, consider other less time-intensive ways of contributing or weighing in (e.g., via email) and ask questions and share input at parent–teacher conferences and the like. If the school tends to ask for volunteers solely at times inconvenient for working parents, consider pointing this out and suggesting alternative times for and types of events or opportunities.

INVESTIGATE POLICIES

Communicate with teachers and school administrators to establish whether the school has policies and procedures in place for dealing with heterosexist, homophobic, and transphobic behavior at school. What are their bullying policies, for example? If sexual and gender identity and expression are not covered in such policies, consider having a conversation with school officials to explain why these are important and to advocate for their inclusion.

TALK TO YOUR CHILDREN

Check in with your children about what they are experiencing at school. In general, it's best to use general questions rather than ask directly if they are being targeted with comments or questions about their family. That might lead to embarrassment or cause them to shut down. Convey that you are there to help them, you can be trusted, you will listen to them if and when something is going on at school, and you will talk together about how to handle it.

EMPOWER YOUR CHILDREN

Build your child's confidence and sense of pride in themselves and their family. If possible, connect them to other children with LGBTQ parents to help them to develop a sense of community and avoid feelings of isolation (e.g., no one else has families like mine). Help them to develop a repertoire of potential responses to general teasing and family-specific teasing—for example, telling a teacher or school support staff member, ignoring the teasing (e.g., brushing it off, walking away), and responding with a simple and straightforward set of facts (e.g., to an insensitive question). Consider role-playing scenarios to practice potential responses (Gays With Kids, 2020).

RESPOND PROMPTLY

It may be appropriate for you to go to your child's school and talk to teachers or administrators directly, especially if you sense that the general climate is hostile or insensitive, as opposed to hearing about an isolated incident with a specific peer, for example. For one parent in the LGBTQ Family Building Project, an incident with a "homophobic teacher" led them to pursue discussions with the principal and teacher in question. Another parent said that they "reported to the school board about the actions of homophobic teachers and consulted with parents about their children's hurtful comments."

BE SELF-REFLECTIVE

Be thoughtful about how your own internalized homophobia/biphobia/queer-phobia/transphobia may be affecting both your anticipation of and response to bullying or negative treatment. For example, if your child is teased because of your gender identity, you may experience a sense of intense guilt, fear, or panic. Try to manage your distress and not let it control how you respond. Seek support and help from other LGBTQ parents (e.g., online, in person) or from a therapist. Remember that these internalized stigmas have been learned from society and are not connected to your actual self-worth or value.

The level of "work" that you will need to do to try to ensure LGBTQ inclusiveness, sensitivity, and representation is partly related to the community in which you live as well as the school or day care's history with LGBTQ-parent families. If some other LGBTQ-parent families have come before you and already done the hard work of being visible, making suggestions, and educating, your job will likely be easier. If there are other LGBTQ-parent families at the school with whom you feel or can form a connection, you are that much more powerful in your efforts at advocacy and inclusivity. If, however, you are fairly isolated as an LGBTQ parent (or, perhaps, the school has had lesbian parents, but you're the first gay dad family; or, you are the school's first visible nonbinary or trans parent), your job may be more challenging, especially if you are the kind of person who would prefer to fade into the woodwork and dislike drawing attention to yourself or your family. Perhaps you can find allies in other parents, even if they are not LGBTQ. Maybe you can gain support and ideas for advocacy from other LGBTQ parents— either online or in your social network. Possibly, you have the option to switch day cares or schools. Explore your options and consider your choices while being mindful of the potential risks of speaking out in certain contexts (e.g., do you have reason to fear repercussions or backlash from teachers or other parents?).

Also, importantly, LGBTQ inclusion may not be the primary issue you will face as a parent in choosing and navigating day cares and schools. Concerns about adequate accommodations, including medication and therapies, for your children's special needs or mental health issues may demand far more of your energy and time than LGBTQ-inclusive paperwork. One parent in the LGBTQ Family Building Project offered these details:

> Both of our sons are diagnosed with ADHD [attention-deficit/hyperactivity disorder], and the oldest has severe anxiety, [which] has been difficult managing in the school environment. It was really, really hard when he first went to school, but with meds, he's gotten a lot better.

Likewise, race may be more of an issue than LGBTQ family-related issues in terms of addressing systemic bias within the day care or school and empowering your child to understand and address racism by peers and teachers. One parent said,

> Our child is mixed race, Black, Indigenous, and White. In day care, specifically, and in other settings as well, people have said or done things that we have had to correct, [like] descriptions that are outdated or racist terms when talking about him or other people, and people making comments about hair.

"We know we will be judged if he doesn't conform to male norms, that people will think it is because he has two moms. That said, he is very much his own person with healthy and flexible ideas about gender, and we love him for it."

"My children happen to be gender conforming. Although I hope that we would be accepting of less gender conforming behavior, I have a feeling that I would have experienced some shame/worry about people thinking less of two moms."

"With our first child, when gay parenting was less common, I felt more conscious of having a 'perfect' child to show to the world that gay parenting was a good idea. By the time we had my son . . . I was more mellow. We are lucky that we have kids who mostly get positive responses from the world. It might be different if we lived [elsewhere]."

"We gave them traditional 'girl' first names and 'boy' middle names so [that] they have options. We dress them in a mix of clothes. We have TGNC [transgender, gender-expansive, and gender nonconforming] friends and took them to a pregnant trans male friend's baby shower, sign them up for feminine and masculine activities, and follow their lead on clothes. They know one of [us] moms shops in the men's department and has short hair, and the other one has long hair and likes feminine clothes. They know that shaving, or not, are both options."

—COMMENTS FROM PARTICIPANTS IN THE
LGBTQ FAMILY BUILDING PROJECT

Gender Roles and Norms: Navigating Possibility and Accountability

Children who are raised by two women or two men are often regarded as "lacking" representation of one gender within the parental unit. This perception is based on a binary, essentialist conception of gender: There are only two genders that are contained "within" people and that correspond to each person's assigned gender as well as align with the sex designation of one's reproductive organs, chromosomes, and genitalia. LGBQ people, however, tend to have more expansive ideas about gender than heterosexual individuals in that they are less likely to conform to gender norms with regard to behavior, interests, appearance, and attraction. Indeed, heterosexuality is a key component of gender normativity. Perhaps it goes without saying that trans and nonbinary folks also tend to have more expansive notions of gender. Research on LGBTQ parents suggests that this expansiveness pertains to parenting as well, such that LGBTQ parents tend to be more likely to be tolerant of, and more likely to even encourage, gender nonconformity in activities, toys, dress, and so on (Averett, 2016; Biblarz & Stacey, 2010; Goldberg, Kashy, & Smith, 2012).

Such expansiveness, however, may be limited or constrained by awareness that, as parents who deviate from sexuality and gender norms, they are under scrutiny regarding their children's gender. Subsequently, they will be held accountable if their children stray too far from established gender norms in terms of appearance, self-expression, behavior, and identity, and such "deviation" from accepted norms will be used as evidence that they should not be parenting children in the first place. Some LGBTQ parents may be more concerned with outsider scrutiny than others—for example, those who are marginalized on the basis of race, class, and immigration status, and who may be especially fearful of discrimination or victimization (e.g., loss of children to social services). Notably, LGBTQ parents who are highly concerned with maintaining privileged positions in society may also be preoccupied with avoiding critique or scrutiny of their families, which may translate into behaviors that are aimed to encourage their children's conformity to gender norms and roles.

In the LGBTQ Family Building Project (Goldberg, 2021), just 3% of parents said that they were "very" invested in their children's conforming to gender norms (e.g., wearing clothes stereotypical of their assigned gender, having interests stereotypical of their assigned gender, using a particular set of pronouns). An additional 16% said they were "somewhat" invested, and the remainder were "not really" invested (31%) and "not at all invested" (50%). Most said that they had approached parenting in such a way that encouraged gender creativity or expansiveness "very much so" (38%) or "somewhat" (44%).

Many parents highlighted their awareness of outsiders' (e.g., extended family, peers) expectations or pressures related to gender and their own efforts to counteract these larger forces. "We are trying hard not to force gender norms, but my mother-in-law makes it hard by always buying pink and girly stuff," said one parent. "I am hoping to provide an environment for our children to explore gender for themselves; I know the world will impose gender norms," said another. One parent commented,

> Gender expression is my child's choice, but I realize how hard it can be to make choices from within a society that enforces strict gender roles. . . . I celebrate the ways my son breaks gender norms: He . . . cries, wears nail polish, and loves singing along to female pop stars.

Nonbinary parents were especially firm in their commitment to gender-inclusive or degendered parenting. Said one parent: "As a nonbinary parent, I work to make sure the kids are aware of many ways of understanding gender and options for expressing or identifying."

A minority of LGBTQ parents experienced a sense of caution or worry related to how outsiders might respond to and punish gender nonconformity in their children. In turn, while they wanted to allow their children to express themselves freely, they also struggled with the competing desire to minimize negative outsider reactions and safety risks. "Part of me doesn't want them to stand out too much in what society would see as a negative," said one parent. "I worry about others' reactions," said another, adding, "This is particularly the case for my son, who loves to wear dresses and princess costumes since he is being raised by two women." Given that masculinity is more heavily regulated and enforced in society, it is unsurprising—and consistent with prior research (Averett, 2016; Berkowitz & Ryan, 2011; Biblarz & Stacey, 2010)—that parents of sons worried that "feminine" appearance or behavior might invite harassment. Such concerns about safety were amplified in the context of raising boys of color, and especially Black boys: "I don't want my Black son to wear a dress outside of home/school."

Gay, bisexual, and queer men more often expressed concern about conforming to gender norms compared with LGBQ women and trans/nonbinary parents. Stated one gay dad,

> I have to admit that we want our son to conform a bit so that he doesn't face bullying. We generally try to be open to what he wants, but we tend to buy him "boy" clothes and toys, which he likes. I guess we are going with "boy" things unless/until he tells us otherwise.

Men, in particular, may need to explore their own internalized homophobia and ideas about gender normativity (and perhaps their own histories of being teased for not conforming to gender norms) vis-à-vis their parenting concerns and behaviors. One gay father reflected, "I think as a gay man, I feared raising a straight son for fear I wasn't adequate enough [but then] realized that I was playing into internalized homophobia."

Regardless of how LGBTQ parents feel about their children's (non)conformity to dominant gender norms, they may see value in their children's having exposure to adults of genders that are not represented within the parental unit. Most parents in two-mom and two-dad families say that they have sought out adult male or female role models for their children—both in prior research (Goldberg & Allen, 2007) and the LGBTQ Family Building Project (Goldberg, 2021). More than half of the parents in the LGBTQ Family Building Project sought out their own or their partner's siblings (52%) or their own or their partner's parents (51%) as gender role models. In addition, 45% indicated that they had sought out teachers of a particular gender, 41% had sought out babysitters, 38% had sought out coaches, and 34% said they had sought out pediatricians. Two thirds of parents identified other adults—most often friends but also neighbors, mentors (e.g., via Big Brothers or Big Sisters), sperm donors, therapists or counselors, other medical providers (e.g., dentist, endocrinologist), camp counselors, extracurricular teachers (e.g., music, dance), and religious community members—as gender role models.

Generally speaking, LGBTQ parents may balk, rightly so, at the notion that their children will not grow up with a healthy sense of their own gender without a same-gender role model. This idea, which is lobbed at LGBTQ parents in many settings, including fertility clinics, pediatricians' offices, and schools, often in the form of questions (e.g., "But who will provide a male role model?") presupposes a few things. First, it assumes that LGBTQ parents "deprive" their children of people of a particular gender—for example, a two-mom family must be parenting in an all-female vacuum, whereby their children and, in particular, their sons are not exposed to men or boys. Second, it is predicated on a binary gender system, whereby both parents and children can only be male or female. Third, it presumes that there is a fairly singular and agreed on way to be an adult man or adult woman and that a child can only learn this with regular exposure to an adult figure or figures who embody arguably stereotypical qualities. Fourth, it prioritizes gender (and, arguably, conformity to a particular set of gender roles) over all other characteristics in identifying suitable or ideal role models for children (e.g., a man without much in common with one's child is more valuable than a nonbinary person or a woman with tons in common with one's child).

LGBTQ parents generally do not live their lives in separatist communities or gender vacuums. Not all parents or children identify as male or female; indeed, there are many ways to embody maleness and femaleness and masculinity and femininity, including simultaneously within the same person. Furthermore, children need role models of all types, including same-race role models, role models who embody certain sets of values and beliefs, and role models who have dealt with similar challenges (e.g., learning disabilities) and succeeded in life. Thus, it is important for parents to think about role models holistically and to not feel pressured to embrace less-than-fabulous humans who happen to be of a certain gender. Rather, emphasis should be placed on surrounding your child with diverse individuals who reflect different aspects of your child, who embody aspirational qualities or values, or who will love your child unconditionally.

All that being said, however, you may still value having relationships with certain individuals because they have been socialized as a particular gender, have particular reproductive anatomy and genitals, and so on. If you are queer mom partnered with another queer mom, and you have a son (or, more accurately, a child who was assigned male at birth), it may be helpful to have support from, and maintain regular contact with, a brother, male friend, or male parent. Some

LGBTQ parents, for example, feel well equipped to handle pretty much all aspects of parenthood—except, for example, teaching a child how to pee standing up or talking about menstruation when a child gets their period. It is good to recognize where you—and your child—might need some extra help and support. But don't worry too much if you don't have a male friend "on call." Do not worry too much that children "need" a male or female role model to be compassionate, happy, independent adults. Research suggests that, compared with children with a mom and a dad, children with two moms and children with two dads may be less gender-stereotyped in their play, especially boys with two moms (Goldberg & Garcia, 2016; Goldberg, Kashy, et al., 2012). So, that can easily be seen as a strength rather than a deficit such that children who play with a variety of toys and activities may be "set up" for a broader and more flexible set of interests and abilities, for example.

Gender-Expansive Parenting Practices

Participants named various practices they engaged in that they saw as actively challenging gender norms and expanding gender possibilities for their young children. These included the following:

- avoiding pronouns or using "they" pronouns for people they don't know or when referring to someone in the abstract (e.g., the doctor, the teacher)
- actively challenging gender stereotypes (e.g., boys can't have long hair or wear makeup)
- offering a variety of toys, clothes, and activities
- avoiding highly gendered hand-me-downs
- reading books that show gender diversity and individuals in nongender-stereotyped roles
- introducing the idea that gender is not a binary, and neither is sexual orientation or attraction
- modeling gender nonconformity in dress, behaviors, and profession

BEYOND HETERONORMATIVITY AND GENDER NORMS: NAVIGATING EARLY PARENTING CHALLENGES

It goes without saying that parenting is a wild ride. Regardless of your gender, sexual orientation, and relationship configuration, parenting is an adventure filled with twists and turns; highs and lows; feats of endurance; and plateaus of uncertainty, frustration, or helplessness. If you have never screamed into a pillow, are you even really a parent? Your status as a nonbinary parent, a bisexual parent, or a lesbian parent may not feel immediately relevant when it comes to navigating the "typical" or universal issues of parenthood—for example, children's emotional or behavioral challenges, learning-related issues, and social issues. Yet, these identities can come into play—for example, in terms of how you feel that teachers, pediatricians, mental health care providers, and others respond to you (e.g., as a visibly gender nonconforming parent, as a member of a two-dad family). You may feel that some providers implicitly or explicitly attribute your children's challenges to your sexual orientation or gender identity—for example, they believe that you "caused" your child's depression or anxiety by getting a divorce from your same-sex partner or taking steps toward gender transition.

It is essential that you know the research literature in this area so that you can be mentally and emotionally prepared to handle outsiders' critiques and assumptions—and, perhaps, your own internalized fears and stigmas. Dozens of studies have been conducted that indicate that children do not experience elevated emotional, behavioral, or developmental issues as a result of being raised by LGBTQ parents (Goldberg & Allen, 2020; Goldberg, Gartrell, & Gates, 2014; Goldberg et al., 2010). Children who are adopted by LGBTQ parents may have elevated mental health, attachment, cognitive, developmental, and medical challenges compared with children in the general population—but this is a reflection of LGBTQ parents' greater tendency to adopt children with such challenges as compared with heterosexual couples. Also, children raised by LGBTQ parents may actually show greater improvements than children in adoptive heterosexual-parent families, possibly reflecting LGBTQ parents' high level of motivation for and preparation for parenthood as well as high levels of resources devoted to these children (Lavner et al., 2012). So, do approach any insinuations that you are an inadequate parent because of your sexual orientation or gender identity with confidence that this is not the case, and feel free to share resources that clearly establish this, such as summaries of the research that are available online for all to read (Goldberg, Gartrell, & Gates, 2014; Perrin et al., 2013).

Navigating universal parenting issues can also be challenging when you have limited support from other LGBTQ parents but also parents in general or family or friends. Some parents find social media and online support groups to be effective in providing them with needed support—for example, groups like "Special Needs Parents Support & Discussion Group" on Facebook (which, as of May 2021, had about 50,700 followers; see https://www.facebook.com/groups/1855573214536750). There are also more specialized Facebook groups, such as those for parents with anxious children, parents of children with sensory needs, and parents of trans children.

To get a sense of the range of issues that LGBTQ parents deal with related to their children, consider the findings from the LGBTQ Family Building Project. Participants were asked about the issues that their children (and, in turn, family) had dealt with over the past year. The most frequently endorsed challenges were child emotional/behavioral issues (50%) and learning or developmental issues (32%).

Such issues were often emphasized as causing family or intimate relationship strain. As one parent said,

> Having two kids with high needs, one on the autism spectrum, one with serious mental health [issues], stuttering, and epilepsy... has been the main source of strain over the years, [along with] a lack of support for us as a family/couple.

A total of 19% of parents identified child health issues as a stressor. Said one parent, "Our kids have chronic health issues due to prematurity, and it can take a toll." Less frequently endorsed issues were social issues or bullying (15%), sexuality/gender identity issues (12%), issues with racial identity or racism (9%), issues with adoption or attachment (7%), and substance use (3%). Twelve percent of parents identified "other" issues, which included COVID-19–related isolation; challenges with online learning; difficulties receiving appropriate assessment, diagnosis, and services for mental health or developmental issues; adjustment to parental divorce; adjustment to new partners/stepparents; tensions or stress related to extended family; and trauma/victimization. Often, parents were dealing with multiple issues: "One of our sons has a learning disability. . . . Our adopted son has some issues with attachment and behavior," said one parent. Another said,

> Our children all have learning and health issues that have to be constantly managed. . . . They all have underlying issues with insecure attachment. With one multiracial child, the issues of raising a Black child in the U.S. are constantly in the background.

Significant, too, is remembering that parents may struggle with mental health or relationship issues that create chronic stress, exacerbating the day-to-day stressors of parenthood. Addressing these issues requires a healthy dose of self-compassion and, ideally, strategies and resources that can facilitate wellness and growth. As one parent in the LGBTQ Family Building Project said, "We both have mental health issues, but we have come up with many communication tools that have helped keep our home peaceful and happy." If you are partnered, know that your relationship may ride many waves during parenthood related to parenting disagreements, lack of intimacy, stress, grief, and other issues. In some cases, riding out these waves will not be possible. But, in many cases, you will be able to sustain your relationship knowing that these dips are normal, expected, and won't last forever. As one parent said, "We had significant challenges regarding talking about parenting early on because we both had so much self-judgment. We also grew very far apart because of two high needs children and stressful jobs. [But things] are much better now."

CONCLUSION

This chapter addressed just a few of the early parenting issues and challenges that you might face as an LGBTQ parent, including choosing a school and advocating for your child in school as well as navigating expectations and pressures surrounding gender conformity and expectations in your children. To be clear: These types of issues and challenges are a direct result of cis/heteronormativity. We all parent within a society that continues to hold fast to certain ideas and ideals related to families, gender, and parenthood. Consider yourself part of the not-so-quiet revolution of destabilizing these ideas and ideals, which only serve to keep families and people in boxes and limit our agency and autonomy as human beings.

When asked how they think their children might benefit from having LGBTQ parents and asked to choose from a preset list of possibilities, parents in the LGBTQ Family Building Project (Goldberg, 2021) reported a number of positive benefits. Here are the benefits they believe their children might receive:

- 84%: more open to people with diverse gender/identities/ expressions
- 83%: more open to people with diverse sexual orientations
- 81%: more tolerant of differences
- 71%: more open to exploring their gender identity or expression
- 63%: more independent-minded
- 61%: more open to exploring their sexuality
- 51%: more confident in who they are
- 11%: something else, including being very much planned, wanted, and loved; being empathic and sensitive; and benefiting from early and consistent education about body parts, anatomy, and sexuality

Thus, parents as a whole endorsed a variety of positive aspects of growing up with LGBTQ parents. These positive aspects echo what we know from previous research about the outcomes of children raised by LGBTQ parents. For example, children with LGBTQ parents may have more expansive ideas about gender and sexuality as well as be more accepting of others, including peers, who deviate from cisnormative and heteronormative identities, behaviors, and appearance. They may also be more tolerant and accepting of other aspects of diversity (e.g., racial, ethnic, cultural) and seek out careers and volunteer opportunities that are grounded in values of equality and inclusion (Goldberg, 2007, 2017; Goldberg & Allen, 2020; Patterson & Goldberg, 2016). These positive elements are at least partly related to what we know about LGBTQ parents as a group, namely, that they themselves may be especially likely to resist (and thus model and teach their children to resist) gender and sexuality binaries and cisnormative and heteronormative ideas, and to embrace values of equality and inclusion. Furthermore, LGBTQ parents have other important strengths, such as showing high levels of motivation, effort, and planning to becoming parents and demonstrating a willingness to advocate for their children and seek out supports and services in academic, mental health, and other arenas (Goldberg, 2017; Goldberg, Frost, et al., 2020).

As you chart your path forward, either in becoming an LGBTQ parent or making your way as an LGBTQ parent, it is important to know that you have every right to be a parent. It is also important to know that you have resources—like this book—to support your decision making in relation to whether, when, and how to become a parent. It is currently much easier to become a parent as an LGBTQ person that it was in decades past—and hopefully the laws, visibility, and resources surrounding LGBTQ parenthood will continue to advance. As one participant in the LGBTQ Family Building Project said,

> I think we didn't act earlier because we had no role models to talk to about getting started. We knew so few male couples with kids. Well, maybe it was none. It's our kids that have caused us to meet lots of gay parents. I hope the next generation of queer young people will think that more is possible because gay parents are more visible.

As you take the next steps in your parenthood journey, consider these words of participants in the LGBTQ Family Building Project about why they wanted to become parents and what finally made them take "the leap":

> We always knew we both wanted kids. My wife would have gotten started sooner, but I didn't feel ready. One day, a straight friend told me she was trying to conceive, and it was like flipping a switch: All of a sudden, I felt ready.

We both wanted to be parents and felt confident in our ability to raise kids in a loving, supportive environment in spite of the challenges that we—the parents and the kids—might face.

We wanted to share our love with a little being and make a good person to put light out into the world!

I always wanted to be a parent. It hasn't been easy—but I have no regrets.

RESOURCES

The following is a range of resources for early childhood educators interfacing with LGBTQ-parent families as well as resources for LGBTQ parents and their families, including children's books and resources for parenting children and teenagers.

Resources for Day Cares and Early Childhood Settings: LGBTQ Family Inclusiveness

As an LGBTQ parent, you can feel free to direct your children's day care to these resources.

Early Childhood Resources

Frost, R. L., & Goldberg, A. E. (n.d.). *The ABCs of diversity and inclusion: Developing an inclusive environment for diverse families in early childhood education.* Zero to Three. https://www.zerotothree.org/resources/3391-the-abcs-of-diversity-and-inclusion-developing-an-inclusive-environment-for-diverse-families-in-early-childhood-education

Head Start/ECLKC. (n.d.). *Creating a welcoming early childhood program for LGBT-headed families.* https://eclkc.ohs.acf.hhs.gov/family-engagement/article/creating-welcoming-early-childhood-program-lgbt-headed-families

Aimed at elementary schools and beyond:

GLSEN. (n.d.). *Best practice: Inclusive and affirming curriculum for all students.* https://www.glsen.org/activity/inclusive-curriculum-guide
Teach All Families: https://www.teachallfamilies.com

Books for Preschool-Aged Children About LGBTQ Parent Families

Newman, L. (2009). *Daddy, Papa, and me.* Tricycle Press.
Newman, L. (2011). *Donovan's big day.* Tricycle Press.
Parr, T. (2003). *The family book.* Little, Brown.
Parr, T. (2009). *We belong together: A book about adoption and families.* Little, Brown and Co.
Polacco, P. (2009). *In our mothers' house.* Philomel Books.
Richardson, J., & Parnell, P. (2005). *And Tango makes three.* Simon & Schuster.
Silverberg, C. (2012). *What makes a baby.* Seven Stories Press.

General Resources on LGBTQ Parenting Research

My website: http://www.abbiegoldberg.com

Goldberg, A. E., Gartrell, N., & Gates, G. J. (2014, July). *Research report on LGB-parent families.* The Williams Institute. https://williamsinstitute.law.ucla.edu/publications/report-lgb-parent-families/
Patterson, C. J., & Goldberg, A. E. (2016, November). *Lesbian and gay parents and their children* [Policy brief]. National Council on Family Relations. https://www.ncfr.org/sites/default/files/2017-01/ncfr_policy_brief_november_final.pdf

Resources for Parenting Children and Teenagers

Child Welfare Information Gateway. (n.d.). *Parenting resources.* https://www.childwelfare.gov/topics/preventing/promoting/parenting/

For children/youth with one or more LGBTQ parents: COLAGE, https://www.colage.org

Creating a Family (the national infertility, adoption, and foster care education and support nonprofit), https://www.creatingafamily.org

Goldberg, A. E. (2019). *Open adoption and diverse families: Complex relationships in the digital age.* Oxford University Press. https://doi.org/10.1093/oso/9780190692032.001.0001

For American Academy of Pediatrics parenting resources: HealthyChildren.org, https://www.healthychildren.org

Roszia, S. K., & Maxon, A. D. (2019). *Seven core issues in adoption and permanency: A comprehensive guide to promoting understanding and healing in adoption, foster care, kinship families and third party reproduction.* Jessica Kingsley Publishers.

APPENDIX A

THE LGBTQ FAMILY BUILDING PROJECT

DESCRIPTION OF THE LGBTQ FAMILY BUILDING PROJECT AND KEY DETAILS ABOUT THE PARTICIPANTS

People were invited to participate in the LGBTQ Family Building Project (Goldberg, 2021) if they were a lesbian, gay, bisexual, transgender (trans), and queer (LGBTQ) parent of at least one child aged 18 years or younger. They were told that the survey took about 20 to 25 minutes to complete and focused mostly on family building and parenting. Participants were entered into a drawing for a $25 Amazon gift card; 25 gift cards in total were awarded.

The total sample was 543 participants—that is, 543 participants who provided full and complete information. Participants were excluded from this final group if they did not complete the whole survey (i.e., dropped out early) or, based on a number of checks and careful scrutiny of the patterns of responding, provided suspicious, inconsistent, or questionable responses—basically anything that undermined my confidence in the validity of the information they provided.

The following are details about this sample of LGBTQ parents. The book provides more detailed information about these parents.

PARENTS' GENDER AND SEXUAL ORIENTATION

- Of the total sample of 543 participants, 68.0% were cisgender (cis) women; 17.5%, cis men; and 14.5%, trans or nonbinary (TNB). Within the TNB umbrella, 23.5% were trans men; 8.5%, trans women; and 68.0%, were nonbinary, genderqueer, or agender or identified in other ways beyond the gender binary.
- Considering participants' sexual orientation, 42% identified as lesbians; 19%, as gay; 14%, as bisexual; 20%, as queer; 3%, as pansexual; 1%, as asexual; and the remainder, as something else (e.g., two-spirit).

Here is a breakdown of the preceding information, by gender:

- Of cis men, 95% identified as gay, and the remainder, as bisexual or queer.
- Among cis women, 56.5% identified as lesbians; 19.0%, as queer; 18.0%, as bisexual; 2.0%, as gay; 2.0%, as pansexual; and the remainder, as asexual (four participants) or two-spirit (one participant).
- Among trans and nonbinary participants, 45.5% identified as queer; 26.5%, as lesbian; 10.0%, as bisexual; 9.0%, as pansexual; 6.0%, as gay; and 3.0%, as straight.

PARENTS' RELATIONSHIP CONTEXTS

- Of the participants, 88% were partnered. And of those, 3% had previously been divorced or separated. Of the 15% of single participants, 6% had previously been divorced or separated. Thus, 9% of the sample had been previously divorced or separated.

- Participants' gender and their partners' gender were as follows:
  - Of the participants, 54.1% were cis women partnered with cis women, 7.2% were cis women with TNB partners, and 6.5% were cis women with cis men partners (all identified as bisexual, pansexual, or queer).
  - Of the participants, 16.0% were cis men partnered with cis men, 1.1% were cis men with TNB partners, and 0.5% were cis men with cis women partners (all identified as bisexual).
  - Of the participants, 8.0% were TNB people partnered with cis women, 4.0% were TNB with TNB partners, and 2.1% were TNB with cis men partners.
  - Of the participants, 0.5% (two participants) were cis women or nonbinary people with partners of multiple genders.

PARTICIPANTS' INCOME, EDUCATION, EMPLOYMENT STATUS, POLITICAL AFFILIATION, AND GEOGRAPHIC LOCATION

- Just 10% of the sample had less than a college education, and just 8% had a family (household) income of under $50,000 a year. Notably, TNB participants were more likely to say that they made less than $50,000 per year (19%) than cis women (8%) or cis men (2%).
- Of the participants, 75.5% worked full time, 12.5% worked part-time, 4.0% were unemployed, and the remainder endorsed something else (e.g., student, retired, homemaker).
- Most participants identified their political affiliation as Democrat (80%), with 8% saying that they were independent or unaffiliated and 4% identifying their political affiliation as Republican. The remainder indicated that they identified in some other way, including Democratic Socialist (4%) and "left-leaning" (3%).

- Participants lived in 44 states, with a small number living outside of the United States. Namely, 19.0% lived in Massachusetts; 12.0%, in California; 7.2%, in Washington State; 6.3%, in Colorado; 5.5%, in New York; 3.5%, in Maryland; 3.0%, in Oregon; 2.7%, in Texas; 2.5%, in North Carolina; 2.5%, in Pennsylvania; 2.3%, in Minnesota; 2.3%, in New Jersey; 2.1%, in Illinois; and fewer than 2.0% in the remaining states. Fifteen participants (2.9%) lived in Canada, and 12 resided in other places outside of the United States—most frequently, Europe.
- Most participants described their communities as either suburban (45%) or urban (41%), with 10% describing their communities as rural, and the remainder, as something else (e.g., college town, small city).

PARTICIPANTS' RACE (AND PARTNERS' RACE)

- Of the participants, 82% were White and 18% were of color, including biracial and multiracial. Breaking this information down further (and keeping in mind that participants could identify with more than one race), 88% identified as White; 6%, as Black/African American; 6%, as Latinx; 5%, as Hispanic; 3%, as Asian; 1%, as American Indian/Alaska Native; 1%, as Native Hawaiian/Other Pacific Islander; and 1%, as some other race (e.g., Middle Eastern).
- Among those who had partners, 72% identified them as White, and 28% identified them as of color. Breaking this information down further (and keeping in mind that participants could endorse multiple race categories for their partners), 74% identified as White; 7%, as Black/African American; 5%, as Hispanic; 5%, as Latinx; 4%, as Asian; 1%, as American Indian/Alaska Native; 1%, as Native Hawaiian/Other Pacific Islander; and 2%, as some other race (e.g., Middle Eastern).

- A total of 22% of participants were in an interracial relationship (one partner was White and one partner was of color). In 10% of cases, both partners were of color. In 68% of cases, both partners were White.

CHILDREN'S AGE, GENDER, AND RACE

- On average, parents had 1.7 children (including step- and foster children), with a range of one to six children. Specifically, 47.5% had one child, 40.5% had two children, 7.0% had three children, and the remainder had between four and six children.
- A total of 42.5% had at least one child age 5 years and under, 36.0% had at least one child aged 6 to 10 years old, 35.0% had at least one child aged 11 to 15 years old, 10.5% had at least one child aged 16 to 18 years old, and 9.0% had at least one child older than age 18. (All parents were required to have at least one child under age 18 to participate, so all parents of children older than age 18 had at least one younger child.)
- Regarding child gender, 52.5% of participants stated that they had at least one girl, and 54.0% said they had at least one boy. In addition, 1.3% reported having at least one trans girl; 1.1%, at least one trans boy; 5.0%, at least one nonbinary child; and 3.5%, at least one child of another gender (e.g., "We're not sure yet," "Our child hasn't told us").
- A total of 41.0% of parents had at least one child who was of color; 59.0% of parents had only White children. Breaking this information down further (keeping in mind that parents could identify their children as occupying multiple race categories), at least one child was identified by 82.0% of parents as White; 17.0%, as Black; 12.0%, as Latinx; 11.0%, as Hispanic; 8.0%, as Asian; 2.0%, as American Indian/Alaska Native;

1.0%, as Native Hawaiian/Other Pacific Islander; and 3.5%, as some other race.

- In terms of race of parent and child, among White parents, 32% were parenting at least one child of color, and the remaining 68% were parenting only White children. Among parents of color, 80% were parenting at least one child of color, and 20% of parents of color had only White children.

FAMILY-BUILDING ROUTES

- Participants became parents through a variety of routes, often more than one. Of the participants, 60% used donor insemination (DI) or surrogacy to become parents, 32% used adoption or foster care, 6% used cis/heteronormative sex (penile–vaginal intercourse), and 5% were stepparents.
- Of the participants, 71.0% indicated that all of their children were born or adopted into their current relationship. Another 12.5% said that all of their children were born or adopted into a prior relationship; 4.3% said some children were born/adopted into their current relationship, whereas others were from a prior relationship; 3.0% said that they were single parents by choice and that they had birthed/adopted all children on their own; and 2.5% said that they and their current partners had both brought children into their union from a prior relationship. Just 1.5% said that some of their children were born or adopted into their current relationship, others were from a prior relationship, and their partner had also brought children into their current relationship. A total of 5.0% indicated that some other description applied (e.g., "My wife and I were dating but not yet married when I was adopting as a single parent," "We are fostering children, and I am carrying").

- A total of 15% of the sample reported at least one private, domestic, open adoption and 8% reported at least one public, domestic adoption (i.e., from the foster care/child welfare system). Three percent had at least one foster child; 3% said they had at least one child adopted via a private, domestic, closed adoption; and 3% of parents said that they had at least one child adopted internationally/from abroad.

Additionally, looking at parent gender by family-building route revealed the following:

- A total of 73.0% of cis women and 21.0% of cis men had used DI or surrogacy (i.e., reproductive technologies) to build their families. A total of 57.5% of TNB participants had used DI or surrogacy.
- Of the participants, 75% of cis men and 21% of cis women had used adoption or foster care to build their families— almost a total reversal or "flip" of the gender breakdown for DI or surrogacy. Just 13% of TNB participants had used adoption or foster care.
- Cis/heteronormative sex (intercourse) was used by 1% of cis men, 4% of cis women, and 18% of TNB participants.
- Becoming parents via repartnering (i.e., stepparenting) was endorsed by 4% of cis men, 5% of cis women, and 5% of TNB participants.

KEY HISTORICAL EVENTS IN U.S. LGBTQ PARENTING HISTORY

MILESTONES IN LGBTQ PARENTING HISTORY OR, THE NOT-SO-MODERN FAMILY

Dana Rudolph

1956: The lesbian organization Daughters of Bilitis holds the first known discussion groups on lesbian motherhood.

1968: Bill Jones, a gay man, became the first single father to adopt a child in California and among the first nationally.

1971: Formation of the first lesbian mothers' activist group, the Lesbian Mothers Union.

Note. This list of key historical events celebrates and acknowledge key historical milestones of laws, visibility, and community related to lesbian, gay, bisexual, transgender (trans), and queer (LGBTQ) parents in the United States. From "Milestones in LGBT Parenting History," by D. Rudolph, Mombian, October 13, 2015 (https://mombian.com/2015/10/13/milestones-in-lgbt-parenting-history-3/). Copyright 2015 by Dana Rudolph. Reprinted with permission by Dana Rudolph. Dana Rudolph has since updated this list (2015–2021) to reflect recent events.

1972: *That Certain Summer*, the first television movie to depict a gay dad, airs on ABC, starring Hal Holbrook as a dad who comes out to his teenage son, and Martin Sheen as his partner. Scott Jacoby, who played the son, won a Best Supporting Actor Emmy.

1973: *Sandy and Madeleine's Family* becomes the first U.S. documentary about a lesbian-headed family.

1973: A Colorado court issues the country's first known opinion involving a transgender parent, upholding his right to retain child custody.

1974: A New Jersey superior court judge rules that a father's sexual orientation is not in itself a reason to deny him child visitation, the first time a U.S. court has acknowledged the constitutional rights of gay fathers.

1974: Several lesbian mothers and friends in Seattle form the Lesbian Mothers National Defense Fund to help lesbian mothers in custody disputes.

1976: Washington, DC, becomes the first jurisdiction in the country to prohibit judges from making custody decisions based solely on sexual orientation.

1977: Lawyers Donna Hitchens and Roberta Achtenberg in San Francisco form the Lesbian Rights Project (LRP), which evolves into the National Center for Lesbian Rights (NCLR), still helping LGBTQ parents (and others) today.

1978: The Washington Supreme Court issues the country's first custody ruling in favor of a lesbian couple (Sandy Schuster and Madeleine Isaacson of the 1973 film [mentioned earlier]).

1978: New York becomes the first state to say it will not reject adoption applicants solely because of "homosexuality."

1979: A gay couple in California becomes the first in the country known to have jointly adopted a child.

1979: The Gay Fathers Coalition forms—a precursor to Family Equality, the national organization for LGBTQ parents and their children.

1979: Jane Severance's *When Megan Went Away* becomes the first picture book in the U.S. to show a lesbian relationship.

1982: The Sperm Bank of California begins operations, the first in the country to serve lesbian couples and single women.

1985: A court for the first time allows a nonbiological mother to adopt the biological child of her female partner. The ruling, in Alaska, also allows the biological father to maintain a relationship with the child.

1988: A group of youth with LGBTQ parents meets at a conference organized by a precursor to Family Equality and begins the organizing that in 1999 leads to Children of Lesbians and Gays Everywhere (COLAGE) as an independent national organization.

1989: Author Lesléa Newman self-publishes *Heather Has Two Mommies*, the first children's book in the U.S. to show a lesbian couple planning and raising a child together.

1990: The *Newsweek* article, "The Future of Gay America," includes the first documented use of the term "gayby boom" to describe the rise in lesbians and gay men having children.

1990: LGBTQ publisher Alyson Publications launches the Alyson Wonderland imprint for children's titles. It publishes *Daddy's Roommate*, by Michael Willhoite, the first children's book published in the U.S. to depict gay male parents, and mass produces *Heather Has Two Mommies*.

1993: Vermont and Massachusetts begin allowing same-sex couples to adopt jointly statewide.

1994: The San Francisco Gay and Lesbian Parents Association produces *Both of My Moms' Names Are Judy: Children of Lesbians* *and Gays Speak Out*, the first educational film for elementary school teachers about LGBTQ families.

1995: A state's highest court (Wisconsin) rules for the first time that a nonbiological mother may try and show that it would be in the best interests of her child for her to remain in the child's life after parental separation.

1997: New Jersey makes it explicit in its adoption policy that same-sex couples may adopt jointly.

2005: The PBS show *Postcards From Buster* airs the first depiction of a two-mom family in a television show for young children.

2008: Marcus Ewert publishes *10,000 Dresses*, the first children's book to show a clearly transgender child.

2009: First explicit mention of same-sex parents [is made] in a presidential proclamation. In announcing September 28 as Family Day, President [Barack] Obama says, "Whether children are raised by two parents, a single parent, grandparents, a same-sex couple, or a guardian, families encourage us to do our best and enable us to accomplish great things."

2010: *The Kids Are All Right*, starring Annette Bening and Julianne Moore, becomes the first major feature film to focus on an LGBTQ couple and their children. It wins Golden Globe Awards for Best Motion Picture and Best Actress (Bening), and four Academy Award nominations, including Best Picture.

2010: President Obama revises hospital visitation rules so patients may designate their own visitors, including same-sex partners. He was motivated in part by the story of Janice Langbehn and her three children, who in 2007 were denied access to her dying partner and the children's other mother, Lisa Pond. Langbehn in 2011 receives the Presidential Citizens Medal, the nation's second-highest civilian honor.

2010: Florida is the last state to end a law explicitly banning gay men and lesbians from adopting. Several other states continue to forbid unmarried couples in those states, by definition (at the time) same-sex couples, from adopting.

2011: The U.S. State Department updates passport applications to say "Mother or Parent 1" and "Father or Parent 2" instead of just "Mother" and "Father."

2011: U.S. Rep. Jared Polis of Colorado becomes the first out LGBTQ parent in Congress with the birth of a son to him and partner, Marlon Reis.

2012: When President Obama announces his support for marriage equality, he explains that his daughters have friends with same-sex parents, and "I know it wouldn't dawn on them that their friends' parents should be treated differently."

2013: The U.S. Supreme Court rules a key part of the Defense of Marriage Act (DOMA) is unconstitutional, citing children's well-being as a key argument.

2015: The U.S. Supreme Court again uses children's well-being as a key argument in overturning bans on marriage for same-sex couples across the country. Among other things, this opens up joint and second-parent adoption for same-sex couples in several additional states.

2015: Kate Brown becomes governor of Oregon, the first bisexual (and bisexual parent) governor, and first LGBTQ governor overall.

2017: The U.S. Supreme Court rules in *Pavan v. Smith* that married same-sex couples have the right to both be on their children's birth certificates.

2018: Jared Polis is elected governor of Colorado, making him the first out gay (and gay parent) governor.

2018: Angie Craig is elected to the U.S. House of Representatives from Minnesota, making her the first out lesbian parent in Congress.

2021: Dr. Rachel Levine becomes the first openly transgender person (and transgender parent) to be confirmed by the Senate. Her position as assistant secretary for health in the Department of Health and Human Service also makes her the country's highest-ranking transgender official.

(I have compiled these items from a number of sources; special recognition goes to Carlos Ball's *The Right to Be Parents*, Jaime Campbell Naidoo's *Rainbow Family Collections*, and Daniel Winunwe Rivers' *Radical Relations: Lesbian Mothers, Gay Fathers, and Their Children in the United States Since World War II.* Any errors remain my own.)

REFERENCES

Acosta, K. L. (2021). *Queer stepfamilies: The path to social and legal recognition*. New York University Press.

Adamsons, K. (2013). Predictors of relationship quality during the transition to parenthood. *Journal of Reproductive and Infant Psychology, 31*(2), 160–171. https://doi.org/10.1080/02646838.2013.791919

Adeleye, A. J., Reid, G., Kao, C.-N., Mok-Lin, E., & Smith, J. F. (2019). Semen parameters among transgender women with a history of hormonal treatment. *Urology, 124*, 136–141. https://doi.org/10.1016/j.urology.2018.10.005

Adopt Connect. (2021, April 14). *Questions to ask yourself when considering a transracial adoption*. https://adopt-connect.com/questions-to-ask-yourself-when-considering-a-transracial-adoption

The Adopted Ones Blog. (2013, August 3). *Adoption and breastfeeding—Touchy subject*. https://theadoptedones.wordpress.com/2019/08/03/adoption-and-breastfeeding-touchy-subject/

Adoption Agencies. (n.d.). *Adoption agency information: Agency vs. independent adoption*. https://adoptionagencies.com/adoption-agency-information/agency-vs-independent-adoption/

Adoption Connection. (n.d.-a). *Adopting a drug-exposed baby: Making the decision*. https://adoptionconnection.jfcs.org/adopting-a-drug-exposed-baby-making-the-decision/#

Adoption Connection. (n.d.-b). *12 tips in adopting a drug-exposed baby*. https://adoptionconnection.jfcs.org/12-tips-when-considering-adopting-a-drug-exposed-baby/#

Adoptions Together. (n.d.). *Gay, lesbian, same-sex adoption (LGBTQ adoption)*. https://www.adoptionstogether.org/adopting/lgbt-adoption/

Adoptive Families. (n.d.-a). *Ask AF: How to choose a school for our transracially adopted child?* https://www.adoptivefamilies.com/transracial-adoption/how-to-choose-school-transracially-adopted-child-weighing-diversity-academics-proximity/

Adoptive Families. (n.d.-b). *5 tips for writing to expectant mothers*. https://www.adoptivefamilies.com/adoption-process/expectant-mothers-letter/

AFTH Marketing. (2020, June 10). *Same sex couple adoptions*. Adoptions from the Heart. https://afth.org/same-sex-couples-adopting/

Ainsworth, A. J., Allyse, M., & Khan, Z. (2020). Fertility preservation for transgender individuals: A review. *Mayo Clinic Proceedings, 95*(4), 784–792. https://doi.org/10.1016/j.mayocp.2019.10.040

Alang, S. M., & Fomotar, M. (2015). Postpartum depression in an online community of lesbian mothers: Implications for clinical practice. *Journal of Gay & Lesbian Mental Health, 19*(1), 21–39. https://doi.org/10.1080/19359705.2014.910853

America Adopts. (n.d.). *Open adoption myths and facts*. https://www.americaadopts.com/resources/open-adoption-myths-and-facts/

American Adoptions. (n.d.). *Adoption without an agency: What is independent adoption? The pros and cons of each path*. https://www.americanadoptions.com/adoption/independent_adoption

Armuand, G., Dhejne, C., Olofsson, J. I., & Rodriguez-Wallberg, K. A. (2017). Transgender men's experiences of fertility preservation: A qualitative study. *Human Reproduction, 32*(2), 383–390. https://doi.org/10.1093/humrep/dew323

Averett, K. H. (2016). The gender buffet: LGBTQ parents resisting heteronormativity. *Gender & Society, 30*(2), 189–212. https://doi.org/10.1177/0891243215611370

Baden, A. L., & Steward, R. J. (2000). A framework for use with racially and culturally integrated families: The cultural-racial identity model as applied to transracial adoption. *Journal of Social Distress and the Homeless, 9*(4), 309–337. https://doi.org/10.1023/A:1009493827019

Baden, A. L., & Steward, R. J. (2007). The cultural-racial identity model: A theoretical framework for studying transracial adoptees. In R. A. Javier, A. L. Baden, F. A. Biafora, & A. Camacho-Gingerich (Eds.),

Handbook of adoption: Implications for researchers, practitioners, and families (pp. 90–112). Sage Publications, Inc. https://doi.org/10.4135/9781412976633.n7

Baden-Lasar, E. (2019, June 26). A family portrait: Brothers, sisters, strangers. *The New York Times.* https://www.nytimes.com/interactive/2019/06/26/magazine/sperm-donor-siblings.html

Baetens, P., Camus, M., & Devroey, P. (2003). Counselling lesbian couples: Requests for donor insemination on social grounds. *Reproductive BioMedicine Online, 6*(1), 75–83. https://doi.org/10.1016/S1472-6483(10)62059-7

Ball, S. J., Bowe, R., & Gewirtz, S. (1996). School choice, social class and distinction: The realization of social advantage in education. *Journal of Education Policy, 11*(1), 89–112. https://doi.org/10.1080/0268093960110105

Bayless, K. (2018, November 5). Gay adoption: How to start the process. *Parents Magazine.* https://www.parents.com/parenting/adoption/facts/gay-adoption-how-to-start-the-process/

Belsky, J. (1990). Children and marriage. In F. D. Fincham & T. N. Bradbury (Eds.), *The psychology of marriage: Basic issues and applications* (pp. 172–200). Guilford Press.

Belsky, J., & Kelly, J. (1994). *The transition to parenthood: How a first child changes a marriage. Why some couples grow closer and others apart.* Delacorte Press.

Belsky, J., & Rovine, M. (1984). Social-network contact, family support, and the transition to parenthood. *Journal of Marriage and Family, 46*(2), 455–467. https://doi.org/10.2307/352477

Ben-Ari, A., & Weinburg-Kurnik, G. (2007). The dialectics between the personal and the interpersonal in the experiences of single mothers by choice. *Sex Roles, 56*(11–12), 823–833. https://doi.org/10.1007/s11199-007-9241-1

Bergman, K., Rubio, R. J., Green, R.-J., & Padrón, E. (2010). Gay men who become fathers via surrogacy: The transition to parenthood. *Journal of GLBT Family Studies, 6*(2), 111–141. https://doi.org/10.1080/15504281003704942

Berkowitz, D. (2020). Gay men and surrogacy. In A. E. Goldberg & K. R. Allen (Eds.), *LGBTQ-parent families: Innovations in research and implications for practice* (2nd ed., pp. 143–160). Springer. https://doi.org/10.1007/978-3-030-35610-1_8

Berkowitz, D., & Ryan, M. (2011). Bathrooms, baseball, and bra shopping: Lesbian and gay parents talk about engendering their children. *Sociological Perspectives*, *54*(3), 329–350. https://doi.org/10.1525/sop.2011.54.3.329

Besse, M., Lampe, N. M., & Mann, E. S. (2020). Experiences with achieving pregnancy and giving birth among transgender men: A narrative literature review. *Yale Journal of Biology and Medicine*, *93*(4), 517–528.

Bewkes, F. J., Mirza, S. A., Rooney, C., Durso, L. E., Kroll, J., & Wong, E. (2018, November 20). *Welcoming all families*. Center for American Progress. https://www.americanprogress.org/issues/lgbtq-rights/reports/2018/11/20/461199/welcoming-all-families/

Bhattacharya, N., Budge, S. L., Pantalone, D. W., & Katz-Wise, S. L. (2021). Conceptualizing relationships among transgender and gender diverse youth and their caregivers. *Journal of Family Psychology*, *35*(5), 595–605. https://doi.org/10.1037/fam0000815

Biblarz, T. J., & Stacey, J. (2010). How does the gender of parents matter? *Journal of Marriage and Family*, *72*(1), 3–22. https://doi.org/10.1111/j.1741-3737.2009.00678.x

Birth for Every Body. (n.d.). *About gender*. https://www.birthforeverybody.org/what-we-do

Blackwell, L., Hardy, J., Ammari, T., Veinot, T., Lampe, C., & Schoenebeck, S. (2016). LGBT parents and social media: Advocacy, privacy, and disclosure during shifting social movements. In *Proceedings of the 2016 CHI Conference on Human Factors in Computing Systems* (pp. 610–622). Association for Computing Machinery. https://doi.org/10.1145/2858036.2858342

Blake, L., Carone, N., Raffanello, E., Slutsky, J., Ehrhardt, A. A., & Golombok, S. (2017). Gay fathers' motivations for and feelings about surrogacy as a path to parenthood. *Human Reproduction*, *32*(4), 860–867. https://doi.org/10.1093/humrep/dex026

Bock, J. D. (2000). Doing the right thing? Single mothers by choice and the struggle for legitimacy. *Gender & Society*, *14*(1), 62–86. https://doi.org/10.1177/089124300014001005

Bos, H. M. W. (2010). Planned gay father families in kinship arrangements. *Australian and New Zealand Journal of Family Therapy*, *31*(4), 356–371. https://doi.org/10.1375/anft.31.4.356

Bos, H. M. W., & Gartrell, N. K. (2020). Lesbian-mother families formed through donor insemination. In A. E. Goldberg & K. R. Allen (Eds.),

LGBTQ-parent families: Innovations in research and implications for practice (2nd ed., pp. 25–44). Springer. https://doi.org/10.1007/978-3-030-35610-1_2

Bos, H. M. W., van Balen, F., & van den Boom, D. C. (2003). Planned lesbian families: Their desire and motivation to have children. *Human Reproduction, 18*(10), 2216–2224. https://doi.org/10.1093/humrep/deg427

Boston IVF. (n.d.). *Assisted reproduction using donor sperm.* http://www.gayivf.com/lgbtq-fertility-education-center/donor-sperm.cfm

Brainer, A., Moore, M. R., & Banerjee, P. (2020). Race and ethnicity in the lives of LGBTQ parents and their children: Perspectives from and beyond North America. In A. E. Goldberg & K. R. Allen (Eds.), *LGBTQ-parent families: Innovations in research and implications for practice* (2nd ed., pp. 85–103). Springer. https://doi.org/10.1007/978-3-030-35610-1_5

Brennan, R., & Sell, R. L. (2014). The effect of language on lesbian nonbirth mothers. *Journal of Obstetric, Gynecologic & Neonatal Nursing, 43*(4), 531–538. https://doi.org/10.1111/1552-6909.12471

Bright, K., Kauffman, M., Crane, D., Goldberg-Meehan, S., Cohen, T., Malins, G., & Chase, A. (Executive Producers). (1994–2004). *Friends* [TV series]. Bright/Kauffman/Crane Productions; Warner Bros. Television.

Brill, S. (2006). *The new essential guide to lesbian conception, pregnancy, & birth.* Alyson Books.

Brodzinsky, D. (1997). Infertility and adoption adjustment: Considerations and clinical issues. In S. R. Leiblum (Ed.), *Infertility: Psychological issues and counseling strategies* (pp. 246–262). John Wiley & Sons.

Brown, S., Smalling, S., Groza, V., & Ryan, S. (2009). The experiences of gay men and lesbians in becoming and being adoptive parents. *Adoption Quarterly, 12*(3–4), 229–246. https://doi.org/10.1080/10926750903313294

Brydum, S. (2015, July 31). The true meaning of the word "cisgender." *The Advocate.* https://www.advocate.com/transgender/2015/07/31/true-meaning-word-cisgender

Cacciatore, J., & Raffo, Z. (2011). An exploration of lesbian maternal bereavement. *Social Work, 56*(2), 169–177. https://doi.org/10.1093/sw/56.2.169

Cahn, N. R. (2013). *The new kinship: Constructing donor-conceived families* [Ebook]. New York University Press. https://doi.org/10.18574/nyu/9780814772034.001.0001

Campaign for Southern Equality v. Mississippi Department of Human Services, et al. 175 F. Supp. 3d 691 (S. D. Miss. 2016).

Cao, H., Mills-Koonce, W. R., Wood, C., & Fine, M. A. (2016). Identity transformation during the transition to parenthood among same-sex couples: An ecological, stress-strategy-adaptation perspective. *Journal of Family Theory & Review, 8*(1), 30–59. https://doi.org/10.1111/jftr.12124

Carone, N., Baiocco, R., & Lingiardi, V. (2017). Single fathers by choice using surrogacy: Why men decide to have a child as a single parent. *Human Reproduction, 32*(9), 1871–1879. https://doi.org/10.1093/humrep/dex245

Carroll, M. (2018). Gay fathers on the margins: Race, class, marital status, and pathway to parenthood. *Family Relations, 67*(1), 104–117. https://doi.org/10.1111/fare.12300

Caughman, S., & Motley, I. (n.d.-a). *The basics: Which type of adoption is right for you?* Adoptive Families. https://www.adoptivefamilies.com/how-to-adopt/type-of-adoption/

Caughman, S., & Motley, I. (n.d.-b). *Questions to ask your potential adoption attorney.* Adoptive Families. https://www.adoptivefamilies.com/adoption-process/questions-for-potential-adoption-attorney/

Center for Advanced Reproductive Services. (n.d.). *LGBTQ family building.* https://www.uconnfertility.com/lgbtq-family-building/

Centers for Disease Control and Prevention. (n.d.). *About opioid use during pregnancy.* https://www.cdc.gov/pregnancy/opioids/basics.html

Chabot, J. M., & Ames, B. D. (2004). "It wasn't 'let's get pregnant and go do it'": Decision making in lesbian couples planning motherhood via donor insemination. *Family Relations, 53*(4), 348–356. https://doi.org/10.1111/j.0197-6664.2004.00041.x

Chaiken, I., Lam, R., Golin, S., & Kennar, L. (Executive Producers). (2004–2009). *The L word* [TV series]. Anonymous Content; Dufferin Gate Productions; Showtime Networks; Viacom Productions.

Chan, R. W., Brooks, R. C., Raboy, B., & Patterson, C. J. (1998). Division of labor among lesbian and heterosexual parents: Associations with children's adjustment. *Journal of Family Psychology, 12*(3), 402–419. https://doi.org/10.1037/0893-3200.12.3.402

Cherney, K., & Frost, A. (2020, April 16). Infertility treatments: 9 questions to ask your doctor. *Healthline.* https://www.healthline.com/health/infertility/doctor-discussion-guide-infertility-treatments#success-rate

Child Welfare Information Gateway. (n.d.-a). *Family support services.* U.S. Department of Health and Human Services. https://www.childwelfare.gov/topics/supporting/support-services/

Child Welfare Information Gateway. (n.d.-b). *Ongoing contact with birth families in adoption.* U.S. Department of Health and Human Services. https://www.childwelfare.gov/topics/adoption/adoptive/before-adoption/openness/

Child Welfare Information Gateway. (2013). *Supporting your LGBTQ youth: A guide for foster parents.* U.S. Department of Health and Human Services, Children's Bureau. https://www.childwelfare.gov/pubPDFs/LGBTQyouth.pdf

Child Welfare Information Gateway. (2015). *Adoption options: Where do I start?* U.S. Department of Health and Human Services, Children's Bureau. https://www.childwelfare.gov/pubPDFs/f_adoptoption.pdf

Child Welfare Information Gateway. (2016). *Frequently asked questions from lesbian, gay, bisexual, transgender, and questioning (LGBTQ) prospective foster and adoptive parents.* U.S. Department of Health and Human Services, Children's Bureau. https://www.childwelfare.gov/pubPDFs/faq_lgbt.pdf

Child Welfare Information Gateway. (2018). *Addressing the needs of young children in child welfare: Part C—Early intervention services.* U.S. Department of Health and Human Services, Children's Bureau. https://www.childwelfare.gov/pubPDFs/partc.pdf

Child Welfare Information Gateway. (2019). *Helping children and youth maintain relationships with birth families and caregivers.* Department of Health and Human Services, Administration for Children & Families, Children's Bureau. https://www.childwelfare.gov/pubPDFs/bulletins_maintainrelationships.pdf

Circle Surrogacy. (n.d.). *Surrogacy by state: Get the facts.* https://www.circlesurrogacy.com/surrogacy/surrogacy-by-state-surrogacy-laws

Clunis, D. M., & Green, G. D. (2004). *The lesbian parenting book: A guide to creating families and raising children* (2nd ed.). Seal Press.

Considering Adoption. (n.d.). *LGBT international adoption: Is it possible?* https://consideringadoption.com/adopting/can-same-sex-couples-adopt/international-gay-adoption/

Corbett, S. L., Frecker, H. M., Shapiro, H. M., & Yudin, M. H. (2013). Access to fertility services for lesbian women in Canada. *Fertility and Sterility, 100*(4), 1077–1080. https://doi.org/10.1016/j.fertnstert. 2013.05.048

Craven, C. (2019). *Reproductive losses: Challenges to LGBTQ family-making.* Routledge. https://doi.org/10.4324/9780429431715

Creating a Family. (n.d.). *Is breastfeeding your adopted baby a lie?* https://creatingafamily.org/adoption-category/is-breastfeeding-your-adopted-baby-a-lie/

Creative Family Connections. (n.d.). *The United States surrogacy law map: State-by-state gestational surrogacy law & statutes.* https://www.creativefamilyconnections.com/us-surrogacy-law-map/

Daley, K. (2019, October 28). What to expect at your 20-week ultrasound appointment. *Today's Parent.* https://www.todaysparent.com/pregnancy/being-pregnant/your-20-week-ultrasound/

Daniels, K. R. (1994). Adoption and donor insemination: Factors influencing couples' choices. *Child Welfare, 73*(1), 5–14.

DeMino, K. A., Appleby, G., & Fisk, D. (2007). Lesbian mothers with planned families: A comparative study of internalized homophobia and social support. *American Journal of Orthopsychiatry, 77*(1), 165–173. https://doi.org/10.1037/0002-9432.77.1.165

Dion, K. K. (1995). Delayed parenthood and women's expectations about the transition to parenthood. *International Journal of Behavioral Development, 18*(2), 315–333. https://doi.org/10.1177/016502549501800208

Dodge, D. (2020, April 17). Legal basics for L.G.B.T.Q. parents. *The New York Times.* https://www.nytimes.com/article/legal-basics-for-lgbtq-parents.html

Doss, B. D., Rhoades, G. K., Stanley, S. M., & Markman, H. J. (2009). The effect of the transition to parenthood on relationship quality: An 8-year prospective study. *Journal of Personality and Social Psychology, 96*(3), 601–619. https://doi.org/10.1037/a0013969

Downing, J. B., & Goldberg, A. E. (2011). Lesbian mothers' constructions of the division of paid and unpaid labor. *Feminism & Psychology, 21*(1), 100–120. https://doi.org/10.1177/0959353510375869

Downing, J. B., Richardson, H. B., Kinkler, L. A., & Goldberg, A. E. (2009). Making the decision: Factors influencing gay men's choice of an adoption path. *Adoption Quarterly, 12*(3–4), 247–271. https://doi.org/10.1080/10926750903313310

Ehrensaft, D. (2005). *Mommies, daddies, donors, surrogates: Answering tough questions and building strong families.* Guilford Press.

Eliason, M. J., & Schope, R. (2007). Shifting sands or solid foundation? Lesbian, gay, bisexual, and transgender identity formation. In I. H. Meyer & M. E. Northridge (Eds.), *The health of sexual minorities: Public health perspectives on lesbian, gay, bisexual, and transgender populations* (pp. 3–26). Springer. https://doi.org/10.1007/978-0-387-31334-4_1

Ellis, S. A., Wojnar, D. M., & Pettinato, M. (2015). Conception, pregnancy, and birth experiences of male and gender variant gestational parents: It's how we could have a family. *Journal of Midwifery & Women's Health, 60*(1), 62–69. https://doi.org/10.1111/jmwh.12213

Erera, P. I., & Segal-Engelchin, D. (2014). Gay men choosing to co-parent with heterosexual women. *Journal of GLBT Family Studies, 10*(5), 449–474. https://doi.org/10.1080/1550428X.2013.858611

Fairfax Cryobank. (n.d.). *Sperm banking background fundamentals.* https://fairfaxcryobank.com/sperm-banking-background-fundamentals

Faisal-Cury, A., Tabb, K., & Matijasevich, A. (2021). Partner relationship quality predicts later postpartum depression independently of the chronicity of depressive symptoms. *Brazilian Journal of Psychiatry, 43*(1), 12–21. https://doi.org/10.1590/1516-4446-2019-0764

Family Equality. (n.d.). *Questions to ask at your first fertility clinic visit.* https://www.familyequality.org/resources/questions-to-ask-at-your-initial-consultation-at-a-fertility-clinic/

Family Equality Council. (2021a). *Adoption options for the LGBTQ+ community.* Family Equality. https://www.familyequality.org/wp-content/uploads/2019/06/AdoptionOptions_FEC_Handbook_REV.pdf

Family Equality Council. (2021b). *Choosing between a known and unknown sperm donor.* Family Equality. https://www.familyequality.org/resources/choosing-between-a-known-and-unknown-sperm-donor/

Farr, R. H., & Goldberg, A. E. (2018). Sexual orientation, gender identity, and adoption law. *Family Court Review, 56*(3), 374–383. https://doi.org/10.1111/fcre.12354

Farr, R. H., & Patterson, C. J. (2009). Transracial adoption by lesbian, gay, and heterosexual couples: Who completes transracial adoptions and with what results? *Adoption Quarterly, 12*(3–4), 187–204. https://doi.org/10.1080/10926750903313328

Fauntleroy, G. (2017, June). The big chill: Do sperm banks need stricter regulations? *Endocrine News.* https://endocrinenews.endocrine.org/big-chill-sperm-banks-need-stricter-regulations/

Fisher, P. A., Ellis, B. H., & Chamberlain, P. (1999). Early intervention foster care: A model for preventing risk in young children who have been maltreated. *Children's Services, 2*(3), 159–182. https://doi.org/10.1207/s15326918cs0203_3

Fitzpatrick, K. (2018, May 7). What it's like when your wife is pregnant—at the same time as you. *Popsugar.* https://www.popsugar.com/news/Lesbian-Couple-Pregnant-Same-Time-43303404

Florida Department of Children and Families, Appellant, v. IN RE: Matter of Adoption of X. X. G. and N. R. G., Appellees, 45 So.3d 79 (Fla. 2010).

Fong, R., & McRoy, R. (Eds.). (2016). *Transracial and intercountry adoptions: Cultural guidance for professionals.* Columbia University Press.

Forenza, B., Dashew, B. L., & Bergeson, C. (2021). LGB + moms and dads: "My primary identity . . . is being a parent." *Journal of GLBT Family Studies, 17*(1), 18–29. https://doi.org/10.1080/1550428X.2019.1688215

Frost, D. M., & Meyer, I. H. (2009). Internalized homophobia and relationship quality among lesbians, gay men, and bisexuals. *Journal of Counseling Psychology, 56*(1), 97–109. https://doi.org/10.1037/a0012844

Frost, R. L., & Goldberg, A. E. (2020). Adopting again: A qualitative study of the second transition to parenthood in adoptive families. *Adoption Quarterly, 23*(2), 85–109. https://doi.org/10.1080/10926755.2019.1627450

Gartrell, N., Banks, A., Hamilton, J., Reed, N., Bishop, H., & Rodas, C. (1999). The National Lesbian Family Study: 2. Interviews with mothers of toddlers. *American Journal of Orthopsychiatry, 69*(3), 362–369. https://doi.org/10.1037/h0080410

Gartrell, N., Hamilton, J., Banks, A., Mosbacher, D., Reed, N., Sparks, C. H., & Bishop, H. (1996). The National Lesbian Family Study: 1. Interviews with prospective mothers. *American Journal of Orthopsychiatry, 66*(2), 272–281. https://doi.org/10.1037/h0080178

Gartrell, N., Rodas, C., Deck, A., Peyser, H., & Banks, A. (2006). The USA National Lesbian Family Study: Interviews with mothers of 10-year-olds. *Feminism & Psychology, 16*(2), 175–192. https://doi.org/10.1177/0959-353506062972

Gates, G. J. (2013, February). *LGBT parenting in the United States*. The Williams Institute. http://williamsinstitute.law.ucla.edu/wp-content/uploads/LGBT-Parenting.pdf

Gates, G. J., Badgett, M. V. L., Macomber, J. E., & Chambers, K. (2007, March). *Adoption and foster care by gay and lesbian parents in the United States*. The Williams Institute. https://escholarship.org/uc/item/2v4528cx

Gays With Kids. (2020, September 11). *Teaching your kids how to handle homophobia at school*. https://www.gayswithkids.com/life-plus/education/teaching-your-kids-how-to-handle-homophobia-at-school

Gibson, C. (2019, March 15). Deciding whether to have kids has never been more complex. Enter parenthood-indecision therapists. *The Washington Post*. https://www.washingtonpost.com/lifestyle/on-parenting/deciding-whether-to-have-kids-has-never-been-more-complex-enter-parenthood-indecision-therapists/2019/03/15/e69231da-44d7-11e9-8aab-95b8d80a1e4f_story.html

Gilmour, P. (2018, June 6). Shared motherhood: The amazing way LGBTQ+ couples are having babies. *Cosmopolitan*. https://www.cosmopolitan.com/uk/love-sex/relationships/a17851346/how-lesbian-couples-have-babies/

Goldberg, A. E. (2006). The transition to parenthood for lesbian couples. *Journal of GLBT Family Studies, 2*(1), 13–42. https://doi.org/10.1300/J461v02n01_02

Goldberg, A. E. (2007). (How) does it make a difference? Perspectives of adults with lesbian, gay, and bisexual parents. *American Journal of Orthopsychiatry, 77*(4), 550–562. https://doi.org/10.1037/0002-9432.77.4.550

Goldberg, A. E. (2009a). Heterosexual, lesbian, and gay preadoptive couples' preferences about child gender. *Sex Roles, 61*(1–2), 55–71. https://doi.org/10.1007/s11199-009-9598-4

Goldberg, A. E. (2009b). Lesbian and heterosexual preadoptive couples' openness to transracial adoption. *American Journal of Orthopsychiatry, 79*(1), 103–117. https://doi.org/10.1037/a0015354

Goldberg, A. E. (2010a). *Lesbian and gay parents and their children: Research on the family life cycle*. American Psychological Association. https://doi.org/10.1037/12055-000

Goldberg, A. E. (2010b). The transition to adoptive parenthood. In T. W. Miller (Ed.), *Handbook of stressful transitions across the life span* (pp. 165–184). Springer. https://doi.org/10.1007/978-1-4419-0748-6_9

Goldberg, A. E. (2012). *Gay dads: Transitions to adoptive fatherhood*. New York University Press. https://doi.org/10.18574/nyu/9780814732236.001.0001

Goldberg, A. E. (2013). "Doing" and "undoing" gender: The meaning and division of housework in same-sex couples. *Journal of Family Theory & Review, 5*(2), 85–104. https://doi.org/10.1111/jftr.12009

Goldberg, A. E. (2017). LGB-parent families and the school context. In S. T. Russell & S. S. Horne (Eds.), *Sexual orientation, gender identity, and schooling: The nexus of research, practice, and policy* (pp. 99–114). Oxford University Press.

Goldberg, A. E. (2019). *Open adoption and diverse families: Complex relationships in the digital age*. Oxford University Press. https://doi.org/10.1093/oso/9780190692032.001.0001

Goldberg, A. E. (2021). *The LGBTQ Family Building Project* [Data set]. Clark University.

Goldberg, A. E., & Allen, K. R. (2007). Imagining men: Lesbian mothers' perceptions of male involvement during the transition to parenthood. *Journal of Marriage and Family, 69*(2), 352–365. https://doi.org/10.1111/j.1741-3737.2007.00370.x

Goldberg, A. E., & Allen, K. R. (2013). Donor, dad, or . . .? Young adults with lesbian parents' experiences with known donors. *Family Process, 52*(2), 338–350. https://doi.org/10.1111/famp.12029

Goldberg, A. E., & Allen, K. R. (Eds.). (2020). *LGBTQ-parent families: Innovations in research and implications for practice* (2nd ed.). Springer. https://doi.org/10.1007/978-3-030-35610-1

Goldberg, A. E., Allen, K. R., Black, K., Frost, R., & Manley, M. (2018). "There is no perfect school . . .": The complexity of school decision-making among lesbian and gay adoptive parents. *Journal of Marriage and Family, 80*(3), 684–703. https://doi.org/10.1111/jomf.12478

Goldberg, A. E., Allen, K. R., & Carroll, M. (2020). "We don't exactly fit in, but we can't opt out": Gay fathers' experiences navigating parent communities in schools. *Journal of Marriage and Family, 82*(5), 1655–1676. https://doi.org/10.1111/jomf.12695

Goldberg, A. E., Black, K., Sweeney, K., & Moyer, A. (2017). Lesbian, gay, and heterosexual adoptive parents' perceptions of inclusivity and receptiveness in early childhood education settings. *Journal of Research in Childhood Education, 31*(1), 141–159. https://doi.org/10.1080/

02568543.2016.1244136 (Corrigendum published 2017, *Journal of Research in Childhood Education, 31*(2), p. 312. https://doi.org/10.1080/02568543.2017.1305241)

Goldberg, A. E., Downing, J. B., & Moyer, A. M. (2012). Why parenthood, and why now?: Gay men's motivations for pursuing parenthood. *Family Relations, 61*(1), 157–174. https://doi.org/10.1111/j.1741-3729.2011.00687.x

Goldberg, A. E., Downing, J. B., & Richardson, H. B. (2009). The transition from infertility to adoption: Perceptions of lesbian and heterosexual preadoptive couples. *Journal of Social and Personal Relationships, 26*(6–7), 938–963. https://doi.org/10.1177/0265407509345652

Goldberg, A. E., Downing, J. B., & Sauck, C. C. (2007). Choices, challenges, and tensions: Perspectives of lesbian prospective adoptive parents. *Adoption Quarterly, 10*(2), 33–64. https://doi.org/10.1300/J145v10n02_02

Goldberg, A. E., Downing, J. B., & Sauck, C. C. (2008). Perceptions of children's parental preferences in lesbian two-mother households. *Journal of Marriage and Family, 70*(2), 419–434. https://doi.org/10.1111/j.1741-3737.2008.00491.x

Goldberg, A. E., Frost, R. L., & Black, K. A. (2017). "There is so much to consider": School-related decisions and experiences among families who adopt noninfant children. *Families in Society, 98*(3), 191–200. https://doi.org/10.1606/1044-3894.2017.98.24

Goldberg, A. E., Frost, R. L., Manley, M. H., & Black, K. A. (2018). Meeting other moms: Lesbian adoptive mothers' relationships with other parents at school and beyond. *Journal of Lesbian Studies, 22*(1), 67–84. https://doi.org/10.1080/10894160.2016.1278349

Goldberg, A. E., Frost, R. L., Manley, M. H., McCormick, N. M., Smith, J. Z., & Brodzinsky, D. B. (2020). Lesbian, gay, and heterosexual adoptive parents' experiences with pediatricians: A mixed-methods study. *Adoption Quarterly, 23*(1), 27–62. https://doi.org/10.1080/10926755.2019.1675839

Goldberg, A. E., Frost, R. L., Miranda, L., & Kahn, E. (2019). LGBTQ individuals' experiences with delays and disruptions in the foster and adoption process. *Children and Youth Services Review, 106*, Article 104466. https://doi.org/10.1016/j.childyouth.2019.104466

Goldberg, A. E., & Garcia, R. L. (2016). Gender-typed behavior over time in children with lesbian, gay, and heterosexual parents. *Journal of Family Psychology, 30*(7), 854–865. https://doi.org/10.1037/fam0000226

Goldberg, A. E., Gartrell, N., & Gates, G. J. (2014, July). *Research report on LGB-parent families*. The Williams Institute. https://williamsinstitute. law.ucla.edu/publications/report-lgb-parent-families/

Goldberg, A. E., & Gianino, M. (2012). Lesbian and gay adoptive parent families: Assessment, clinical issues, and intervention. In D. M. Brodzinsky & A. Pertman (Eds.), *Adoption by lesbians and gay men: A new dimension in family diversity* (pp. 204–232). Oxford University Press.

Goldberg, A. E., Kashy, D. A., & Smith, J. Z. (2012). Gender-typed play behavior in early childhood: Adopted children with lesbian, gay, and heterosexual parents. *Sex Roles, 67*(9–10), 503–515. https://doi.org/10.1007/s11199-012-0198-3

Goldberg, A. E., Kinkler, L. A., Moyer, A. M., & Weber, E. (2014). Intimate relationship challenges in early parenthood among lesbian, gay, and heterosexual couples adopting via the child welfare system. *Professional Psychology: Research and Practice, 45*(4), 221–230. https://doi.org/10.1037/a0037443

Goldberg, A. E., Kinkler, L. A., Richardson, H. B., & Downing, J. B. (2011). Lesbian, gay, and heterosexual couples in open adoption arrangements: A qualitative study. *Journal of Marriage and Family, 73*(2), 502–518. https://doi.org/10.1111/j.1741-3737.2010.00821.x

Goldberg, A. E., McCormick, N., & Virginia, H. (2021). Parenting in a pandemic: Work–family arrangements, well-being, and intimate relationships among adoptive parents. *Family Relations, 70*(1), 7–25. https://doi.org/10.1111/fare.12528

Goldberg, A. E., Moyer, A. M., Kinkler, L. A., & Richardson, H. B. (2012). "When you're sitting on the fence, hope's the hardest part": Challenges and experiences of heterosexual and same-sex couples adopting through the child welfare system. *Adoption Quarterly, 15*(4), 288–315. https://doi.org/10.1080/10926755.2012.731032

Goldberg, A. E., Moyer, A. M., Weber, E. R., & Shapiro, J. (2013). What changed when the gay adoption ban was lifted?: Perspectives of lesbian and gay parents in Florida. *Sexuality Research & Social Policy, 10*(2), 110–124. https://doi.org/10.1007/s13178-013-0120-y

Goldberg, A. E., & Perry-Jenkins, M. (2007). The division of labor and perceptions of parental roles: Lesbian couples across the transition to parenthood. *Journal of Social and Personal Relationships, 24*(2), 297–318. https://doi.org/10.1177/0265407507075415

Goldberg, A. E., Ross, L. E., Manley, M. H., & Mohr, J. J. (2017). Male-partnered sexual minority women: Sexual identity disclosure to health care providers during the perinatal period. *Psychology of Sexual Orientation and Gender Diversity, 4*(1), 105–114. https://doi.org/10.1037/sgd0000215

Goldberg, A. E., & Scheib, J. E. (2015). Why donor insemination and not adoption? Narratives of single and female-partnered mothers. *Family Relations, 64*(5), 726–742. https://doi.org/10.1111/fare.12162

Goldberg, A. E., & Smith, J. Z. (2008). The social context of lesbian mothers' anxiety during early parenthood. *Parenting: Science and Practice, 8*(3), 213–239. https://doi.org/10.1080/15295190802204801

Goldberg, A. E., & Smith, J. Z. (2009). Predicting non-African American lesbian and heterosexual preadoptive couples' openness to adopting an African American child. *Family Relations, 58*(3), 346–360. https://doi.org/10.1111/j.1741-3729.2009.00557.x

Goldberg, A. E., & Smith, J. Z. (2011). Stigma, social context, and mental health: Lesbian and gay couples across the transition to adoptive parenthood. *Journal of Counseling Psychology, 58*(1), 139–150. https://doi.org/10.1037/a0021684

Goldberg, A. E., & Smith, J. Z. (2013). Predictors of psychological adjustment in early placed adopted children with lesbian, gay, and heterosexual parents. *Journal of Family Psychology, 27*(3), 431–442. https://doi.org/10.1037/a0032911

Goldberg, A. E., & Smith, J. Z. (2014). Preschool selection considerations and experiences of school mistreatment among lesbian, gay, and heterosexual adoptive parents. *Early Childhood Research Quarterly, 29*(1), 64–75. https://doi.org/10.1016/j.ecresq.2013.09.006

Goldberg, A. E., Smith, J. Z., & Kashy, D. A. (2010). Preadoptive factors predicting lesbian, gay, and heterosexual couples' relationship quality across the transition to adoptive parenthood. *Journal of Family Psychology, 24*(3), 221–232. https://doi.org/10.1037/a0019615

Goldberg, A. E., Smith, J. Z., McCormick, N. M., & Overstreet, N. M. (2019). Health behaviors and outcomes of parents in same-sex couples: An exploratory study. *Psychology of Sexual Orientation and Gender Diversity, 6*(3), 318–335. https://doi.org/10.1037/sgd0000330

Goldberg, A. E., Smith, J. Z., & Perry-Jenkins, M. (2012). The division of labor in lesbian, gay, and heterosexual new adoptive parents. *Journal*

of Marriage and Family, *74*(4), 812–828. https://doi.org/10.1111/
j.1741-3737.2012.00992.x

Goldberg, A. E., Tornello, S., Farr, R., Smith, J. Z., & Miranda, L. (2020).
Barriers to adoption and foster care and openness to child characteristics among transgender adults. *Children and Youth Services
Review*, *109*, Article 104699. https://doi.org/10.1016/j.childyouth.
2019.104699

Goldberg, A. E., Weber, E. R., Moyer, A. M., & Shapiro, J. (2014). Seeking
to adopt in Florida: Lesbian and gay parents navigate the legal process.
Journal of Gay & Lesbian Social Services, *26*(1), 37–69. https://doi.org/
10.1080/10538720.2013.865576

Green, C. (2015, June 25). "Cisgender" has been added to the Oxford English
Dictionary. *Independent*. https://www.independent.co.uk/incoming/
cisgender-has-been-added-oxford-english-dictionary-10343354.html

Greenblatt, R., Janollari, D., Poul, A., & Ball, A. (Executive Producers).
(2001–2005). *Six feet under* [TV series]. Home Box Office (HBO); The
Greenblatt Janollari Studio; Actual Size Films; Actual Size Productions.

Greenfeld, D. A., & Seli, E. (2011). Gay men choosing parenthood through
assisted reproduction: Medical and psychosocial considerations.
Fertility and Sterility, *95*(1), 225–229. https://doi.org/10.1016/
j.fertnstert.2010.05.053

Greenfield, M., & Darwin, Z. (2021). Trans and non-binary pregnancy,
traumatic birth, and perinatal mental health: A scoping review. *International Journal of Transgender Health*, *22*(1–2), 203–216. https://
doi.org/10.1080/26895269.2020.1841057

Gregg, I. (2018). The health care experiences of lesbian women becoming
mothers. *Nursing for Women's Health*, *22*(1), 40–50. https://doi.org/
10.1016/j.nwh.2017.12.003

Greif, G. L., Leitch, J., & Wooley, M. E. (2019). A preliminary look at relationships between married gay men and lesbians and their parents-
in-law: Five case studies. *Journal of Gay & Lesbian Social Services*,
31(3), 290–313. https://doi.org/10.1080/10538720.2019.1615591

Gurevich, R. (2020, January 30). *Understanding donor arrangements: Having
a baby with third-party reproduction*. Verywell Family. https://www.
verywellfamily.com/understanding-donor-arrangements-4176290

Haines, B. A., Ajayi, A. A., & Boyd, H. (2014). Making trans parents visible:
Intersectionality of trans and parenting identities. *Feminism & Psychology*, *24*(2), 238–247. https://doi.org/10.1177/0959353514526219

Harris, E., & Winn, A. (2019, December). *Building LGBTQ+ families: The price of parenthood.* Family Equality. https://www.familyequality. org/resources/building-lgbtq-families-price-parenthood/

Hatem, A. (2020, September 17). Sperm donors are almost always White, and it's pushing Black parents using IVF to start families that don't look like them. *Insider.* https://www.insider.com/egg-sperm-donor-diversity-lacking-race-2020-9

Herek, G. M. (2007). Confronting sexual stigma and prejudice: Theory and practice. *Journal of Social Issues, 63*(4), 905–925. https://doi.org/ 10.1111/j.1540-4560.2007.00544.x

Hicks, S. (2008). Gender role models . . . Who needs 'em?! *Qualitative Social Work, 7*(1), 43–59. https://doi.org/10.1177/1473325007086415

Hillis, L. (1998). Intercountry adoption under the Hague Convention: Still an attractive option for homosexuals seeking to adopt? *Indiana Journal of Global Legal Studies, 6*(1), 237–256.

Hoffkling, A., Obedin-Maliver, J., & Sevelius, J. (2017). From erasure to opportunity: A qualitative study of the experiences of transgender men around pregnancy and recommendations for providers. *BMC Pregnancy and Childbirth, 17,* Article 332. https://doi.org/10.1186/ s12884-017-1491-5

Hudson, J., Nahata, L., Dietz, E., & Quinn, G. P. (2018). Fertility counseling for transgender AYAs. *Clinical Practice in Pediatric Psychology, 6*(1), 84–92. https://doi.org/10.1037/cpp0000180

Human Rights Campaign. (n.d.-a). *Adoption options overview.* https:// www.hrc.org/resources/adoption-options-overview

Human Rights Campaign. (n.d.-b). *Second parent adoption.* https://www. hrc.org/resources/second-parent-adoption

Human Rights Campaign. (n.d.-c). *Trump's timeline of hate.* https://www. hrc.org/resources/trumps-timeline-of-hate

Human Rights Campaign. (2020a). *Change-makers in child welfare 2020.* https://www.hrc.org/resources/change-makers-in-child-welfare-2020

Human Rights Campaign. (2020b). *Healthcare Equality Index 2020: Promoting equitable and inclusive care for LGBTQ patients and their families.* https://www.hrc.org/resources/healthcare-equality-index

IAC Counseling Center. (n.d.). *Pre-adoption.* https://iaccenter.com/about-iac/ pre-adoption/

Jacobson, H. (2018). A limited market: The recruitment of gay men as surrogacy clients by the infertility industry in the USA. *Reproductive*

BioMedicine and Society Online, 7, 14–23. https://doi.org/10.1016/j.rbms.2018.10.019

Jenkins, D. A. (2013). Boundary ambiguity in gay stepfamilies: Perspectives of gay biological fathers and their same-sex partners. *Journal of Divorce & Remarriage*, 54(4), 329–348. https://doi.org/10.1080/10502556.2013.780501

Jennings, S., Mellish, L., Tasker, F., Lamb, M., & Golombok, S. (2014). Why adoption? Gay, lesbian, and heterosexual adoptive parents' reproductive experiences and reasons for adoption. *Adoption Quarterly*, 17(3), 205–226. https://doi.org/10.1080/10926755.2014.891549

Jin, H., & Dasgupta, S. (2016). Disparities between online assisted reproduction patient education for same-sex and heterosexual couples. *Human Reproduction*, 31(10), 2280–2284. https://doi.org/10.1093/humrep/dew182

Johnson, K. M. (2012). Excluding lesbian and single women? An analysis of U.S. fertility clinic websites. *Women's Studies International Forum*, 35(5), 394–402. https://doi.org/10.1016/j.wsif.2012.05.002

Johnson-Motoyama, M., Moses, M., Conrad-Hiebner, A., & Mariscal, E. S. (2016). Development, CAPTA Part C referral and services among young children in the U.S. child welfare system: Implications for Latino children. *Child Maltreatment*, 21(3), 186–197. https://doi.org/10.1177/1077559516630831

Kashef, Z. (2019, April 6). *How to talk to your child about nontraditional family types*. BabyCenter. https://www.babycenter.com/child/parenting-strategies/how-to-talk-to-your-child-about-nontraditional-family-types_3657068

Kasza, K. (1992). *A mother for Choco*. Putnam.

Katon, W., Russo, J., & Gavin, A. (2014). Predictors of postpartum depression. *Journal of Women's Health*, 23(9), 753–759. Advance online publication. https://doi.org/10.1089/jwh.2014.4824

Kaufman, D. (2020, July 24). The fight for fertility equality. *The New York Times*. https://www.nytimes.com/2020/07/22/style/lgbtq-fertility-surrogacy-coverage.html

Khanna, N., & Killian, C. (2015). "We didn't even think about adopting domestically": The role of race and other factors in shaping parents' decisions to adopt. *Sociological Perspectives*, 58(4), 570–594. https://doi.org/10.1177/0731121415572688

King-Miller, L. (2018, March 22). How doulas and midwives around the country are filling gaps in birth care for queer families. *Rewire News Group.* https://rewirenewsgroup.com/article/2018/03/22/doulas-midwives-around-country-filling-gaps-birth-care-queer-families/

Kinkler, L. A., & Goldberg, A. E. (2011). Working with what we've got: Perceptions of barriers and supports among small-metropolitan-area same-sex adopting couples. *Family Relations, 60*(4), 387–403. https://doi.org/10.1111/j.1741-3729.2011.00654.x

Kohn, J. L., Rholes, S. W., Simpson, J. A., Martin, A. M., III, Tran, S., & Wilson, C. L. (2012). Changes in marital satisfaction across the transition to parenthood: The role of adult attachment orientations. *Personality and Social Psychology Bulletin, 38*(11), 1506–1522. https://doi.org/10.1177/0146167212454548

Lai-Boyd, B. (2020, June 11). *Maternity care for LGBTQ+ people—How can we do better?* All 4 Maternity. https://www.all4maternity.com/maternity-care-for-lgbtq-people-how-can-we-do-better/

La Leche League. (2020, May). *Nursing babies, nursing families: Induced lactation and relactation.* https://lllusa.org/induced-lactation-and-relactation/

Langdridge, D., Sheeran, P., & Connolly, K. (2005). Understanding the reasons for parenthood. *Journal of Reproductive and Infant Psychology, 23*(2), 121–133. https://doi.org/10.1080/02646830500129438

Lash, D. (2017). *"When the welfare people come": Race and class in the US child protection system.* Haymarket Books.

Lavner, J. A., Waterman, J., & Peplau, L. A. (2012). Can gay and lesbian parents promote healthy development in high-risk children adopted from foster care? *American Journal of Orthopsychiatry, 82*(4), 465–472. https://doi.org/10.1111/j.1939-0025.2012.01176.x

Law Office of Brian Esser PLLC. (2014, May 9). *Do I really need a sperm donor agreement?* https://www.esserlawoffice.com/blog/second-parent-adoption/2014/05/09/really-need-sperm-donor-agreement/

Lawrence, E., Rothman, A. D., Cobb, R. J., & Bradbury, T. N. (2010). Marital satisfaction across the transition to parenthood: Three eras of research. In M. S. Schulz, M. K. Pruett, P. K. Kerig, & R. D. Parke (Eds.), *Strengthening couple relationships for optimal child development: Lessons from research and intervention* (pp. 97–114). American Psychological Association. https://doi.org/10.1037/12058-007

Leondires, M. (n.d.). *Finding the right fertility clinic for LGBTQ parents-to-be.* https://www.saythefword.com/archive/finding-the-right-fertility-clinic-for-lgbtq-parents-to-be

Leondires, M. P. (2020, March 19). *Fertility insurance mandates & same-sex couples.* Gay Parents to Be. https://www.gayparentstobe.com/gay-parenting-blog/fertility-insurance-mandates-same-sex-couples/

Leslie, L. K., Gordon, J. N., Lambros, K., Premji, K., Peoples, J., & Gist, K. (2005). Addressing the developmental and mental health needs of young children in foster care. *Journal of Developmental and Behavioral Pediatrics, 26*(2), 140–151. https://doi.org/10.1097/00004703-200504000-00011

Lev, A. I. (2004). *The complete lesbian & gay parenting guide.* Berkeley Books.

Lev, A. I., & Sennott, S. L. (2020). Clinical work with LGBTQ parents and prospective parents. In A. E. Goldberg & K. R. Allen (Eds.), *LGBTQ-parent families* (pp. 383–403). Springer. https://doi.org/10.1007/978-3-030-35610-1_24

Levitan, S., Lloyd, C., Zuker, D. (Writers), & Koch, C. (Director). (2010, April 14). Benched. In S. Levitan, J. Morton, P. Corrigan, B. Walsh, D. Zuker, A. Higginbotham, J. Richman, C. Lloyd, E. Ko, B. Wrubel, S. Lloyd, V. Chandrasekaran, D. O'Shannon, J. Pollack, & J. Burditt (Executive Producers), *Modern family* [TV series, 2009–2020]. Levitan/Lloyd; 20th Century Fox Television; Steven Levitan Productions; Picador Productions.

Levitan, S., Morton, J., Corrigan, P., Walsh, B., Zuker, D., Higginbotham, A., Richman, J., Lloyd, C. Ko, E., Wrubel, B., Lloyd, S., Chandrasekaran, V., O'Shannon, D., Pollack, J., & Burditt, J. (Executive Producers). (2009–2020). *Modern family* [TV series]. Levitan/Lloyd; 20th Century Fox Television; Steven Levitan Productions; Picador Productions.

Lewin, E. (1993). *Lesbian mothers: Accounts of gender in American culture.* Cornell University Press. https://doi.org/10.7591/9781501720031

Lewin, E. (2009). *Gay fatherhood: Narratives of family and citizenship in America.* Chicago University Press. https://doi.org/10.7208/chicago/9780226476599.001.0001

Light, A. D., Obedin-Maliver, J., Sevelius, J. M., & Kerns, J. L. (2014). Transgender men who experienced pregnancy after female-to-male gender transitioning. *Obstetrics & Gynecology, 124*(6), 1120–1127. https://doi.org/10.1097/AOG.0000000000000540

Logsdon, M. C., & McBride, A. B. (1994). Social support and postpartum depression. *Research in Nursing & Health, 17*(6), 449–457. https://doi.org/10.1002/nur.4770170608

Lynch, J. M. (2004a). The identity transformation of biological parents in lesbian/gay stepfamilies. *Journal of Homosexuality, 47*(2), 91–107. https://doi.org/10.1300/J082v47n02_06

Lynch, J. M. (2004b). Integrating identities. *Journal of Homosexuality, 48*(2), 45–60. https://doi.org/10.1300/J082v48n02_03

Mallon, G. P. (2011). The home study assessment process for gay, lesbian, bisexual, and transgender prospective foster and adoptive parents. *Journal of GLBT Family Studies, 7*(1–2), 9–29. https://doi.org/10.1080/1550428X.2011.537229

Malmquist, A., & Nelson, K. Z. (2014). Efforts to maintain a "just great" story: Lesbian parents' talk about encounters with professionals in fertility clinics and maternal and child healthcare services. *Feminism & Psychology, 24*(1), 56–73. https://doi.org/10.1177/0959353513487532

Maltby, A. (2018, July 31). How to split household chores so everyone shares the work. *RealSimple.* https://www.realsimple.com/home-organizing/cleaning/how-to-split-household-chores

Manley, M. H., Goldberg, A. E., & Ross, L. E. (2018). Invisibility and involvement: LGBTQ community connections among plurisexual women during pregnancy and postpartum. *Psychology of Sexual Orientation and Gender Diversity, 5*(2), 169–181. https://doi.org/10.1037/sgd0000285

Manley, M. H., Legge, M. M., Flanders, C. E., Goldberg, A. E., & Ross, L. E. (2018). Consensual nonmonogamy in pregnancy and parenthood: Experiences of bisexual and plurisexual women with different-gender partners. *Journal of Sex & Marital Therapy, 44*(8), 721–736. https://doi.org/10.1080/0092623X.2018.1462277

Marcoux, H. (2018, October 12). This woman and her wife are both pregnant—and due on the same day. *Motherly.* https://www.mother.ly/news/two-moms-two-babies-one-family/particle-1

Marisa N. Pavan, et al. v. Nathaniel Smith, 137 S. Ct. 2075 (2017).

May, A., & Tenzek, K. (2016). "A gift we are unable to create ourselves": Uncertainty reduction in online classified ads posted by gay men pursuing surrogacy. *Journal of GLBT Family Studies, 12*(5), 430–450. https://doi.org/10.1080/1550428X.2015.1128860

Mckenzie, S. K., & Carter, K. (2013). Does transition into parenthood lead to changes in mental health? Findings from three waves of a population based panel study. *Journal of Epidemiology and Community Health,* 67(4), 339–345. https://doi.org/10.1136/jech-2012-201765

Medina, C., & Mahowald, L. (2021, February 11). *Lessening the pandemic's burden on LGBTQ workers and families.* Center for American Progress. https://www.americanprogress.org/issues/lgbtq-rights/news/2021/02/11/495675/lessening-pandemics-burden-lgbtq-workers-families/

Meyer, I. H. (2003). Prejudice, social stress, and mental health in lesbian, gay, and bisexual populations: Conceptual issues and research evidence. *Psychological Bulletin, 129*(5), 674–697. https://doi.org/10.1037/0033-2909.129.5.674

Meyers, D. (2015, April 17). *Designing maternity clothes for genderqueer parents.* The Cut. https://www.thecut.com/2015/04/maternity-clothes-for-genderqueer-parents.html

Mills, B. (2018, September 21). *11 things to remember while writing your "Dear Expectant Parent" letter.* Mills Adoption Law. https://www.millsadoptionlaw.com/blog/11-things-to-remember-while-writing-your-dear-expectant-parent-letter/

Mitnick, D. M., Heyman, R. E., & Smith Slep, A. M. (2009). Changes in relationship satisfaction across the transition to parenthood: A meta-analysis. *Journal of Family Psychology, 23*(6), 848–852. https://doi.org/10.1037/a0017004

Moore, M. R. (2008). Gendered power relations among women: A study of household decision making in Black, lesbian stepfamilies. *American Sociological Review, 73*(2), 335–356. https://doi.org/10.1177/000312240807300208

Moreau, J. (2018, November 22). *Religious exemption laws exacerbating foster and adoption "crisis," report finds.* NBC News. https://www.nbcnews.com/feature/nbc-out/religious-exemption-laws-exacerbating-foster-adoption-crisis-report-finds-n939326

Moreau, J. (2019, April 4). *Anti-LGBTQ adoption bills "snowballing" in state legislatures, rights group says.* NBC News. https://www.nbcnews.com/feature/nbc-out/anti-lgbtq-adoption-bills-snowballing-state-legislatures-rights-group-says-n991156

Moreau, J. (2020, June 4). *Adoption agency should be able to reject gay couples, Trump administration argues.* NBC News. https://www.nbcnews.com/feature/nbc-out/adoption-agency-should-be-able-reject-gay-couples-trump-administration-n1224911

Moreno, C. (2014, October 9). *What Ricky Martin told his son when asked, "Dad, was I in your belly?"* HuffPost. https://www.huffpost.com/entry/ricky-martin-son-questions_n_5882228

Moss, A. R. (2012). Alternative families, alternative lives: Married women doing bisexuality. *Journal of GLBT Family Studies, 8*(5), 405–427. https://doi.org/10.1080/1550428X.2012.729946

Mroz, J. (2011, September 5). One sperm donor, 150 offspring. *The New York Times.* https://www.nytimes.com/2011/09/06/health/06donor.html

Murkoff, H. E., Mazel, S., & Neppe, C. (2018). *What to expect when you're expecting* (5th ed.). HarperCollins.

Murphy, D. A. (2013). The desire for parenthood: Gay men choosing to become parents through surrogacy. *Journal of Family Issues, 34*(8), 1104–1124. https://doi.org/10.1177/0192513X13484272

Musings of a Birthmom. (2015, August 16). *Dying to breastfeed.* https://musingsofabirthmom.com/2015/08/16/dying-to-breastfeed/

National Center for Education Statistics. (2021). *Public and private school comparison.* https://nces.ed.gov/fastfacts/display.asp?id=55

Nayak, R. L. (n.d.). *"Confirmatory" or second-parent adoption: What you need to know.* Family Equality. https://www.familyequality.org/resources/confirmatory-adoption/

Newson, A. J. (2016). Compensated transnational surrogacy in Australia: Time for a comprehensive review. *The Medical Journal of Australia, 204*(1), 33–35. https://doi.org/10.5694/mja15.00166

Nordqvist, P. (2015). "I've redeemed myself by being a 1950s 'housewife'": Parent–grandparent relationships in the context of lesbian childbirth. *Journal of Family Issues, 36*(4), 480–500. https://doi.org/10.1177/0192513X14563798

Obergefell v. Hodges, 576 U.S. ____ (2015). https://www.supremecourt.gov/opinions/14pdf/14-556_3204.pdf

Oswald, R. F. (2002). Resilience within the family networks of lesbian and gay men: Intentionality and redefinition. *Journal of Marriage and Family, 64*(2), 374–383. https://doi.org/10.1111/j.1741-3737.2002.00374.x

Oswald, R. F., Blume, L. B., & Marks, S. R. (2005). Decentering heteronormativity: A model for family studies. In V. L. Bengtson, A. C. Acock, K. R. Allen, P. Dilworth-Anderson, & D. M. Klein (Eds.), *Sourcebook of family theory & research* (pp. 143–165). Sage Publications, Inc.

Otero-Amad, F. (2019, November 2). *A modern family: 20-plus sperm donor siblings find each other.* NBC News. https://www.nbcnews.com/news/us-news/modern-family-20-plus-sperm-donor-siblings-find-each-other-n1071656

Pact. (n.d.). *Private adoption: Also known as independent adoption.* https://www.pactadopt.org/birth/services/placement/independent.html

Paige, P., Gugliotta, G., Bredeweg, B., Ziffren, J., Johnson, J., Lopez, J., Goldsmith-Thomas, E., Medina, B., & Fields, S. (Executive Producers). (2013–2018). *The Fosters* [TV series]. Blazing Elm Entertainment; Nitelite Entertainment; Nuyorican Productions; Prodco.

Pallotta-Chiarolli, M., Sheff, E., & Mountford, R. (2020). Polyamorous parenting in contemporary research: Developments and future directions. In A. E. Goldberg & K. R. Allen (Eds.), *LGBTQ-parent families: Innovations in research and implications for practice* (2nd ed., pp. 171–183). Springer.

Parr, T. (2003). *The family book.* Little, Brown.

Patterson, C. J., & Goldberg, A. E. (2016). *Lesbian and gay parents and their children* [Policy brief]. National Council on Family Relations. https://www.ncfr.org/sites/default/files/2017-01/ncfr_policy_brief_november_final.pdf

Patterson, C. J., Hurt, S., & Mason, C. D. (1998). Families of the lesbian baby boom: Children's contact with grandparents and other adults. *American Journal of Orthopsychiatry, 68*(3), 390–399. https://doi.org/10.1037/h0080348

Patterson, C. J., Sutfin, E. L., & Fulcher, M. (2004). Division of labor among lesbian and heterosexual parenting couples: Correlates of specialized versus shared patterns. *Journal of Adult Development, 11*(3), 179–189. https://doi.org/10.1023/B:JADE.0000035626.90331.47

Peel, E. (2010). Pregnancy loss in lesbian and bisexual women: An online survey of experiences. *Human Reproduction, 25*(3), 721–727. https://doi.org/10.1093/humrep/dep441

Pelka, S. (2009). Sharing motherhood: Maternal jealousy among lesbian co-mothers. *Journal of Homosexuality, 56*(2), 195–217. https://doi.org/10.1080/00918360802623164

Pepper, R. (2005). *The ultimate guide to pregnancy for lesbians: How to stay sane and care for yourself from pre-conception to birth.* Cleis Press.

Perez, M. (2018, November 28). Where are all the sperm donors of color? *Rewire News Group.* https://rewirenewsgroup.com/article/2018/11/28/where-are-all-the-sperm-donors-of-color/

Perrin, E., Siegel, B. S., & the Committee on Psychosocial Aspects of Child and Family Health. (2013). Promoting the well-being of children whose parents are gay or lesbian. *Pediatrics*, *131*(4), e2374–e1383. https://doi.org/10.1542/peds.2013-0377

Perry, J. R. (2017). *Promising practices for serving transgender & non-binary foster and adoptive parents*. The Human Rights Campaign Foundation. https://assets2.hrc.org/files/assets/resources/HRC_ACAF_Promising_ Practices_Serving_Transgender_Non-Binary_Parents.pdf

Power, J., Dempsey, D., Kelly, F., & Lau, M. (2020). Use of fertility services in Australian lesbian, bisexual and queer women's pathways to parenthood. *Australian and New Zealand Journal of Obstetrics & Gynaecology*, *60*(4), 610–615. https://doi.org/10.1111/ajo.13175

The Practice Committee of the American Society for Reproductive Medicine. (2014). Ovarian tissue cryopreservation: A committee opinion. *Fertility and Sterility*, *101*(5), 1237–1243. https://doi.org/10.1016/j.fertnstert. 2014.02.052

Practice Committee of the American Society for Reproductive Medicine and the Practice Committee for the Society of Assisted Reproductive Technology. (2021, June). *Guidance regarding gamete and embryo donation*. https://www.asrm.org/globalassets/asrm/asrm-content/ news-and-publications/practice-guidelines/for-non-members/recs_for_ gamete_and_embryo_donation.pdf

Price, C. A., Bush, K. R., & Price, S. J. (Eds.). (2016). *Families & change: Coping with stressful events and transitions* (5th ed.). Sage Publications.

Prickett, K. C., Martin-Storey, A., & Crosnoe, R. (2015). A research note on time with children in different- and same-sex two-parent families. *Demography*, *52*(3), 905–918. https://doi.org/10.1007/s13524-015-0385-2

Priddle, H. (2015). How well are lesbians treated in UK fertility clinics? *Human Fertility*, *18*(3), 194–199. https://doi.org/10.3109/1464727 3.2015.1043654

Private School Review. (2021). *Average private school tuition cost*. https:// www.privateschoolreview.com/tuition-stats/private-school-cost- by-state

Pyne, J. (2012). *Transforming family: Trans parents and their struggles, strategies, and strengths*. LGBTQ Parenting Network, Sherbourne Health Centre. http://www.academia.edu/7252776/Transforming_Family_ Trans_Parents_and_their_Struggles_Strategies_and_Strengths

Pyne, J., Bauer, G., & Bradley, K. (2015). Transphobia and other stressors impacting trans parents. *Journal of GLBT Family Studies*, *11*(2), 107–126. https://doi.org/10.1080/1550428X.2014.941127

Raleigh, E. (2016). The color line exception: The transracial adoption of foreign-born and biracial Black children. *Women, Gender, and Families of Color*, *4*(1), 86–107. https://doi.org/10.5406/womgenfamcol.4.1.0086

Ramey, C. T., & Ramey, S. L. (1999). Prevention of intellectual disabilities: Early interventions to improve cognitive development. In S. J. Ceci & W. M. Williams (Eds.), *Essential readings in developmental psychology. The nature—nurture debate: The essential readings* (pp. 147–163). Blackwell Publishing.

Reinoso, A. O. (2008). Middle-class families and school choice: Freedom versus equity in the context of a "local education market." *European Educational Research Journal*, *7*(2), 176–194. https://doi.org/10.2304/eerj.2008.7.2.176

Revel & Riot. (n.d.). *Internalized homophobia*. https://www.revelandriot.com/resources/internalized-homophobia/

Riggs, D. W. (2007). *Becoming parent: Lesbians, gay men, and family*. Post Pressed.

Riggs, D. W. (2011). Australian lesbian and gay foster carers negotiating the child protection system: Strengths and challenges. *Sexuality Research & Social Policy*, *8*(3), 215–226. https://doi.org/10.1007/s13178-011-0059-9

Riggs, D. W., Pearce, R., Pfeffer, C. A., Hines, S., White, F. R., & Ruspini, E. (2020). Men, trans/masculine, and non-binary people's experiences of pregnancy loss: An international qualitative study. *BMC Pregnancy and Childbirth*, *20*, Article 482. https://doi.org/10.1186/s12884-020-03166-6

Riskind, R. G., & Tornello, S. L. (2017). Sexual orientation and future parenthood in a 2011–2013 nationally representative United States sample. *Journal of Family Psychology*, *31*(6), 792–798. https://doi.org/10.1037/fam0000316

Rivers, D. W. (2013). *Radical relations: Lesbian mothers, gay fathers, & their children in the United States since World War II*. The University of North Carolina Press.

Roberts, D. (2002). *Shattered bonds: The color of child welfare*. Basic Books.

Robitaille, C., & Saint-Jacques, M.-C. (2009). Social stigma and the situation of young people in lesbian and gay stepfamilies. *Journal of Homosexuality*, *56*(4), 421–442. https://doi.org/10.1080/00918360902821429

Rosenhaus, N. (2020, September 15). *How to know if you are ready to parent your baby: 15 questions to ask*. Adoptions with Love. https://adoptionswithlove.org/birth-parents/are-you-ready-to-parent

Ross, L. E., & Dobinson, C. (2013). Where is the "B" in LGBT parenting? A call for research on bisexual parenting. In A. E. Goldberg & K. R. Allen (Eds.), *LGBTQ-parent families: Innovations in research and implications for practice* (pp. 87–103). Springer. https://doi.org/10.1007/978-1-4614-4556-2_6

Ross, L. E., Dobinson, C., & Eady, A. (2010). Perceived determinants of mental health for bisexual people: A qualitative examination. *American Journal of Public Health*, *100*(3), 496–502. https://doi.org/10.2105/AJPH.2008.156307

Rostosky, S. S., & Riggle, E. D. B. (2017). Same-sex couple relationship strengths: A review and synthesis of the empirical literature (2000–2016). *Psychology of Sexual Orientation and Gender Diversity*, *4*(1), 1–13. https://doi.org/10.1037/sgd0000216

Ryan, M. (2009). Beyond Thomas Beatie: Trans men and the new parenthood. In R. Epstein (Ed.), *Who's your daddy? And other writings on queer parenting* (pp. 139–150). Sumach Press.

Ryan, S., & Whitlock, C. (2007). Becoming parents: Lesbian mothers' adoption experience. *Journal of Gay & Lesbian Social Services*, *19*(2), 1–23. https://doi.org/10.1080/10538720802131642

Savage, D. (2000). *The kid (what happened when my boyfriend and I decided to get pregnant): An adoption story*. Plume.

Scheib, J. E., McCormick, E., Benward, J., & Ruby, A. (2020). Finding people like me: Contact among young adults who share an open-identity sperm donor. *Human Reproduction Open*, *2020*(4), hoaa057. Advance online publication. https://doi.org/10.1093/hropen/hoaa057

Scheib, J. E., Riordan, M., & Shaver, P. R. (2000). Choosing between anonymous and identity-release sperm donors: Recipient and donor characteristics. *Reproductive Technologies*, *10*(1), 50–58.

Schwartz, E. F. (2016). *Before I do: A legal guide to marriage, gay and otherwise*. New Press.

Seattle Sperm Bank. (2021). *SSB connects brings donor siblings and families together.* https://www.seattlespermbank.com/ssb-connects-brings-donor-siblings-and-families-together/

SEEDS. (n.d.). *Standards.* https://www.seedsethics.org/ethical-business-practices-among-agencies

Shenkman, G., Bos, H., & Kogan, S. (2019). Attachment avoidance and parenthood desires in gay men and lesbians and their heterosexual counterparts. *Journal of Reproductive and Infant Psychology, 37*(4), 344–357. https://doi.org/10.1080/02646838.2019.1578872

Siegenthaler, A. L., & Bigner, J. J. (2000). The value of children to lesbian and non-lesbian mothers. *Journal of Homosexuality, 39*(2), 73–91. https://doi.org/10.1300/J082v39n02_04

Silverberg, C. (2013). *What makes a baby.* Seven Stories Press.

Simon, R. J., & Altstein, H. (2000). *Adoption across borders: Serving the children in transracial and intercountry adoptions.* Rowman & Littlefield Publishers.

Skinner, A. L., Perry, S. P., & Gaither, S. (2020). Not quite monoracial: Biracial stereotypes explored. *Personality and Social Psychology Bulletin, 46*(3), 377–392. https://doi.org/10.1177/0146167219858344

Smith, D. E. (1993). The standard North American family: SNAF as an ideological code. *Journal of Family Issues, 14*(1), 50–65. https://doi.org/10.1177/0192513X93014001005

Soloway, J., Hsu, V., Gordon, J., Lewis, J., Sperling, A., Bedard, B., & Soloway, F. (Executive Producers). (2014–2019). *Transparent* [TV series]. Amazon Studios; Picrow.

South, S. C., Lim, E., Jarnecke, A. M., & Foli, K. J. (2019). Relationship quality from pre- to postplacement in adoptive couples. *Journal of Family Psychology, 33*(1), 64–76. https://doi.org/10.1037/fam0000456

Spalding, D. (2019, April 18). IVF, IUI, and IVI: There are so many ways to make a family. *Motherly.* https://www.mother.ly/life/ivf-iui-ici-ivi

Spence-Chapin. (2018, November 3). *7 myths about open adoption.* https://spence-chapin.org/7-myths-open-adoption/

The Sperm Bank of California. (n.d.). *Identity-Release® program.* https://www.thespermbankofca.org/content/identity-release-program

Sweeney, K. A. (2013). Race-conscious adoption choices, multiraciality, and color-blind racial ideology. *Family Relations, 62*(1), 42–57. https://doi.org/10.1111/j.1741-3729.2012.00757.x

Sylvestre-Margolis, G., Vallejo, V., & Rauch, A. (2015). Gestational surrogacy/ egg donation IVF: Behavior of gay men intended parents with respect to numbers of embryos transferred. *Fertility and Sterility, 104*(3), Article e57. Advance online publication. https://doi.org/10.1016/ j.fertnstert.2015.07.173

Szilagyi, M. A., Rosen, D. S., Rubin, D., Zlotnik, S., the Council on Foster Care, Adoption, and Kinship Care, the Committee on Adolescence, & the Council on Early Childhood. (2015). Health care issues for children and adolescents in foster care and kinship care. *Pediatrics, 136*(4), e1142–e1166. https://doi.org/10.1542/peds.2015-2656

Tasker, F., & Gato, J. (2020). Gender identity and future thinking about parenthood: A qualitative analysis of focus group data with transgender and non-binary people in the United Kingdom. *Frontiers in Psychology, 11*, Article 865. https://doi.org/10.3389/fpsyg.2020.00865

Tasker, F., & Lavender-Stott, E. S. (2020). LGBTQ parenting post-heterosexual relationship dissolution. In A. E. Goldberg & K. R. Allen (Eds.), *LGBTQ-parent families: Innovations in research and implications for practice* (2nd ed., pp. 3–23). Springer. https://doi.org/10.1007/978-3-030-35610-1_1

Tate, D. P., & Patterson, C. J. (2019). Desire for parenthood in context of other life aspirations among lesbian, gay, and heterosexual young adults. *Frontiers in Psychology, 10*, Article 2679. https://doi.org/ 10.3389/fpsyg.2019.02679

Tate, D. P., Patterson, C. J., & Levy, A. J. (2019). Predictors of parenting intentions among childless lesbian, gay, and heterosexual adults. *Journal of Family Psychology, 33*(2), 194–202. https://doi.org/ 10.1037/fam0000499

Timm, T. M., Mooradian, J. K., & Hock, R. M. (2011). Exploring core issues in adoption: Individual and marital experience of adoptive mothers. *Adoption Quarterly, 14*(4), 268–283. https://doi.org/10.1080/10926755. 2011.628264

Tinker, B. (2019, June 14). *The top 10 questions about surrogacy for same-sex couples, answered.* CNN. https://www.cnn.com/2019/06/14/health/ same-sex-surrogacy-faq/index.html

Titlestad, A., & Robinson, K. (2019). Navigating parenthood as two women: The positive aspects and strengths of female same-sex parenthood. *Journal of GLBT Family Studies, 15*(2), 186–209. https://doi.org/ 10.1080/1550428X.2018.1423660

Tornello, S. L., Sonnenberg, B. N., & Patterson, C. J. (2015). Division of labor among gay fathers: Associations with parent, couple, and child adjustment. *Psychology of Sexual Orientation and Gender Diversity*, 2(4), 365–375. https://doi.org/10.1037/sgd0000109

Touroni, E., & Coyle, A. (2002). Decision-making in planned lesbian parenting: An interpretative phenomenological analysis. *Journal of Community & Applied Social Psychology*, 12(3), 194–209. https://doi.org/10.1002/casp.672

Turney, K., & Wildeman, C. (2016). Mental and physical health of children in foster care. *Pediatrics*, 138(5), Article e20161118. https://doi.org/10.1542/peds.2016-1118

U.S. Department of Health & Human Services. (2019, October 24). *AFCARS report #26*. https://www.acf.hhs.gov/cb/report/afcars-report-26

Valby, K. (2020). The realities of raising a child of a different race. *Time*. https://time.com/the-realities-of-raising-a-kid-of-a-different-race

Vandivere, S., Malm, K., & Radel, L. (2009). *Adoption USA: A chartbook based on the 2007 National Survey of Adoptive Parents*. U.S. Department of Health & Human Services. https://aspe.hhs.gov/sites/default/files/private/pdf/75911/index.pdf

Vaughn, R. (2021, March 12). *Why is there a shortage of Black egg donors and Black sperm donors?* International Fertility Law Group. https://www.iflg.net/black-egg-donor-sperm-donor-shortage/

Ward, K. O. (2020, October 30). It took a village: Surrogacy made my dream of fatherhood a reality. *Healthline*. https://www.healthline.com/health/parenting/our-surrogacy-story

Ward, M. (1998). Impact of adoption on the new parents' marriage. *Adoption Quarterly*, 2(2), 57–78. https://doi.org/10.1300/J145v02n02_04

Weigel, G., Ranji, U., Long, M., & Salganicoff, A. (2020, September 15). *Coverage and use of fertility services in the U.S.* KFF. https://www.kff.org/womens-health-policy/issue-brief/coverage-and-use-of-fertility-services-in-the-u-s/

Wendland, C. L., Burn, F., & Hill, C. (1996). Donor insemination: A comparison of lesbian couples, heterosexual couples and single women. *Fertility and Sterility*, 65(4), 764–770. https://doi.org/10.1016/S0015-0282(16)58211-9

Wide Horizons for Children. (n.d.). *LGBT adoption*. https://whfc.org/lgbt/

Wilson, B. D., Cooper, K., Kastanis, A., & Nezhad, S. (2014). *Sexual and gender minority youth in foster care: Assessing disproportionality and disparities in Los Angeles*. The Williams Institute.

Witte, R. (n.d.). 4 trans men talk about pregnancy. *Trans Magazine*. https://transmagazine.nl/trans-men-and-pregnancy/

Wojnar, D. M., & Katzenmeyer, A. (2014). Experiences of preconception, pregnancy, and new motherhood for lesbian nonbiological mothers. *Journal of Obstetric, Gynecologic & Neonatal Nursing, 43*(1), 50–60. https://doi.org/10.1111/1552-6909.12270

Wood, K. (2016). "It's all a bit pantomime": An exploratory study of gay and lesbian adopters and foster-carers in England and Wales. *The British Journal of Social Work, 46*(6), 1708–1723. https://doi.org/10.1093/bjsw/bcv115

Wu, H. Y., Yin, O., Monseur, B., Selter, J., Collins, L. J., Lau, B. D., & Christianson, M. S. (2017). Lesbian, gay, bisexual, transgender content on reproductive endocrinology and infertility clinic websites. *Fertility and Sterility, 108*(1), 183–191. https://doi.org/10.1016/j.fertnstert.2017.05.011

You Gotta Believe. (n.d.). *We're proud to make LGBT pride a priority!* https://www.yougottabelieve.org/parenting/ygb-pride/

Zhang, S. (2019, May 13). The trouble with fathering 114 kids. *The Atlantic*. https://www.theatlantic.com/science/archive/2019/05/bachelorette-contestant-114-kids-sperm-donor/589258/v

INDEX

ABOUT THE AUTHOR

Abbie E. Goldberg, PhD, is a professor of psychology at Clark University in Worcester, Massachusetts. She received her doctorate in clinical psychology from the University of Massachusetts Amherst. She is the author of the books *Open Adoption and Diverse Families: Complex Relationships in the Digital Age* (2019), *Gay Dads: Transitions to Adoptive Fatherhood* (2012), and *Lesbian and Gay Parents and Their Children* (2010). Dr. Goldberg also is the editor/coeditor of five books, including *The SAGE Encyclopedia of Trans Studies* (2020) and *LGBTQ Divorce and Relationship Dissolution* (2018). She is the author of more than 130 peer-reviewed articles on lesbian, gay, bisexual, transgender (trans), queer (LGBTQ) parenting, adoption, diverse families, family transitions, and trans students.

Dr. Goldberg has received research funding from the National Institutes of Health, the American Psychological Foundation, the Spencer Foundation, and numerous other private foundations. She has spoken internationally to diverse audiences on topics as wide ranging as transracial adoption, same-sex divorce, and LGBTQ-affirming schools. She has been interviewed by numerous media outlets, including *The New York Times*, *The Washington Post*, *USA Today*, *The Atlantic*, *Real Simple*, and *People.com*. Her website is http://www.abbiegoldberg.com and handle is @DrAbbieG on Twitter.